Terrorism and democratic stability revisited

Manchester University Press

PERSPECTIVES ON DEMOCRATIC PRACTICE

With the ebbing away of the 'third wave' of democratisation, democratic practice is unfolding and consolidating in different ways. While state based representative democracy remains central to our understanding of the concept, we are also conscious of the importance of social movements, non-governmental organisations and governance institutions. New mechanisms of accountability are being developed, together with new political vocabularies to address these elements in democratic practice. The books published in this series focus on three aspects of democratic practice: analytical and normative democratic theory, including processes by which democratic practice can be explained and achieved; new social and protest movements, especially work with a comparative and international focus; and institution-building and practice, including transformations in democratic institutions in response to social and democratic forces. Their importance arises from the fact that they are concerned with key questions about how power can be more fairly distributed and how people can be empowered to have a greater influence on decisions that affect their lives.

This series takes forward the intellectual project of the earlier MUP series, *Perspectives on Democratization*.

Already published

Susan Buckingham and Geraldine Lievesley (eds) *In the hands of women: paradigms of citizenship*

Katherine Fierlbeck *Globalizing democracy (2nd edn)*

Carina Gunnarsan *Cultural warfare and trust: fighting the Mafia in Palermo*

SHIRIN M. RAI and WYN GRANT   series editors

Terrorism and democratic stability revisited

Second edition
JENNIFER S. HOLMES

Manchester University Press

Copyright © Jennifer S. Holmes 2001, 2008

The right of Jenifer S. Holmes to be identified as the author of this work has been asserted by her in accordance with the Copyright, Designs and Patents Act 1988.

Published by Manchester University Press
Altrincham Street, Manchester M1 7JA, UK
www.manchesteruniversitypress.co.uk

British Library Cataloguing-in-Publication Data is available

ISBN 978 0 7190 7566 7 *paperback*

First published by Manchester University Press in 2001

This edition first published 2019

The publisher has no responsibility for the persistence or accuracy of URLs for any external or third-party internet websites referred to in this book, and does not guarantee that any content on such websites is, or will remain, accurate or appropriate.

Printed by Lightning Source

Contents

List of figures	*page* vii
List of tables	ix
Acknowledgements	xi
List of abbreviations	xiii
1 Introduction	1
2 Aristotelian concepts applied to a comparative study of violence and democratic stability	31
3 A historical overview of Uruguay, Peru, and Spain	53
4 Terrorist violence	85
5 State repression and violence	105
6 Testing of hypotheses one and two	132
7 Prospects for stability	189
8 Al Qaeda in *al-Andalus*: lessons learned from domestic terrorism	247
Select bibliography	264
Index	281

Figures

4.1	Uruguay: total incidents of terrorist violence, 1963–1973	*page* 95
4.2	Uruguay: terrorist incidents by category, 1963–1973	95
4.3	Uruguay: monthly terrorist incidents by category, 1972	96
4.4	Peru: non-state terrorist violent incidents, 1980–1992	97
5.1	Uruguay: state violence, spring and summer 1973	112
7.1	Peru: terrorist violent incidents, 1993–2006	211
7.2	Peru: state counterterrorism actions and National Police deaths, 1993–2006	213

Tables

3.1	Uruguayan economic indicators, 1965–1973	page 73
3.2	Peru: economic indicators, 1980–1992	75
3.3	Spanish economic indicators, 1974–1986	78
4.1	Spain: non-state terrorist incidents with attributions of responsibility, 1976–1986	99
4.2	Spain: non-state terrorist incidents by type, 1976–1986	100
5.1	Peru: victim profiles of state violence with attributions of responsibility, 1980–2000	120
5.2	Spain: state counterterror/internal security actions, 1976–1986	126
6.1	Peru: victims of non-state terrorism with attributions of responsibility, 1980–1992	136
6.2	Peru: victim profiles of non-state terrorism with attributions of responsibility, 1980–2000	138
6.3	Peru: four principal problems, 1988–1992	139
6.4	Spain: top problems facing the country, 1977–1986	142
6.5	Spain: deaths due to terrorism, 1976–1986	143
6.6	Peru: average or good rating of institutions, 1990–1992	161
6.7	Peru: choice of regime, 1982–1992	174
7.1	Uruguayan economic indicators, 1980–2005	203
7.2	Views of democracy, 1995–2006	204
7.3	Peruvian economic indicators, 1993–2005	210
7.4	Peru: four principal problems, 1993–2006	216
7.5	Peru: confidence in institutions, 1993–2005	219
7.6	Spanish economic indicators, 1987–2005	224

7.7 Spain: non-state terrorist incidents with attributions of responsibility and by type of attack, 1987–2004 225
7.8 Spain: characteristics of victims of non-state violence 227
7.9 Spanish public opinion, 1993–2006 232

Acknowledgements

After two editions, there are many people to thank. The first edition benefited greatly from the guidance of Robert T. Holt, Mary Dietz, August Nimtz, Norman Dahl, and Carla R. Philips, scholars who exemplify personal integrity and professionalism. Sheila Amin Gutiérrez de Piñeres, Brian J. L. Berry, and Edward J. Harpham provided crucial guidance on the book prospectus and manuscript revisions. Douglas C. Dow gave detailed and insightful comments on chapter two. John Peeler also provided constructive criticism and advice on the project. While I lived in Arkansas, Jaime Malamud Goti was an essential source of friendship, intellect, and sanity. Compensated only by weekly bottles of wine, my family (Rebecca and Willem Bastiaens, Jessica and John Klingler, Natina and Tedd James, and Theodore and Carolyn Smith) graciously hosted me in Minnesota for rotating weeks during much of the writing and research for this book. Rebecca also volunteered as a research assistant, helping photocopy countless Peruvian news articles for me while I was away. For the second edition, I would especially like to thank Tony Mason and Jenny Howard at Manchester University Press for their patience and confidence, and the series editors Shirin Rai and Wyn Grant for the opportunity to revise the manuscript to be part of their new Perspectives on Democratic Practice series. Despite a heavy administrative load, Sheila Amin Gutiérrez de Piñeres took the time to read the entire manuscript. With only a day's notice, Richard Millett gave valuable comments on chapter eight. The manuscript was also greatly improved by comments from anonymous reviewers.

List of abbreviations

AAA	Alianza Apostólica Anticomunista
AP	Acción Popular/Popular Alliance
APRA	Alianza Popular Revolucionaria Americana
APRODEH	Asociación pro Derechos Humanos
BVE	Batallón Vasco-Español
CAEM	Centro de Altos Estudios Militares del Peru
CDC	Convergència Democràtica de Catalunya (Catalan Democratic Convergence Party)
CiU	Convergencia i Unió (Catalan Convergence and Union)
CNI	Consejo Nactional de Inteligencia
CONAE	Consejo Nactional de Educación (Uruguayan National Council on Education)
COSENA	Consejo de Seguridad Nacional
CPI	Consumer Price Index
CRF	Comando Rodrigo Franco
DEA	Drug Enforcement Agency
DSV	double simultaneous vote
EC	European Community
EE	Euskadiko Eskerra
EEC	European Economic Community
ELP	Ejercito de Liberación (Popular National Liberation Army)
ESMACO	Estado Mayor Conjunto (Joint Chiefs of Staff) Uruguayan permanent secretary
ETA	Euzkadi ta Askatasuna
ETA-m	ETA-militar
ETA-pm	ETA-político-militar
EU	European Union
FBIS	Foreign Broadcast Information Service

FONCODES	Fondo Nacional de Compensación y Desarrollo Social
FRAP	Frente Revolucionario Antifascista y Patriótico
GAL	Grupo Antiterrorista de Liberación (Anti-Terrorist Groups of Liberation)
GRAPO	Grupos de Resistencia Antifascista de Octubre (Antifascist Resistance Groups of the First of October)
GSPC	Grupo Salafista para la Predicación y el Combate
HB	Herri Batasuna (People's Unity)
IMF	International Monetary Fund
IMET	International Military Education and Training Programme
INEI	Instituto Nacional de Estadística e Informática
IPA	InterAmerican Police Academy
IU	Izquierda Unida (United Left)
JUJEM	Junta de Jefes de Estado Mayor (Joint Chief of Staffs)
JUP	Juventud Uruguaya de Pie
LOPP	Ley Orgánica de Partidos Políticos
MANO	Movimiento Armado Nacional Oriental
MIR	Movimiento de Izquirda Revolcionaria (Movement of the Revolutionary Left)
MPS	*medidas prontas de seguridad*
MRTA	Movimiento Revolucionario Tupac Amaro
NATO	North Atlantic Treaty Organization
OAS	Organization of American States
OEDC	Organization for Economic Cooperation and Development
PCE	Partido Comunista de España (Spanish Communist Party)
PCP-SL	Partido Comunista del Perú en el Sendero Luminoso de Jose Carlos Mariátegui
PNV	Partido Nacionalista Vasco (Basque Nationalist Party)
PPC	Partido Popular Cristiano (Popular Christian Party)
PSOE	Partido Socialista Obrero Español (Spanish Socialist Workers Party)

SIDE	Secretaría de Inteligencia del Estado (Argentine Information Service)
SIN	Servicio de Inteligencia Nacional
SINAMOS	Sistema Nacional de Movilización Social (National System of Support for Social Mobilization)
UCD	Unión de Centro Democrático (Union of the Democratic Centre)
UDC	Unió Democràtica de Catalunya (Catalan Democratic Union)
USAID	United States Agency for International Development

To Trevor, the one constant in my life.

1
Introduction

The question

Can terrorist and state violence cause democratic breakdown? Typically, the origins of violence are studied, but rarely are the consequences. For example, Ted Gurr states 'on the basis of the record to date, the revolutionary potential of political terrorism is vastly overrated. Where it has had any impact at all, other powerful political forces were pushing in the same direction.'[1] When the consequences of violence are studied, its effects are usually limited to a reflection of the pre-existing conflict that originally spawned the violence. In this study, the claim is made that to understand the consequences of violence on democratic stability, violence coming from terrorist groups and violence emanating from the state must be studied together. Instead of asking what unleashed the violence in Uruguay, Peru, and Spain, the consequences of the violence are examined. Violence is considered as a cause of further instability, instead of merely a manifestation of pre-existing conflict.

In my initial examination of this question, the conventional social science concepts of legitimacy and order appeared to be inadequate for my analysis. As a result, an alternative concept of citizen support is derived from Aristotle's political philosophy and contemporary proponents of his work. The use of these concepts in conjunction with the three case studies articulates both a persuasive defence of this alternative concept of citizen support and a greater understanding of the three case studies.

This work also is one of the few works of case study based comparative analyses of the consequences of terrorism.

Scholars have noted a lack of both 'theoretically grounded case studies'[2] and 'comprehensive historical comparisons'.[3] Frederick Schultz calls for more historically grounded comparisons and stresses the need for researchers to 'become familiar with the history of terrorism'.[4] In-depth analysis of the Peruvian, Spanish, and Uruguayan cases can help to illustrate causal mechanisms and to clarify useful concepts in studying violence.

This book has been extensively revised and expanded for the second edition, taking advantage of new historical sources, an extended time span, and new theories since its original publication. In addition to adding new data sources in the Peruvian and Spanish cases, the time period covered has been expanded from the late 1990s to early 2007, allowing a more comprehensive treatment of the consequences of state and non-state violence on democratic stability and the prospects for stability. Since the publication of the first edition in autumn 2001, a plethora of studies on terrorism has been published. The literature reviews of democratic stability, democratic consolidation, and terrorism have been significantly revised and updated. Finally, chapter eight is an entirely new chapter, which covers the special case of Spain, which faces both a domestic and an international threat.

Organization of the book

The first part of the book is conceptual. The re-emergence of Aristotle's political philosophy into current political thought by contemporary philosophers has introduced new concepts and questions for comparative politics. The pathways linking these two subjects, further explored in chapter two, provide a framework of analysis to investigate the consequences of violence on democratic stability. The Aristotelian framework replaces 'legitimacy' with an evaluation of the state, and ultimately the constitution, based on its rudimentary purposes, and 'order' with the concept of the political community. Aristotelian concepts help illuminate the effects of violence and its consequences on democratic stability, resulting in an approach that works well in a comparative analysis.

The rest of the book is a comparative, empirical analysis of the effects of violence (terrorist and state) on democratic stability in three countries: Uruguay (1965–1984), Peru (1980–1992), and Spain (1975–1986). Chapter three provides a short historical discussion of the challenges facing all three democracies, including economic crisis. Chapter four examines terrorism and the consequences of terrorism for democratic stability. It is theorized that terrorist violence threatens democratic stability by undermining both rudimentary purposes of the state, security, and integration. As the purposes of the state are unfulfilled, then citizen confidence in the state should decline. As citizen confidence decreases, increases in democratic instability are expected. Chapter five examines the consequences of state repression and violence for democratic stability. It is hypothesized that state violence also undermines the rudimentary purposes of the state. A decrease in citizen confidence is expected to follow the decrease in the rudimentary purposes. Chapter six concludes the testing of the two hypotheses by examining changes in citizen confidence in the state and in democratic stability. Overall, this inquiry seeks to explain, with reference to Spain's successful democratic consolidation, the demise of Uruguayan and Peruvian democracies. Specifically, it aims to understand the initial popular support for the military takeover in Uruguay and the support of Alberto Fujimori's *autogolpe* in Peru.

Chapter seven presents the conclusion that although terrorism is a threat to democratic stability, the state reaction to that violence is as least as important in influencing the ultimate outcome of continued democracy or democratic breakdown. The three cases are updated to 2006 to examine the prospects for stability in spite of internal strife.

Chapter eight examines the lessons learned for those three cases and asks how they can be applied to discussions of international terrorism. In this respect, the case of Spain is unique. Initially, Spain faced only an internal threat. Recently, however, it now has an additional international threat from Al Qaeda affiliated groups on Spanish soil. How can general principles of maintaining support based on providing security and maintaining integration guide decision making in democracies facing international threats?

The case studies

Uruguay

Uruguay was 'one of the world's friendliest, most progressive, and most democratic countries' according to Russell Fitzgibbon.[5] Shockingly, in 1973 the peaceful, progressive country of Uruguay crumbled into authoritarian rule. Strategically located between Brazil and Argentina, Uruguay, the 'Switzerland of South America', was considered one of the most stable democracies in Latin America. The small, tranquil country of approximately three million people, which prior to the coup did not even have compulsory military service, became a victim of widespread, military led torture and repression under authoritarian, military rule from 1973–1984. How did the military change from an institution that 'played only a marginal role in the public arena and were mildly despised and indulgently tolerated by a populace that considered them good only for disciplining the unruly sons of the middle classes or for providing relief during natural disasters' to an institution that assumed power with the support of the citizens?[6] In 1965 the Tupamaros began their violent protest, disrupting society and publicizing corruption. As early as 1966, the dismantling of democracy began, including severe censorship of the media. These first steps towards tyranny were mostly unchallenged by the people. In 1973 the military directly assumed power by issuing communiqués and later by occupying the National Assembly (the Uruguayan legislature). Democracy was not restored until 1984. In a country with such a pervasive history of participatory democracy, why the absence of popular protest of the military takeover?

Peru

Unlike Uruguay, Peru has experienced numerous changes of constitution in this century. Politics of the early twentieth century were plagued by faction within the old oligarchy and shifting, unstable political alliances. The military was directly involved in many of these changes. Two early military interventions resulted in the relatively effective rule of President Oscar Raimundo Benavides (1933–1939) and President Manuel Odría (1948–1956). When these leaders were elected by citizens, few Peruvians were eligible to vote. A majority of Peruvians remained excluded from any meaningful participation in politics. A revolutionary coup, led by General Juan Velasco Alvarado, replaced the elected President Belaúnde in 1968. Velasco attempted to radically reform Peruvian society. He succeeded in some agrarian reform, but his proposals were opposed by many. Eventually he was ousted and replaced by General Francisco Morales Bermúdez in 1975. The country was returned to democratic rule in 1980. For the first time, illiterates were granted the right to vote.[7] Newly democratic Peru faced economic crisis and rampant violence. Sendero Luminoso, or the Shining Path, emerged in 1980 and MRTA, the Tupac Amaru Revolutionary Movement, began violent activities in 1984. In 1990 Alberto Fujimori was elected president in an atmosphere of public cynicism, economic crisis, and widespread violence. On 6 April 1992, Fujimori, with the support of the military, committed an *autogolpe* or self-coup, dissolving Congress, dismissing the judiciary, and restricting the press. His action was widely supported by the Peruvian people. What role did violence, both state and terrorist, play in preparing the people to support Fujimori's *autogolpe*?

Spain

Early twentieth-century Spain was chaotic. In a short number of years, Spain had a constitutional monarchy, a benign dictatorship, the re-establishment of a republic and a civil war. The victorious Nationalists, under the command of General Francisco Franco, imposed calm after the civil war. Franco's rule was sanctified by the Catholic Church in the 1953 Concordat and was supported by the military until his death in 1975. Under the guidance of Franco's successor, the new King Juan Carlos, Spain began a transition to democracy. Nonetheless, the military remained a potentially powerful institution. The new democracy was tested and challenged by violent attacks which spanned the ideological spectrum. In addition to the violent threat, Spain faced economic crisis. Violent activity increased between 1975 and 1980. However, the state largely refrained from a broad repressive response. During this time, military conspiracies and plots flourished within the barracks, culminating in a nearly successful coup attempt on 23 February 1981. In response to this attempted coup, citizens demonstrated in favour of democracy. Why did Spaniards remain loyal to their democracy, in spite of such troubles? Later, on 11 March 2004, bombs at the Madrid Atocha train station killed 191 people. Initially, Euzkadi ta Askatasuna (ETA) was blamed, although the responsibility of an Al Qaeda affiliated group became evident within a few days. How can Spain fight both a domestic conflict and protect itself from an international terrorist network?

Case selection

This work builds upon the extensive secondary and primary sources available for these cases. As Collier and Collier state, 'a principal challenge of comparative-historical research is to push the systematic comparison as far as possible without pushing it to a point where it does violence to the distinctive attributes of each case'.[8] This study examines both similarities and differences among cases. First, this study follows the logic of comparative history as the parallel demonstration of theory. The aim of the parallel demonstration of theory is to 'persuade the reader that a given, explicitly delineated hypothesis or theory can repeatedly demonstrate its fruitfulness . . . when applied to a series of relevant historical trajectories'.[9] In this study, the intention is to demonstrate the usefulness of the concept of citizen support in understanding these cases and to probe the strength of the hypotheses. Second, both the most different and most similar designs are used in the case selection with the aim of pursuing macro-causal analysis. In the most different design, which follows Mill's method of agreement, the outcome is the same, despite a series of overall differences. However, the cases share a crucial similarity – in these cases, a repressive government response to non-state violence. This method is used in the comparison between Uruguay and Peru to eliminate the possible explanatory power of overall differences. The two countries differ in respect to features that are speculated by some to be related to stability. The violent movement in Uruguay was mostly urban, whereas in Peru it was mostly rural. Uruguay has had a much more stable history of democratic governance than Peru. The level of industrialization in Uruguay was higher than in Peru. The Uruguayan population includes the original Spanish settlers, plus a large proportion of later Spanish and Italian immigrants, creating a generally homogeneous population.[10] Contrarily, Peru has a large population of indigenous Indians, in addition to people of African and Chinese descent, creating a heterogeneous population. Not only is the country heterogeneous, but the country is geographically divided into three regions. Twelve per cent of the population is white, Catholic and lives on the coast. Of the remaining population, in general, 45 per cent is Indian, 37 per cent is mestizo, and 6 per cent is black. Two-thirds of the population lives in the Andean mountains and consists mostly of non-Spanish speaking, impoverished peasants who adhere to Incan faiths.[11] In total, there are fifty-seven ethnic groups[12] and approximately thirty-one languages spoken in Peru.[13] Uruguay has had a very well established, almost consociational two party system of the Colorados and Blancos since 1904. Peru has an extensive history of military intervention and unstable political parties. Its most popular party, Alianza Popular Revolucionaria Americana (APRA), was excluded from electoral competition for much of the twentieth century. In addition, the coup and *autogolpe* occurred in very different time periods. US intervention to deter leftist guerrillas was common in many Latin American countries, although in Uruguay the US involvement was indirect, limited to aid and intelligence assistance. Peru's later instability was in the context of a radically different international post cold war environment. However, instead of US intervention to counter leftist guerrillas, at this time, the United States was more interested in combating the drug trade. However, it should also be noted that there are three main similarities between Uruguay and Peru. First, both countries experienced violence followed by a change of constitution. In Uruguay, the Tupamaros began their violent protest in 1965. In 1973, the military assumed power. Democracy was not restored until 1984. In Peru, the most recent violent political movement is Sendero Luminoso, which emerged in 1980. President Fujimori conducted his *autogolpe* in 1992. Second, neither country had extensive United States intervention in their national politics. Third, both states responded to the threat with repression. The last similarity is theorized to be crucial to explaining the breakdown of democracy in these cases. Finally, Spain is introduced as an exploratory case within the most similar design, which follows Mill's method of difference. In the most similar design, although there are overall similarities, a crucial difference explains the difference in outcome. Spain, like Uruguay and Peru, faced terrorist violence. Not only is Spain heterogeneous, but it is also geographically divided, as is Peru. In addition to a violence threat, Spain faced economic crisis and a politicized military. The case of Spain is important for illustrating an alternative state response to terrorist violence. Despite being challenged by a plethora of violent groups from across the ideological spectrum, Spain did not implement policies of indiscriminate state violence and repression. Spain's democracy consolidated. Today, Spanish democracy continues to counter domestic terrorism from Basque separatists, in addition to violence from an Al Qaeda affiliated group. What can we learn from the intersection of international and domestic threats to democracy?

Traditional explanations

There are four dominant factors in the literature of democratic breakdown and democratic consolidation: economic, leadership, political, and international. Some literature on consolidation is included because, presumably, a lack of factors that encourage consolidation could also undermine stability. However, the explanatory power of these factors is mixed.

Economic crisis

Some scholars blame economic crisis and tension for democratic breakdown. Both Peru and Uruguay experienced prolonged economic crisis preceding democratic breakdown. Uruguay began having negative economic growth in the mid-1950s. Peru had declining growth from 1975–1992 with a 50 per cent decline between 1988 and 1992. Both countries had high inflation, while Peru experienced hyperinflation of up to 7650 per cent in 1991. Spain's economy also suffered from inflation and higher unemployment in the late 1970s. A sophisticated example of this type of argument can be found in Adam Przeworski, Michael Alvarez, José Cheibub, and Fernando Limongi's 'What Makes Democracies Endure?'. They state:

> democracy is more likely to survive in a growing economy with less than $1,000 per capita income than in a country where per-capita income is between $1,000 and $4,000, but which is declining economically... When poor countries stagnate, whatever democracies happen to spring up tend to die quickly... we have found that once a country is sufficiently wealthy, with per-capita income of more than $6,000 a year, democracy is certain to survive.[14]

Two years after the coup, in 1975, Uruguay had a per capita income of $2144. Two years before Fujimori's *autogolpe*, in 1990, Peru's level was $849. Spain's level in 1980, one year before the attempted coup, was $6657.[15] Indeed, at first glance this looks consistent with the economic situations of the three countries. However, an exclusive focus on economic factors cannot explain democratic breakdown or lack thereof. Economic problems need to be considered in a broader context to understand their effects on democratic stability.[16]

Leadership

Many scholars have followed the focus of Juan Linz by studying leadership. Linz asks 'what causes a regime to move beyond its functional range to become a disrupted or semicoercive regime that ends in repudiation by large or critical segments of the population?'[17] Linz argues against deterministic analysis, stressing that factors create opportunities and constraints for the agents involved, while still leaving room for meaningful action. Leadership choices were important in all three cases.

Some scholars have blamed poor leadership for Uruguay's troubles. With hindsight, leadership errors can be identified. This is a sentiment echoed by General Liber Seregni, presidential candidate for the Frente Amplio, who during the 1971 elections called the Colorado and Blanco parties dead and void of leadership.[18] Charles Gillespie also believes the 'final complicity of the politicians was to abandon Bordaberry when he appealed for help during the military rebellion of February 1973'.[19] Kaufman commented that negotiations between the Blanco leader and the military to propose new elections and the establishment of a broad national coalition 'endorsed the principle of military involvement within the government machinery'.[20] Wilson was not the only politician to court the military. Julio Sanguinetti, later president of Uruguay, commented that the Uruguayan left courted the military as well.[21] Ronald McDonald also finds fault with the political leadership in the National Assembly.[22]

In the study of Peru, some scholars have blamed Fujimori for the *autogolpe*. Jaime de Althaus concluded that Fujimori conducted his *autogolpe* to prevent the re-election of Alan García. Maxwell Cameron believed Fujimori instituted a coup to eliminate Congress and García as rivals. Moreover, according to Cameron, Fujimori personally preferred to rule by decree, not by building coalitions.[23]

In contrast, the astute leadership of King Juan Carlos is widely noted as an important explanation for the successful democratization in Spain. Joel Podolny credits him for the successful transition to democracy.[24] Richard Gunther believed that the King's personal legitimacy was transferred to the new regime.[25] Charles Powell states, 'while in the thirties the establishment of democracy had forced the prior elimination of the monarchy, four decades later only the monarchy seemed capable of guaranteeing the continuation of democracy'.[26] Indeed, on the night of the attempted coup in February 1981, the King succeeded in securing the loyalty of many otherwise disgruntled and potentially seditious officers. The focus on leadership as a primary means of explanation is tricky.

The problem with this style of analysis is that it is very difficult to craft a definition of good leadership. Juan Linz's definition of good leadership is tautological in the sense that good leadership is leadership that prevents breakdown, while poor leadership is leadership that results in breakdown. Moreover, the focus on leadership privileges the actions of the elites over those of the citizens. Elites are not leaders if people do not follow them.[27] In Uruguay and Peru, the public broadly supported, or at the very least, calmly acquiesced to the overthrow of their democracies. In Spain, the people demonstrated against the coup attempt. Although the actions of the elites were important, the granting or withholding of mass support from potential coups is very important to understand the success or failure of coups.

Other scholars focus on the presence or absence of cooperation or pacting among competing politicians. In Spain, the tendency towards conciliation among Spaniards and fear of the previous faction were cited as a factor in the successful transition.[28] In Uruguay, cooperation among the main political parties was common in regard to policy and power. However, instead of stability, cooperation led to stagnation and crisis in Uruguay. Since the late nineteenth century there had been a tradition of peaceful sharing of political and informal bureaucratic power, including opposition presence in governments and bureaucracy. The Uruguayan system of *coparticipación*, that had guaranteed stability for early Uruguay, may have become debilitating towards the end of democratic rule. According to Martin Weinstein, *coparticipación* is 'an integrating mechanism perverted by the sectarianism of party politics into jockeying for advantage by factions of the two traditional parties. What was left an orphan was the "national interest" and the effective policies to promote it.'[29]

Political system and parties

Many scholars link democratic stability to either the strength of political parties or the type of political system to indicate future stability. For example, Larry Diamond and Juan Linz state, 'An important element in the institutional resilience of democracy has been the strength of the party system and the high degree of institutionalization and popular loyalty achieved by the major parties.'[30] Uruguay had very well established political parties, the Blancos and Colorados. These two main political parties dominated Uruguayan politics from 1904 until 1971, and have fairly coherent memberships.[31] In the 1971 presidential elections, a new leftist coalition, the Frente Amplio party, gained one third of the presidential votes. Peru's parties were poorly established compared with Uruguay. Peru's APRA was established in 1930, but had been excluded from participation for much of its existence. Acción Popular (or Popular Action; AP) was founded in 1956; the Partido Popular Cristiano (or Popular Christian Party; PPC) was founded in 1967. According to A. Adrianzén, a party system does not exist in Peru; Presidents Belaúnde, Garcia, and Fujimori lacked coherent programmes, and few party loyalties have been generated.[32] Joseph Tulchin found a severe difficulty in crafting stable alliances in his analysis of Peru.[33] The weakness of the Peruvian political parties was highlighted by the success of a new independent party, Fujimori's Cambio 90 party, in the 1990 presidential election. Although the Peruvian party system portended problems, so did the new Spanish party system. In Spain, after the death of Franco in 1975, more than two hundred groups emerged, proclaiming themselves political parties. Some of these parties had emerged from parties active during the Second Republic, but many more were completely new groups.[34] In the founding election,[35] two parties dominated. The Partido Socialista Obrero Español (Spanish Socialist Workers Party; PSOE) and the Unión de Centro Democrático (Union of the Democratic Centre; UCD) were the main recipients of votes. The UCD was a newly formed centrist party, established in 1977, and led by Adolfo Suárez. The UCD carried Spain through the first years of democracy. Three of the main parties, the PSOE, the Partido Comunista de España (Spanish Communist Party; PCE), and the Partido Nocionalista Vasco (Basque Nationalist Party; PNV), had existed since the Second Republic and continued underground under Franco. Another important party, the AP (Popular Alliance) was formed of mostly former Francoist officials and founded in 1976. Although there was some continuity among parties from the Second Republic, many major political forces from that period were not represented after 1975. For example, the bourgeois republican parties of the centre left, the anarchist parties, and the conservative clerical party (CEDA or the Confederación Española de Derecha Autónoma) had disappeared.[36] In spite of the emergence of two main political parties, the party system was unstable and top heavy.[37] After 1982, the UCD lost its electoral support and was formally dissolved in February 1983. From this brief discussion of main political parties, it appears that the strength of party systems is not helpful in understanding the outcomes in Uruguay and in Spain.

Other scholars have tried to explain the Uruguayan and Peruvian breakdowns as failures of the political system.

Both countries had multi-party presidential political systems that tended to produce presidents without stable majorities in the legislative bodies.[38] Moreover, both countries had unique aspects that further complicated presidents being elected with electoral majorities. In Uruguay, the lema system produced electoral fragmentation. Uruguay's unique double simultaneous vote (DSV) entails a presidential election in which the equivalent of primary and presidential elections is held simultaneously. The DSV encourages party fragmentation, since the law allows factions to combine their votes in favour of the candidate who received the most votes. The more candidates a party has, the more votes the party can potentially receive. The resulting party system in Uruguay had become increasingly fragmented. In 1946, there were only 45 lists for deputy in the Blanco party and 108 in the Colorado party. By 1971, there were 308 lists for the Blancos and 246 for the Colorados.[39] In nine years the number of lists for deputy increased by approximately one hundred for each party. According to Kaufman, the lack of party cohesion and increasing fragmentation, the authoritarian personality of Bordaberry, and the emergence of the Frente Amplio, 'hampered the placement of a solid civilian obstacle to the military drive'.[40] In the case of Uruguay, President Bordaberry did lose his majority in the National Assembly before the coup which made him more dependent upon military support.[41] However, a fragmented political system does not explain the public apathy towards the dissolution of Uruguay's constitutional institutions in 1973. In Peru, the party system was faulted for creating conditions that hindered stable and effective political control. For example, Maxwell Cameron notes that the Peruvian system of a runoff election between the two most popular candidates to ensure a president gained at least 50 per cent popularity also made it difficult to achieve a Congressional majority.[42]

International influences

Some scholars privilege international influences to explain the breakdown or stability of democracies or a demonstration effect.[43] Many scholars of Uruguay blame the involvement of the United States for the breakdown of democracy. Foreign influence was also theorized to be important in Peru and in Spain. Undoubtedly, international pressures account for opportunities and constraints on national events. Even scholars who believe that international forces can influence democratic outcomes acknowledge the limitation of the effectiveness of international forces. For example, P. Nikiforos Diamandorus states,

> First, by mobilizing effectively in support of forces favoring a democratic outcome, nondomestic structures can enhance the democratization dynamic and thus contribute to eventual consolidation. Second, and perhaps more important, international influences play a role that can only be described as complementary and secondary to that of domestic forces.[44]

A brief discussion of international influences in the breakdown of Uruguay and Peru, in addition to the successful democracy in Spain, reveals an incompleteness of this factor as an explanatory cause.

Uruguay

International factors were blamed frequently in the Uruguayan breakdown. For example, Weinstein cites a diffusion effect in the importance of international factors for the breakdown of Uruguayan democracy. He states:

> One shoe dropped for Uruguay when the dynamics of the bureaucratic authoritarian regime in Brazil brought hard-line elements to power in the late 1960's; the other dropped with the accentuated belief by successive military governments in Argentina that liberal, civilian run Uruguay provided too much of a safe haven for their domestic foes.[45]

Although there were rumours of a possible Brazilian intervention, actual linkages between Argentina and Brazil are unclear in causing the Uruguayan breakdown. There is some evidence of an Argentine influence. For instance, in February 1971 Uruguayan president pacheco met with Argentine president General Roberto Marcelo Levingston to discuss how to deal with terrorists, in addition to economic matters.[46] On 9 June 1972, *Marcha* published the declaration of former policeman Nelson Benítez, who revealed that Pacheco was cooperating with Argentina on the training of Uruguayan para-police groups in Argentina.[47] A. J. Langguth and Wilson Fernandez blame US involvement for the Uruguayan breakdown.[48] Others blame the influence of the

National Security Doctrine for the demise of Uruguayan democracy. The United States gave Uruguay police and military aid through the Agency for International Development (USAID), International Military Education and Training (IMET) programme, the InterAmerican Police Academy (IPA), and through other training programmes. During 1962–1970, through the Agency for International Development's Office of Public Safety, Uruguay's police force received money and training. Through USAID, the US gave an additional $225,000 in 1972.[49] Additionally, the United States gave significant amounts of aid through the IMET. Between 1968 and 1972, the US gave $1,703,000.[50] The IPA was established to train police to fight communism wherever it existed.[51] US public safety technicians and consultants, including undercover CIA agents,[52] were hired to train Uruguayan police officers. As of 1971, 113 policemen had been trained in the United States with an additional 700 trained in Uruguay by American advisors.[53] The total amount of police aid from 1961–1971 was $1,936,000. From 1946–1982, 920 Uruguayan officers attended courses at Fort Gulick in the Panama Canal Zone.[54] US influence is also felt through officer training at the School of the Americas at Fort Sherman.[55] The United States was involved in the training of Uruguayan police and military, but how influential was the involvement?

Carina Perelli argues forcibly against attributing military interventions to the National Security Doctrine of the United States or training at the School of the Americas or other training courses attended by Latin American officers in the United States. Perelli rejects the contention that the adoption of this doctrine reinforced a historical tendency to intervene in politics. She states, 'by this view, the armed forces act as mindless instruments that simultaneously obey the dominant demands of their societies and of the creators of the doctrine'.[56] Instead, she calls for an examination of the context in which the military operated, noting the wide social unrest. She argues that the military intervened due to three factors. First, the divisions in the political class, scandal, inefficiency, and corruption led to the existence of a belief in a void of power. In addition, the poor economic performance and use of violence primed the military to rethink its role and intervene.[57] Two factors weaken the argument that United States influenced security doctrine was responsible for the Uruguayan breakdown. First, General Liber Seregni, who later was the presidential candidate for the Frente Amplio, had been director of the officer school, Instituto Military de Estudios Superiores. The fact that a progressive, constitutionalist officer was in charge of officer training for years casts doubt on this explanation, especially that of the National Security Doctrine. In addition, Uruguay's National Security and Defence School was established five years after the coup, unlike Brazil's Escola Superior de Guerra, which was established before the coup.[58]

Peru

The effect of international factors in Peru is inconsistent. In Peru, instead of US involvement under the pretence of fighting subversion, as in Uruguay, US involvement was directed towards curbing the drug trade. Beginning in 1983, the Peruvian army emulated the US army's strategic hamlet campaign plan used in Vietnam. However, this plan only succeeded in allowing Sendero to exploit the economic dislocation. Later, the United States pressured for investigation of human rights violations. However, unlike Uruguay, among Peruvians, especially those in the military leadership, there was a distrust of US involvement. Economic and military aid to Peru from the United States was inconsistent and encumbered with negotiation of terms. In 1985 a new policy of drug interdiction was introduced, called 'Operation Condor', in which US military pilots and Drug Enforcement Agency (DEA) officials cooperated with the Peruvians.[59] Under Peruvian president Alan García, the United States was involved in drug enforcement through the DEA. The operation was called 'Operation Snowcap' and was developed in 1987 to increase crop eradications and drug interdiction. US army Green Berets were also involved in training and established a base in the Upper Huallaga Valley. However, President García rejected a five year $701,000,000 plan of economic and military assistance because it was conditional upon Peru's focusing on a military counternarcotics strategy. Likewise, President Fujimori rejected an initial aid package in 1990. Many in the state and military were hesitant to involve the military in the counter-drug operations.⁶⁰ Eventually an agreement was signed in May 1991 that recognized Peru's security and economic needs in addition to the anti-drug campaign pushed by the United States.⁶¹ The international reaction to the coup was negative and in fact encouraged Fujimori to quickly call new elections. Despite military aid to Peru, the US reaction to Fujimori's coup was negative. The US suspended all economic and military assistance and used its influence to delay loans from the Peru Support Group and the Inter-American Development Bank.⁶² In addition, the International Monetary Fund (IMF) held a $222 million loan. International pressure succeeded in moving up Fujimori's plan for the re-introduction of elections, but did not diminish Fujimori's domestic support.

Some scholars, such as Abraham Lowenthal, have noted the importance of international pressure, especially the actions of the Organization of American States (OAS), in pressuring for a return to electoral politics in Peru, Guatemala, and Haiti.⁶³ Previously, the OAS had been committed to a doctrine of non-intervention, as stated in Articles 18 and 19.⁶⁴ However, in June 1991 Resolution 1080 requested that the OAS respond to 'violations of the democratic process'. The General Assembly responded with a change in policy and what has now become known as the Santiago Commitment to Democracy, which laid the foundations for collective action in response to the interruption of the democratic institutional process. Moreover, with the Protocol of Washington of 1993, the OAS has been changed to allow the suspension of delinquent states.⁶⁵ Moreover, the OAS issued resolutions on restoring democracy in Haiti, Peru, and Venezuela. The OAS stated in its resolution that 'representative democracy can be promoted and defended only by democratic means, any other course being rejected as contrary to the fundamental principles established in the Charter of the OAS'. It also resolved to hold Fujimori to his pledge of calling elections for a Constitutional Congress, to urge Peru to respect the separation of powers, human rights and the rule of law, and offered to provide electoral observation.⁶⁶ The results of OAS actions are uneven. The OAS condemned the attempted coup in Guatemala, which failed eight days later when Serrano was ousted by the military and a new president was installed. In Haiti, the OAS failed to convince the military to restore President Aristide. In Peru, critics accuse the OAS of being a 'midwife to a process by which an authoritarian system is being established under the guise of formal democracy'.[67]

Spain

International factors seemed to both help and hinder the new Spanish democracy. Spain began to integrate itself into European institutions after Franco's death. Spain tried to gain associate membership of the EEC in 1962, but was turned down since it was a dictatorship. '[Although] the EEC Treaty said that "any European State may apply to become a member of the Community", democracy has – in practice – been a basic precondition. Spain was given a preferential trade agreement in 1970 and Portugal in 1973, but ... only with ... the death of Franco in Spain in 1975 was EEC membership' taken as a real possibility.[68] In June 1977, Spain again applied for membership to the European Community. Two months later, in October 1977, Spain was admitted to the Council of Europe. In 1982, despite objections from the PSOE and negative public opinion, UCD leader Leopoldo Calvo Sotelo gained approval for entry into NATO.[69] Initially, the PSOE opposed joining NATO. However, Spain eventually joined under the Socialist government, hoping that joining NATO would 'democratize military thinking through international contact'.[70] In addition to desires to re-educate the military, pressures for modernization came from budgetary and technological concerns, which helped to convince many European governments, including the Spanish, that cooperation can increase efficiency.[71]

Finally, EU membership was allowed in 1986. The symbolism of EU membership was critical to Spanish democracy. According to Carlos Closa, it meant 'a return to the western world ... The EC had a legitimizing effect on the new Spanish democracy because of Community members' permanent criticism and rejection and occasional condemnation of Franco's regime'.[72] The symbolism of the Spaniards was equalled by the expectations of other Europeans. Despite problems with Spain's membership, such as its relative poverty, controversy over fishing rights, and fear of excessive worker migration, 'the EEC felt membership would encourage democracy in the Iberian Peninsula and help link the two countries more closely to NATO and Western Europe'.[73]

Moreover, with the direction of integration of security and crime fighting, it is easier for Spain to apprehend and investigate terrorism abroad and to extradite suspects. After Spain joined the EU, it participated in the attempts to create a coordinated security and defence policy and integration. The Common Foreign and Security Policy commits member states 'to defining and implementing a common policy that includes all questions related to the security of the Union, including the eventual framing of a common defence policy'.[74] Recently, member states have agreed to cooperate in the investigation and prosecution of criminals who are participating in a criminal organization.[75] To that end, Europol has been directed to deal with crimes 'committed or likely to be committed in the course of terrorist activities against life, limb, personal freedom or property'.[76] One of the objectives of Europol is to increase the effectiveness of cooperation among different authorities in combating and preventing terrorism when there is evidence that two or more member states are involved. Since 1993, countering terrorism and other organized crime has been given top priority, even when the different countries lack the same legal provisions making an action an offence. Now, different legal traditions or specific differences in legal provisions are insufficient to prevent extradition. In effect, an exception has been made to previous requirements of dual criminality.[77] Furthermore, efforts to improve the cooperation among member states to combat terrorism have been highlighted in a Council Recommendation on 9 December 1999; specifically, the sharing of intelligence, creation of joint initiatives, and participation by Europol were discussed. The importance of these actions should not be understated. Spain was able to prosecute ETA members more effectively when France started to cooperate with the Spanish authorities, no longer allowing ETA members to flee to safety in southern France.

In addition to helping with law enforcement, joining the EU also set certain standards of conduct. In the Single European Act signed in February 1986 and implemented in July 1987, the promotion of democracy, human rights, and the fundamental freedoms, including equity and social justice, were prominently placed in the preamble.[78] These standards have been recently reaffirmed in actions taken against Indonesia and Yugoslavia to prohibit the sales of items that could be used for repression or state terror.[79]

Some scholars, such as Richard Gillespie, credit this integration into the EU for an increasing stability. Gillespie states: 'the new regime benefited from EC solidarity and the process of European integration made it increasingly difficult for anti-democratic elements in Spain to offer a credible scenario for the future'.[80] Ultimately, however, the ability of the EU to impose its influence is limited by an implementation deficit. Although member states that do not comply with EU policies can be tried before the European Court of Justice and can be fined, the EU lacks a coherent and powerful administration that is capable of enforcing and implementing policies. Instead, the EU relies of the national and sub-national administrations to enforce EU policies.[81] The strength of its effects seems to be on the symbolic effect and commitment to the organization on the part of Spaniards.

However, some international influences were negative for Spanish democracy. Under Franco, in 1953, Spain signed an agreement with the United States to establish American bases in Spain in return for economic aid. Many cite this aid as crucial in sustaining Franco's regime when it may have otherwise failed. Through this agreement, the Spanish military had much contact with the US military. Moreover, even later, democratic Spain was not helped by the United States during the attempted coup.[82] During the crisis, US Secretary of State Alexander Haig commented that the attempted coup was an internal matter for Spaniards.[83]

The military

In each of the three cases, the military played an important role. In Uruguay, the military directly dismantled democracy. In Peru, Fujimori conducted his *autogolpe*, or self-coup, with the support of the military. In Spain, the military remained a threat to the new democracy throughout the democratic consolidation. In his review of security and democracy in Latin America, J. Samuel Fitch warns 'at a minimum, democratic governments must clearly delineate the lines between police and military roles in internal security. Insofar as possible, the armed forces should be removed from primary responsibility for internal security, without denying the need for trained counterinsurgency forces to intervene when antidemocratic forces attempt to establish a territorial base.'[84] Historically, a major issue in Latin American politics has been figuring out how to stop politicians from 'knocking on the barrack doors' and how to convince the military that they are not the ultimate protectors of the constitution, as they interpret it.

What motivates a military institution or particular officer to move against the state and to seize power? In each of the three case studies, some military officers viewed the armed forces as a source of power to be used to assume control of the country or to promote someone who could. This propensity towards power among some in the military was present in all three cases yet should not account for the differences in outcome among the cases. Instead of analysing internal factors within the military to explain intervention, this study asks what makes public support for military intervention possible, by focusing on the problems facing the state which could undermine citizen support for democracy. In the cases of authoritarian takeovers of democracies, the military entered the political scene because the officers believed the civilian politicians to be incompetent. Aspects about the performance of the previous state were unacceptable.[85] Considering that many interventions are popularly supported, it appears that some citizens also believed that the performance of the state was lacking. The successful coups in Uruguay and in Peru were supported, at least initially, by the people. Instead of merely focusing on the actors in the destruction of a state, it is also necessary to ask why the government lost the support of a large number of citizens.

The explanatory power of these factors is mixed. In terms of economic crisis, all three countries faced significant challenges, although the Spanish democracy had a more developed economy, which could have made it more resilient. A focus on leadership directs attention to particular choices and actions, but is difficult to use as a predictor because of problems of a priori definition. The presence of cooperation to create and maintain democracy among political leaders may have aided democracy in Spain, but an excess of cooperation in regard to policy and power sharing frustrated problem solving in Uruguay. In Spain, many parties were new, although others had been established prior to the civil war. In two of the three case studies, the factor of strength or weakness of the political parties did not predict the ultimate outcome of democratic stability. Uruguayan democracy broke down, in spite of a stable party system and Spain's democracy consolidated despite its unstable party system. A focus on political systems predicted trouble for Uruguay and Peru. Both democracies that were overthrown, Uruguay and Peru, were multi-party presidential systems. The case of a successful, stable democracy, Spain, was a parliamentary system. The argument of parliamentary versus presidential system cannot be ruled out as a contributing factor to the ability of leaders to successfully address problems. In terms of international factors, no consistent pattern of effect can be seen. In both Uruguay and Peru, there was some foreign influence, but the evidence is contradictory. In Spain, international factors were both positive and negative.

The treatment of violence in the literature

One theme is recurrent in the literature. When violence is discussed as a possible threat to democratic stability, it is usually discussed in the context of legitimacy.[86] For example, in the case of Peru, Carol Graham states that under García, 'the political violence emanating from within the ranks of the governing party clearly demonstrated the lack of agreement on commitment to democratic practices and principles within the party, undermined the legitimacy of the state and surely exacerbated the political polarization process'.[87] In the case of Uruguay, Charles Gillespie believed that labour unrest alone probably would not have toppled the regime, but

> Labor militants had begun to scare managers and owners quite badly (especially when the factory occupations became violent and the Tupamaros began to kidnap businessmen). Uruguayan democracy became delegitimated in the eyes of businessmen for failing to protect their personal safety, liberty and property. Just as it appeared hollow to strike leaders who were detained in the barracks by the military.[88]

For Graham, the violence of the state undermined the legitimacy. For Gillespie, both the state violence and Tupamaro violence undermined legitimacy.

In the literature that discusses violence more generally, the tie to legitimacy is also important. Martha Crenshaw points out, 'in examining both the causes and consequences of terrorism, a central question is the relation between terrorism and political legitimacy, particularly in democratic states'.[89] Typically in the literature, the democratic response is analysed in the following manner. According to Cynthia McClintock, terrorist violence affects legitimacy because

> Government officials perceive a contradiction between respect for human rights and the defeat of the subversives. Civilian and military officials argue over the correct policy response. The democratic state loses its legitimacy both by reacting aggressively, without concern for the constitution, and by reacting more cautiously, and thereby possibly appearing ineffectual.[90]

In terms of the results of state violence, G. Bingham Powell also connects violence to legitimacy. Powell states:

> It is hard to escape the conclusion that the reactions of the democratic parties are at least as important as the terrorist strategies or the military sympathies. This point is emphasized when we consider another form of the use of violence: its employment by electoral parties or their supporters to intimidate opponents and mobilize backing... Such electoral violence also undermines the claim of democracy to be able to manage conflict through peaceful electoral processes, justifying the use of various coercive resources by any groups possessing them.[91]

However, how exactly does violence affect popular support? Wilkinson hints to performance versus process, stating that 'if the government, judiciary and police prove incapable of upholding the law and protecting life and property, its whole credibility and authority will be undermined'.[92] Is legitimacy the best concept to address this question?

Conclusion

This study is a comparative study of the consequences of state and terrorist violence on democratic stability in Uruguay, Peru, and Spain. How do people react to attacks and threats of state and terrorist violence? Does violence affect the citizen support of democracies? What is the basis of the citizen support of democracies? These are compelling questions. The Aristotelian approach described in the following chapters illuminates these issues in ways that other approaches to violence have not. The Aristotelian approach can explain how state and terrorist violence has effects more insidious and long lasting than previously thought, by referring to the purposes of the state and to the importance of the political community. Finally, the book will conclude with a discussion of the relevance of lessons learned from domestic terrorism to democracies facing an international terrorist threat.

Notes

1 Ted Gurr, 'Some Characteristics of Political Terrorism in the 1960s', in Michael Stohl (ed.), *Politics of Terrorism* (West Lafayette: Purdue University, 1988), p. 51.

2 Frederick Schultz, 'Breaking the Cycle: Empirical Research and Postgraduate Studies on Terrorism', in Andre Silke (ed.), *Research on Terrorism: Trends, Achievements and Failures* (New York: Routledge, 2004), pp. 183-184.

3 David Rapoport, 'General Introduction', David Rapoport (ed.), *Terrorism: Critical Concepts in Political Science* (New York: Routledge, 2006), p. xxvii.

4 Schultz, p. 183.

5 Russell Fitzgibbon, *Uruguay: Portrait of a Democracy* (New Brunswick: Rutgers University Press, 1954), p. vii.

6 Carina Perelli, 'From Counterrevolutionary Warfare to Political Awakening: The Uruguayan and Argentine Armed Forces in the 1970's', *Armed Forces and Society* Vol. 20, No. 1, Fall 1993, pp. 25-49, p. 35.

7 David Scott Palmer, 'Rebellion in Rural Peru', *Comparative Politics* Vol. 18, No. 2, January 1986, pp. 127-146, p. 130.

8 Ruth Berins Collier and David Collier, *Shaping the Political Arena* (Princeton: Princeton University Press, 1991), p. 13.

9 Theda Skopol and Margaret Somer, 'The Uses of Comparative History in Macrosocial Inquiry', *Comparative Studies in Society and History* Vol. 22, No. 2, April 1980, pp. 174-197, p. 176.

10 In Uruguay, the original Indian population fled or was killed off during colonization; no pure Churrúa and Chana Indians were left by 1850. Approximately 5-8 per cent of the population is mestizo, and this population is clustered along the northern border. Another small ethnic group of about forty to sixty thousand blacks lives in the north and is employed mainly in the meat packing 'Cerro' area. Martin Weinstein,

Uruguay: Democracy at the Crossroads (Boulder: Westview Press, 1988), p. 3.

11 Cynthia McClintock, 'The Prospects for Democratic Consolidation in a "Least Likely" Case: Peru', *Comparative Politics* Vol. 21, No. 2, January 1989, pp. 127–149, p. 129. See also Peter Klaren, 'Peru's Great Divide', *The Wilson Quarterly* Vol. 14, Summer 1990, No. 3, pp. 23–33, p. 29.

12 Alberto Adrianzén, *Democracia, etnicidad y violencia política en los países andinos* (Lima: IEP, 1993), p. 111.

13 James W. Wilke (ed.), *Statistical Abstract of Latin America*, Volume 23. (Los Angeles: UCLA Latin American Center Publications), p. 151.

14 Adam Przeworski, Michael Alvarez, José Cheibub, and Fernando Limongi, 'What Makes Democracies Endure?', *Journal of Democracy* Vol. 7, No. 1, January 1996, p. 49.

15 United Nations Development Programme, *Human Development Report 1999* (New York: Oxford University Press, 1999), pp. 151–152.

16 Kurt Weyland, in 'Latin America's Four Political Models', *Journal of Democracy* Vol. 6, No. 4, October 1995, pp. 125–140, highlights this connection. 'Poverty and inequality thus pose more urgent problems for democratic stability... The quality of democracy and indeed its very survival in the long run may require that poverty be reduced and popular hopes for social improvements be satisfied' (Weyland, p. 137). Nancy Bermeo concurs, stating 'economic crises might be a necessary though not sufficient incentive for the breakdown of authoritarian regimes'. Nancy Bermeo, 'Rethinking Regime Change', *Comparative Politics* April 1990, pp. 359–377, p. 366.

17 Juan Linz, *The Breakdown of Democratic Regimes: Crisis, Breakdown and Reequilibration* (Baltimore: Johns Hopkins, 1978), p. 10.

18 General Liber Seregni, *Discursos* (Montevideo: Bolsilibros ARCA 86, 1971), p. 14.

19 Charles Guy Gillespie, *Negotiating Democracy: Politicians and Generals in Uruguay* (Cambridge: Cambridge University Press, 1991), p. 44.

20 Edy Kaufman, *Uruguay in Transition: From Civilian to Military Rule* (New Brunswick: Transaction Books, 1979), p. 28.

21 *La Opinión* 18 July 1973.

22 Ronald H. McDonald, 'Electoral Politics and Uruguayan Political Decay', *Inter-American Economic Affairs* Vol. 26, No. 1, Summer 1972, pp. 25–46, p. 34.

23 Maxwell Cameron, *Democracy and Authoritarianism in Peru* (New York: St. Martin's Press, 1995), pp. 150–153.

24 Joel Podolny, 'The Role of Juan Carlos I and the Consolidation of the Parliamentary Democracy' in Richard Gunther, (ed.), Politics, Society and Democracy: The Case of Spain (Boulder: Westview Press, 1993), p. 90.

25 Podolny, p. 104.

26 Charles Powell, *El piloto del cambio* (Barcelona: Editorial Planeta, 1991), p. 17. Also see Charles Powell's book, *Juan Carlos of Spain* (Oxford: St. Anthony's College, 1996).

27 This criticism is analogous to Daniel Levine's criticism of the focus on elite pacts in the literature on redemocratization, such as in Guillermo O'Donnell, Phillippe Schmitter, and Laurence Whitehead's *Transitions*

from *Authoritarian Rule*: Tentative Conclusions about Uncertain Democracies (Baltimore: Johns Hopkins University Press, 1986). For example, 'the stress on pacts as antidemocratic manipulation ignores the ties that link the elites who make the pacts to popular groups, and thus obscures the reasons why the latter give them a grant of legitimacy.' Daniel Levine, 'Paradigm Lost: Dependence to Democracy', *World Politics* April 1988, p. 379.

28 See Raymond Carr and Juan Pablo Fusi, *Spain: Dictatorship to Democracy* (London: Unwin Hyman, 1981); José Maravall, *The Transition to Democracy in Spain* (London: St. Martin's Press, 1982); E. Ramón, Arango, *Spain: Democracy Regained* (Boulder: Westview Press, 1995). Other scholars focusing on cooperation include Donald Share, *The Making of Spanish Democracy* (New York: Westport, 1986). See also Omar Encarnacion, 'Social Concertation in Democratic and Market Transactions: Comparative Lessons from Spain', *Comparative Political Studies* Vol. 30, No. 4, August 1997, pp. 387–420; and Paloma Aguilar, 'The Memory of the Civil War in the Transition to Democracy: The Peculiarity of the Basque Case', *West European Politics* Vol. 21, No. 4, October 1998, pp. 5–25.

29 Weinstein, 1988, p. 34. See McDonald 1972, p. 44.

30 Larry Diamond and Juan Linz, 'Introduction', in Larry Diamond, Juan Linz, and S. M. Lipset (eds), *Democracy in Developing Countries: Latin America* (Boulder: Lynne Rienner, 1989), pp. 20–21. See also Scott Mainwaring, 'Political Parties and Democratization in Brazil and the Southern Cone', *Comparative Politics* Vol. 21, No. 1, pp. 91–120; Samuel Huntington, *Political Order in Changing Societies* (New Haven: Yale University Press, 1969); Robert Dix, 'Democratization and the Institutionalization of Latin American Political Parties', *Comparative Politics* Vol. 24, No. 4, January 1992, pp. 488–511; and Liliana de Riz, 'Política y partidos: ejercicio de análisis comparado: Argentina, Chile, Brasil y Uruguay', *Desarrollo Económico* Vol. 25, 1986, pp. 659–682.

31 Gillespie, 1991, p. 18.

32 See Adrianzén.

33 Francisco Sagasti and Max Hernandez, 'Crisis of Governance', in Joseph Tulchin and Gary Bland (eds), *Peru in Crisis: Dictatorship or Democracy* (Boulder: Lynne Rienner, 1994), p. 26.

34 Andrea Bonime-Blanc, *Spain's Transition to Democracy* (Boulder: Westview Press, 1986), p. 27.

35 Many scholars have argued that the order of founding elections was crucial to the new Spanish democracy. For example, Linz and Stepan argue: 'if the first elections in Spain had been regional, rather than union-wide, the incentives for the creation of all-union parties and an all-union agenda would have been greatly reduced'. Juan Linz and Alfred Stepan, 'Political Identities and Electoral Sequences: Spain, the Soviet Union, and Yugoslavia', *Daedalus* Vol. 121, No. 2, Spring 1992, pp. 123–140, p. 127. See also Fred A. Lopez III, 'Bourgeois State and the Rise of Social Democracy in Spain', in Ronald Chilcote (ed.), *Transitions from Dictatorship to Democracy* (New York: Crane Russak, 1990), p. 57 and Richard Gunther, P. Nikiforos Diamandouros, and Hans-Jurgen Puhle (eds), *The Politics of Democratic Consolidation* (Baltimore: Johns Hopkins University Press, 1995).

36 Mario Caciagli, 'Spain: Parties and the Party System in the Transition', in Geoffrey Pridham (ed.), *The New Mediterranean Democracies* (London: Frank Cass, 1984), pp. 85–87.
37 Caciagli, p. 85.
38 See Scott Mainwaring, 'Presidentialism, Multipartism, and Democracy', *Comparative Political Studies* Vol. 26, No. 2. 1993, pp. 198–228 for the argument that the combination of a multi-party system and presidentialism is detrimental to a stable democracy. See also César Cansino, 'Party Government in Latin America: Theoretical Guidelines for an Empirical Analysis', *International Political Science Review* Vol. 16, No. 2, 1995, pp. 169–182 and Juan Linz and Arturo Valenzuela (eds), *The Failure of Presidential Democracy* (Baltimore: Johns Hopkins University Press, 1994).
39 Gillespie, 1991, p. 31; also Cesar Aguiar, *Uruguay de los setenta: balance de una decada* (Montevideo: CIEDUR, 1981).
40 Kaufman, pp. 22–23. For a complete description and analysis of the Uruguayan electoral system, see Oscar Bottinelli's *El sistema electoral uruguayo: descripción y análisis*, Working Paper No. 1. (Montevideo: PIETHO, 1991).
41 Kaufman, pp. 26–27.
42 Cameron, 1995, p. 197.
43 For example, George Lopez, 'The National Security Ideology as an Impetus to State Terror', in Michael Stohl and George A. Lopez (eds), *Government Violence and Repression: An Agenda for Research* (New York: Greenwood Press, 1986). See also Richard Millet, 'Beyond Sovereignty: International Efforts to Support Latin American Democracy', *Journal of Interamerican Studies and World Affairs* Vol. 36, No. 3, Fall 1994, pp. 1–23.
44 P. Nikiforos Diamandorus, 'Southern Europe: A Third Wave Success Story', in Larry Diamond, Marc Plattner, Yun-han Chu, and Hung-mao Tien (eds), *Consolidating the Third World Democracies* (Baltimore: Johns Hopkins University Press, 1997), p. 7.
45 Weinstein, p. xiii.
46 *Generals and Tupamaros: The Struggle for Power in Uruguay 1969–1973* (London: Latin American Review of Books, 1974), p. 21.
47 Inter-Church Committee on Human Rights in Latin America *Violations of Human Rights in Uruguay (1972–1976)* (Toronto: Inter-Church Committee on Human Rights in Latin America, 1978), p. 16.
48 See Wilson Fernández, *El Gran Culpable: la responsabilidad de los E.E.U.I. en el proceso militar uruguayo* (Montevideo: Ediciones Atenea, 1986); and A. J. Langguth, *Hidden Terrors* (New York: Pantheon, 1978).
49 Arturo Porzencanski, *Uruguay's Tupamaros* (New York: Praeger, 1973), p. 54.
50 Fernández, p. 175.
51 Langguth, p. 131.
52 William Cantrell, Adolfo Saenz and later Dan Mitrione.
53 Porzencanski, p. 53.

54 Weinstein, p. 48.
55 Langguth, pp. 242, 96.
56 Perelli, pp. 25–26.
57 Perelli, p. 31.
58 Gillespie, 1991, p. 53, n. 11.
59 Cynthia McClintock, 'The War on Drugs: The Peruvian Case', *Journal of Interamerican Studies and World Affairs* Vol. 30, No. 23, Summer/Fall 1988, pp. 127–142, p. 132. This alliance nets Sendero as much as $30,000,000 annually. Henry Dietz, 'Peru's Sendero Luminoso As a Revolutionary Movement', *Journal of Political and Military Sociology* Vol. 18, Summer 1990, 123–150, p. 136. Not only did the policy result in a lucrative alliance for Sendero, it failed to reduce the amount of coca grown. Since 1988, the growers have shifted their activities north and anti-drug activity has become more dangerous for the individuals in the anti-drug campaign. The amount of coca produced has again increased. Another strategy was proposed in which strong herbicides would be sprayed on coca fields. However, this strategy met with resistance due to fears of reprisals on the South American operations of the companies that produced the herbicide and possible product liability. McClintock, 1988, p. 133.
60 Kenneth Roberts and Mark Peceny, 'Human Rights and United States Policy Toward Peru', in Maxwell Cameron and Philip Mauceri (eds), *Peruvian Labyrinth: Polity, Society, and Economy* (University Park, Pa.: Pennsylvania State University Press, 1997), pp. 213–217.
61 David Scott Palmer, 'Peru, the Drug Business and Shining Path: Between Scylla and Charybdis?', *Journal of Interamerican Studies and World Affairs* Vol. 34, No. 3, Fall 1992, pp. 65–89, p. 73. For a complete overview of the amount of economic and military aid, see the *Statistical Abstract of Latin America* (Wilke (ed.), p. 885.
62 David Scott Palmer, 'Collectively Defending Democracy in the Western Hemisphere', in Tom Farer (ed.), *Beyond Sovereignty: Collectively Defending Democracy in the Americas* (Baltimore: Johns Hopkins University Press, 1996), p. 273.
63 Abraham Lowenthal, 'Battling the Undertow in Latin America', in Larry Diamond, Marc Plattner, Yun-han Chu, and Hung-ao Tien (eds), *Consolidating the Third Wave Democracies: Themes and Perspectives* (Baltimore: Johns Hopkins University Press, 1997), pp. 58–59.
64 Tom Farer, 'Collectively Defending Democracy in the Western Hemisphere: Introduction and Overview', in Tom Farer (ed.), *Beyond Sovereignty: Collectively Defending Democracy in the Americas* (Baltimore: Johns Hopkins University Press, 1996), p. 7.
65 Claudio Grossman, 'The Organization of American States and the Protection of Democracy', in Tom Farer (ed.), *Beyond Sovereignty: Collectively Defending Democracy in the Americas* (Baltimore: Johns Hopkins University Press, 1996), p. 133.
66 'OAS Resolutions', US Department of State Dispatch, Washington; 29 Jun 1992, *US Department of State Dispatch* Vol. 3, No. 2, pp. 525–528.
67 *Washington Quarterly* Vol. 17, No. 2, Spring 1994, pp. 157–170.

68 John McCormick, *The European Union: Politics and Policies* (Boulder: Westview, 1999), p. 59.
69 Michael T. Newton with Peter J. Donaghy, *Institutions of Modern Spain* (Cambridge: Cambridge University Press, 1997), p. 6.
70 Richard Gillespie, 'Regime Consolidation in Spain', in Geoffrey Pridham (ed.), *Securing Democracy: Political Parties and Democratic Consolidation in Southern Europe* (London: Routledge, 1990), p. 132.
71 William Wallace, 'Rescue or Retreat? The Nation State in Western Europe, 1945-1993', in Peter Gowan and Perry Anderson (eds), *The Question of Europe* (New York: Verso, 1997), p. 42.
72 Carlos Closa, 'Spain: The Cortes and the EU – A Growing Together', *Journal of Legislative Studies* Vol. 1, No. 3, Fall 1995, pp. 136–150, p. 136.
73 McCormick, p. 59.
74 McCormick, p. 266.
75 Joint Action of 21 December 1998 adopted by the Council on the basis of Article K.3 of the Treaty on European Union, on making it a criminal offence to participate in a criminal organization in the member states of the European Union, *Official Journal* L 351 29/12/1998 pp. 0001–0003.
76 Council Decision of 3 December 1998, Article 1, EU Document 399D0130(02). See also EU Document 497Y0623(01).
77 Article 3, Convention relating to extradition between the member states of the European Union – Explanatory Report *Official Journal* C 191, 23/06/1997 pp. 0013–0026.
78 Brent Nelsen and Alexander C.-G. Stubb (eds), 'Preamble to the Single European Union Act' in *The European Union: Readings on the Theory and Practice of European Integration* (Boulder: Lynne Rienner, 1994), p. 46.
79 See EU proposal, 20 June 1999.
80 Richard Gillespie, 'The Continuing Debate on Democratization in Spain', *Parliamentary Affairs* Vol. 46, October 1993, pp. 534–548, p. 536.
81 Tanja A. Borzel, 'Shifting or Sharing the Burden? The Implementation of EU Environmental Policy in Spain and Germany', *European Planning Studies* Vol. 6, No. 5, 1998, pp. 537–553.
82 Gregory Treverton, *Spain: Domestic Politics and Security Policy* (Adelphi Papers 204, London: International Institute for Strategic Studies, 1986), p. 6.
83 Anatoly Krasikov, *From Dictatorship to Democracy: Spanish Reportage* (Oxford: Pergamon Press, 1984), p. 165.
84 J. Samuel Fitch, *The Armed Forces and Democracy in Latin America* (Baltimore: Johns Hopkins University Press, 1998), pp. 132–133.
85 An excellent, recent example of a study of military intervention is Peter Calvert and Susan Milibank, 'The Ebb and Flow of Military Government in Latin America', in William Gutteridge (ed.), *Latin America and the Caribbean: Prospects for Democracy* (Aldershot: Ashgate, 1997).

86 Some scholars have discussed the plausibility of violence as a cause of democratic breakdown in Uruguay, Peru, and Spain within the context of a combination of factors which weakened democracy. Certain scholars in particular have examined Uruguay in this way. For example, see Kaufman, p. 95; Ronald H. McDonald. 'The Rise of Militery Politics in Uruguay', *Inter-American Economic Affairs* Vol. 27, No. 4, Spring 1975, pp. 25–44, p. 27. Gillespie, 1991, p. 34; Cameron, 1995, pp. 147–148; Maravall, p. 62; Howard Wiarda, *The Transition to Democracy in Spain and Portugal* (Washington, D.C.: American Enterprise Institute for Public Policy Research, 1988), p. 14; Felipe Aguero, *Soldiers, Civilians, and Democracy* (Baltimore: Johns Hopkins Press, 1995). In general, one recent study has addressed the consequences of repression. Will Moore, 'Repression and Dissent: Substitution, Context and Timing', *American Journal of Political Science* Vol. 42, No. 3, July 1998, pp. 851–873, finds that dissidents will substitute violent protest for nonviolent protest and vice versa when faced with government repression. He found no evidence that contextual factors of authoritarian or democratic regimes affect this relationship or that there is a difference in effectiveness of repression in the short or long term.

87 Carol Graham, *Peru's APRA* (Boulder: L. Rienner Publishers, 1992), p. 137.

88 Gillespie, 1991, p. 39.

89 Martha Crenshaw, 'Thoughts on Relating Terrorism to Historical Contexts', in Martha Crenshaw (ed.), *Terrorism in Context* (University Park: Pennsylvania University Press, 1995), p. 7.

90 McClintock, 1989, p. 129.

91 G. Bingham Powell, *Contemporary Democracies: Participation, Stability and Violence* (Cambridge: Harvard University Press, 1982), p. 167.

92 Paul Wilkinson, 'Maintaining the Democratic Process and Public Support', in Richard Clutterbuck (ed.), *The Future of Political Violence* (New York: St. Martin's Press, 1986), pp. 177–178.

2
Aristotelian concepts applied to a comparative study of violence and democratic stability

Introduction

Some scholars in the philosophy of science argue for an Aristotelian approach to politics.[1] Certain Aristotelian concepts, approaches, and categories are useful to examine instability and are applicable to a comparative study of violence, repression, and democratic stability in Uruguay, Peru, and Spain. After the usefulness of these concepts and approaches is established, scholars may wish to revisit the more fundamental arguments raised by the Aristotelian approach. Without rejecting the importance of studies on the origin of violence, this study focuses on the possible consequences of the violence, once established.[2]

The limitations of conventional contemporary comparative politics

In terms of conceptualizing citizen support, most scholars of contemporary comparative politics operate within the general framework outlined by Max Weber. Typically, the state is defined by process or means, instead of ends or purposes. Max Weber provided a general definition of the state that has continued to influence contemporary scholars:

> Sociologically, the state cannot be defined in terms of its ends. There is scarcely any task that some political association has not taken in hand ... Ultimately, one can define the modern state sociologically only in terms of the specific means peculiar to it, ... we have to say that a state is a human community that claims the monopoly of the legitimate use of physical force.[3]

An example of a contemporary scholar following this tradition is Juan Linz, who defines the state in the following manner: 'a chief characteristic of the modern state is the monopoly of legitimate force in the hands of police and the military under the direction of political authorities'.[4]

According to Weber, there are three basic legitimations of domination: traditional, which would include habit and 'ancient recognition', charisma, and virtue of legality, which includes a 'belief in the validity of legal statute and functional "competence" based on rationally created rules'.[5] Today, the three main contemporary concepts of legitimacy (socialization, procedural, and evaluative) fit within the bounds espoused by Weber. David Easton's definition of legitimacy typifies concepts that are based on socialization. He identifies the objects of legitimacy, the political authorities, or the regime. Easton identifies three sources of legitimacy: ideological, structural, and personal.[6] Legitimacy is transmitted through socialization. An exemplar of the importance of process, Robert A. Dahl, in *A Preface to Democratic Theory*, defines legitimacy 'not in an ethical but in a psychological sense, *i.e.*, a belief in the rightness of the decision or the process of decision making'.[7] He identifies three areas of consensus necessary for a functioning polyarchy: procedural rules, scope of policy options, and range of legitimate political activity. He views legitimacy as a belief in the procedures of rule.

The conventional wisdom within the study of democracy is to conceptualize democracy based on procedural aspects of democracy and/or political liberties.[8] Beyond a minimalist definition based on elections, scholars disagree about what additional attributes should be included as part of the minimal standard for democracy.[9] A drawback of minimalist positions is that they may include authoritarian regimes as long as they have elections, even if they are not free. Because of this, some advocate including other aspects of procedural democracy, such as civil liberties or an expanded notion of accountability. Without these basic protections, elections can be easily subverted.[10] For example, in the influential work *Transitions from Authoritarian Rule*, Guillermo O'Donnell and Philippe Schmitter focus on a definition of democracy that builds upon a procedural minimum, including free and fair elections, universal suffrage, and political and civil liberties, to define democracy.[11] The inclusion of other attributes leads to a further differentiation of the concept, such as concepts of hybrid regimes, electoral democracy, semi-democracy, semi-authoritarianism, etc.[12] Although the advantages and disadvantages of a minimalist, subminimalist, liberal, and electoral democracy are discussed, rarely does the debate progress beyond proceduralism.

In the literature that deals with democratic breakdown or democratic consolidation, the concept of legitimacy used by Linz in his 1978 *Breakdown of Democratic Regimes* dominates the discussion. In general, legitimacy is considered to be a positive attitude towards the democracy and a belief that the democratic form of constitution is most appropriate for that nation.[13] Linz identifies three ways to anchor legitimacy: through a belief in the legitimacy of a regime, through habit, or through rational calculation. Linz highlights that the belief in a regime's legitimacy is particularly important in times of crisis. Habit in obeying a particular regime grows with time. Rational calculation involves evaluations of a regime's basic functions of efficacy and efficiency. These evaluations of a regime's effectiveness and efficacy seem to be biased 'by initial commitments to legitimacy'.[14] Linz defines the relationship between legitimacy and effectiveness and efficacy as circular. Efficacy is the 'capacity of a regime to find solutions to the basic problems facing any political system'. Effectiveness is the 'capacity actually to implement the policies formulated, with the desired results'. The basic functions are economic and social policies, the 'maintenance of civil order, personal security, the adjudication, and arbitration of conflicts, and a minimum of predictability in the making and implementation of decisions'.[15] The public evaluates a regime and awards legitimacy on the basis of these two functions: regime efficacy and effectiveness. In this discussion, there is no statement of why some things seem to matter more than others. Mentions of the need to 'maintain public order' and 'promote economic growth' are fragmentary and unconnected.

Process based concepts of legitimacy may be helpful to illuminate the origin of violence. In most of the studies that discuss terrorism, the discussion is focused on explaining the origin of this violence, not the consequences of it.

Perhaps this is a function of 'legitimacy'. In one example, Linz addresses the issue of political violence. He states that, typically, a challenger to a regime will dispute a regime's authority and its ability to maintain order. Linz suggests that political violence is usually not enough to explain regime breakdown, although he believes that the cause and effect overlap. In another example, Jorge Nef and Jokelee Vanderkop cite a system of violence to explain Peruvian conflict.

> In Peru, and for that matter in most of Latin America, violence is a manifestation of profound conflicts that exist in the society, the international system and within the state itself. It involves the inability of the contending social forces to reach political consensus – a lack of legitimation – as well as the incapacity of the government to exercise effective control. In this context, violence should not be perceived necessarily as abnormal or irrational, but as a particular form of conflict management coexisting with other non-violent forms.[16]

They believe that Peruvian society 'has tended to nurture ideologies which justify violence'.[17] Thus, violence may be expected to emerge when regimes are considered illegitimate. Moreover, many rebels, guerrillas, and revolutionaries justify their violence by attacking the legitimacy of the targeted regime.

However, to understand the consequences of violence, it is critical to identify exactly what the state is supposed to be doing. This link is largely absent in the concept of legitimacy, which fits with a notion of a state without ends. Within these contemporary definitions, there is little independent basis for the evaluation of whether a state, legitimate or illegitimate, is good or bad. The socialization based concepts do not help with questions of citizen evaluation of the state. The efficiency based concepts cannot satisfactorily explain what functions the state is expected to fulfil. The concept of legitimacy, while attempting to measure degrees of acceptance or rejection of authority which is helpful in understanding the emergence of terrorist groups, does not aid in understanding the consequences of violence.

Much of the field tries to eschew any normative dimensions in analysis. For example, Samuel Huntington states, 'Fuzzy norms do not yield useful analysis.'[18] Others, such as

Robert Keohane, have recognized a duty for political scientists to ask these types of questions. 'We need to reflect on what we, as political scientists, know that could help actors in global society design and maintain institutions that would make possible the good life in our descendants ... What normative standards should institutions meet, and what categories should we use to evaluate institutions according to those standards?'[19] Indeed, a focus on procedure alone may quickly produce sceptics among citizens. For example, the increasing disillusionment with democracy, thinly understood, is a growing problem in Latin America.[20]

Legitimacy rarely includes standards of evaluation necessary to understand these consequences. Evaluation becomes a critical foundation for state, and ultimately constitutional support, when history provides a choice of constitutional type and when habit based legitimacy is not strong. The Aristotelian approach provides a purpose or end based concept that is essential to understanding the consequences of terrorist and state violence.

The Aristotelian approach defined

Stephen Salkever describes the Aristotelian approach to politics not as a particular method, but rather as a series of questions which define the task of the social scientist. He states that the approach stems from three fundamental questions which

> have to do with how, given our specific nature and the various environmental circumstances we confront, communities can best solve the three great problems, which as *problems* are unique to the experience of human being: living, living together and living well.[21]

In order to answer the three questions, the scholar must call on many resources, philosophical and empirical, to pursue answers.

The Aristotelian approach, with its aim of achieving the highest good possible and its requirements of virtue, is inherently purpose or end oriented, while utilizing hypothesis testing, which is directed by the ends oriented nature of the work.[22] Salkever presents the approach as deliberation oriented as opposed to dogmatic. Accordingly, the Aristotelian approach is a way of thinking about political problems that encourages a conversation from various forms of inquiry.[23] The approach is a type of practical philosophy that is 'necessarily imprecise and in the form of an outline, and thus should be treated not as a source of definite answers to definite questions about how to act but rather as a preparation for informed deliberation in cases where no such answers are available'.[24] What this challenges the scholar to do is to consider problems and solutions within broader goals, such as a healthy, stable state, not just focusing on ending terrorism by any means.

How the Aristotelian approach differs from conventional comparative politics

According to Aristotle, the most practicable form of constitution is not always a form of rule by the many. This idea is rejected by many contemporary scholars.[25] He also believed that there were good forms of rule by one and rule by few. His standard is absolute justice: 'those constitutions which consider the common interest are right constitutions, judged by the standard of absolute justice. Those constitutions which consider only the personal interest of the rulers are all wrong constitutions, or perversions of the right forms' (*Pol.* p. 112). In cases of a corrupt form, instead of advocating revolution, Aristotle advocated reform. (He also suggests self-imposed exile.) Aristotle counsels us to examine each particular state, as is, and try to improve it in order to achieve the most possible stability, even if the best possible in that case is an inferior type.

This notion that there are better and worse forms of different forms is more acceptable in Latin America. For example, as Guillermo O'Donnell noted, there is a differentiation between the terms *dictadura* and *dictablanda*. A *dictadura* is a dictatorship that is particularly repressive. On the contrary, a *dictablanda* is seen as a more benign, sometimes even a partially good form of constitution. In the cases of Uruguay and Peru, the people abandoned their loyalty to their democratic constitutions in favour of a change to what they hoped would be a more practicable form of rule. In Peru, they supported Fujimori, who forcibly reformed their democracy with his *autogolpe*. In Uruguay, they supported the military, at least initially. Peruvians and Uruguayans had different expectations for the alternate constitutional forms; however, they had one thing in common: hopes for a more practicable form of rule. There was optimism that the new forms would be better. These hopes can be betrayed. Citizens can be misled or misunderstood. These hopes were betrayed in the case of Uruguay. There were hopes that the Uruguayan military would act as an aristocracy not as a tyrannous oligarchy that ruled by fear. In Peru, Fujimori ultimately lost power due to corruption scandals. It seems that the concept of acceptable forms of rule other than democracy is well established in many countries.

Instead of labelling states as corrupt based on principles of rule, Aristotle asks if they are oriented to the good.[26] Can this conception be compatible with a political science that predominantly believes that the science of politics should be value-neutral? Most contemporary scholars reject the teleological vision based on two objections: first that the teleological end cannot be demonstrated scientifically and could be used oppressively, and second that the teleological vision is hopelessly idealistic and therefore irrelevant to actual politics.

If something cannot be demonstrated scientifically, does that necessarily mean that it cannot be supported rationally? Even though the first principles may not be deduced from other principles, the teleology may be supported by argument, by inference, or by reason. Without falling back on dogmatism, it can be argued that some conceptions of the good are better or worse than others. Moreover, it is entirely possible that most, if not all, political scientists are committed to some conception of the good that implicitly guides their work. This can be shown by asking political scientists why they are interested in politics. If the practice of political science is only one intellectual curiosity among others, then the Aristotelian approach is not appropriate. However, if one believes that political science may be useful, perhaps that some genuine good may come out of it, then the individual probably has some conception of good behind their work, and this approach may not be inappropriate. Alasdair MacIntyre argues that teleology is not as uncommon as one may first suspect: 'there is no present which is not informed by some image of some future and an image of the future which always presents itself in the form of telos – or of a variety of ends or goals – towards which we are either moving or failing to move in the present.'[27]

Other critics may reject Aristotelian teleology on the basis that it is idealistic and irrelevant to the everyday imperfect politics and societies. Bernard Yack, in *Problems of a Political Animal*, counters this charge. The Aristotelian approach 'shows how even the imperfect politics of actual political communities can make human flourishing possible, it encourages us to use our understanding of the problems of a political community to identify the real possibilities for a good human life.'[28] Aristotle himself, in book IV, chapter 1 of the *Politics*, stresses the need to look for the practicable and the appropriate, as well as what would be ideally best in general and best given the circumstances (*Pol.* pp. 155–156).

What concepts and tools does the Aristotelian approach offer?

Certain Aristotelian concepts and tools can help to illuminate the consequences of terrorism and state repression on democratic stability in the political community. The evaluation of whether or not a state works for the common good and aims to help its citizens to flourish are issues that move to the forefront of the discussion when legitimacy is replaced by an Aristotelian approach. This Aristotelian concept of the purposes of the state provides explanatory power to understand the consequences of terrorism and state repression on democratic stability.

Specifically, the concept of a polis leads the scholar to look at a state in terms of its purposes. The political community upon which Aristotle bases his discussion is the *polis*. It is 'an association of households and clans in the good life ... The end and purpose of a polis is the good life, and the institutions of social life are means to that end' (*Pol.* p. 120). Aristotle criticizes those who view the state as an end for factors other than the cardinal factor of the good life, while still acknowledging the importance of the rudimentary purposes of the state. While the polis '*grows* for the sake of mere life, it *exists* for the sake of a good life' (*Pol.* p. 5).

Accordingly, Aristotle asks three questions of the constitution of a polis: what kind of authority is used, what is the end of the constitution, and is it well ordered (*Pol.* p. 156)? In asking this question, he seems to incorporate the other two factors (authority and end) and matches those factors with the particular body of people that makes up the state. Whether or not a state is well ordered is indicated by at least two factors: general approval and stability.

> The maintenance of a constitution is the thing which really matters... Legislators... must be on their guard against all the elements of destruction;... they must believe that the true policy, for democracy and oligarchy alike, is not one which ensures the greatest possible amount of either, but one which will ensure the longest possible life for both. (*Pol.* p. 267)

Again, Aristotle stresses citizen approval: 'the proper policy, wherever it can be pursued, is to keep all citizens alike attached to the constitution and the government under it, or at any rate, failing that, to prevent any citizen from regarding the government as his enemy' (*Pol.* p. 268). Even though it is difficult to measure the balance of forces within a state to determine whether or not the state is well balanced, stability and general approval are user friendly indicators of a well balanced state.

In most societies, the predominant notion of justice is based on reciprocity. Aristotle recognizes that the vast majority of political associations are not true *poleis*, that is they have not progressed to the second level of achieving human flourishing or complete virtue. Instead, these societies are based on exchange instead of virtue. Aristotle acknowledges that many people think that mere reciprocity is, without qualification, just (*NE* 1132b21-22, p. 117). Aristotle states:

> in associations for exchange this sort of justice does hold men together –... Men seek to return either evil for evil – and if they cannot do so, think their position mere slavery – or good for

good – and if they cannot there is no exchange, but it is by exchange that they hold together. (*NE* 1132b31-34, p. 118)

In these exchange based societies, the justice common, reciprocal, to them is also less stable and whole than other types of justice.

A new concept of citizen support derived from the Aristotelian approach

Instead of focusing on legitimacy, the notion that is so central to contemporary accounts, to explain political stability and instability, the Aristotelian approach looks to the purposes of the state to understand popular support, or lack thereof. This approach fundamentally differs from a process oriented understanding of legitimacy. This approach does not just ask whether or not the majority of the people acquiesce to authority or to an agreed upon process, but it attempts to introduce some broad standards, the purposes of the state, in terms of which to understand support of the state, and ultimately of the form of constitution. The notion of purposes of the state introduces two questions: are the rudimentary purposes being fulfilled and is the state attempting to move beyond the rudimentary purposes to achieve human flourishing? This linkage of purposes of the state with citizen evaluations is particularly applicable to the study of the granting or withdrawal of support for various regimes.

In the *Politics*, Aristotle draws a distinction between living and living well in political life. Stephen Salkever, in his commentary on the *Politics*, identifies two levels of the purposes of the polis. In the first level, some rudimentary conditions must be guaranteed before more ultimate purposes are even proposed. Salkever states, 'before it is possible to live well, it is necessary for us to live and to live together'.[29] To achieve this, stability and integration are necessary. 'Survival and internal tranquillity ... are only necessary conditions of virtue, but they are very necessary.'[30] The first level of purpose involves the achievement of the proximate goals of security and integration. As Leo Strauss says, 'the most urgent and primary task is self-preservation.' The second level entails achieving the goal of developing flourishing and virtuous citizens, or self-improvement.[31] Ultimately, however, the second threshold needs to be attempted, even if never achieved.[32] Aristotle recognizes that most political associations will never become true *poleis*; however, that does not mean they can abrogate their attempts to progress towards the ultimate end. However, in his emphasis on the second threshold, he does not minimize the importance of the first: 'for perhaps there is some simple element of the good in just living, so long as the evils of existence do not preponderate too heavily' (*Pol.* p. 111).

Sometimes the requirements of each level conflict with one another. Salkever characterizes the tension in Aristotelian thought as a conflict between stability and virtue, stating:

> Political organization and authority are not fully justified unless the laws and customs of that organization are reasonable means towards the development of healthy personalities, but the organization cannot continue to exist unless those same nomoi (laws and norms) are also reasonable means toward the stability and integration of the polis.[33]

More importantly, these purposes are not independent, tradable commodities. One cannot make up a lack of liberty, or any other benefit, with an excess of order or vice versa. To have a healthy state, one needs an appropriate balance of all these features.[34] Comparative judgments can be made among different goods but certain tradeoffs between various goods are unacceptable. For example, even if indiscriminate repression could quell terrorism, it would eliminate more than 'subversives', by destroying community, friendship, and justice and preventing any possibility of promoting the common good. This distinguishes the concept of purposes of the state from merely a list of functions necessary to maintain legitimacy. When it is a matter of the ends that constitute the good for human beings, it is not satisfactory to the Aristotelian to imagine a tradeoff between them in purely quantitative terms. This is especially relevant to a discussion of appropriate responses to terrorism, which are often dominated by the rhetoric of tradeoffs.

How can these rudimentary purposes be applied to a comparative study? It is possible to ask whether or not most people believe that their form of constitution is most appropriate. The good in politics implies asking what the state is supposed to be doing. Does the state exist to maintain a monopoly of the forces of coercion, or is it supposed to do something for its people? If a state should be doing something, what then should it be doing? What do its citizens expect of the state? The rudimentary purposes of the state, security and integration, can be quantified. This conceptualization enables the scholar to see the effects of terrorism and state repression on security and integration. Instead of other concepts that look to procedural grounds or to belief, this concept relates to purposes instead of processes. Using these ideas, it can be shown that if the state is not fulfilling its rudimentary purposes and making no effort to fulfil its ultimate purpose, then the citizens look to other forms of constitution that can. An idea of a well ordered constitution, the purposes of the state, and competing notions of justice are all important things to examine when studying instability. The Aristotelian approach provides a coherent framework within which to ask these questions.

Aristotle's contemporary applicability

Some political theorists and others have argued that the Aristotelian approach is inappropriate for incorporation into the contemporary study of politics. First of all, some charge, it is old and thus, presumably, out of date. Aristotle wrote approximately twenty-five hundred years ago. How could his theory be relevant today, in a context much different from that in which Aristotle lived and wrote?[35]

One critic of the application of classical Greek theory to contemporary problems is Stephen Holmes. Holmes attacks two claims of classical thought: that there are 'true' purposes and that 'individuals, being thoroughly "political animals" can fully realize themselves in political participation'.[36] Moreover, he claims that modern politics cannot be conceived of as a whole.[37] Undeniably, the ancient definition of politics was more encompassing than the modern. However, that does not mean that the connections which the ancients more readily recognized do not exist in modern life. Nichols responds to the charges of Holmes by elaborating three levels of political thought set out earlier by Leo Strauss in 1964. They are 'philosophic principles, analysis of a given society, and immediately available prescriptions for political action'.[38] Nichols claims that any failure to recognize these different levels would make any political theory, from any foreign or temporally distinct context, obsolete. Nichols defends proposing philosophic principles from other times and contexts as possibly helpful. This illumination is not automatic, but relies on the analysis of given societies and an analysis of their principles. Whether or not prescriptions for action can be drawn from them is a matter of prudence, moderation, and empirical analysis. Another possible objection to using an approach inspired by Aristotle and contemporary commentators on his work is that contemporary democracy is significantly different from ancient democracy. Aristotle broadly defines democracy as a constitution in which 'the freeborn and poor control the government – being at the same time a majority'. (*Pol.* p. 164). Although the modern democracy is different in that the citizens do not directly rule but instead vote for representatives, the modern democratic state would still be considered a democracy for Aristotle since the poor majority has the same rights to vote and participate in the government as do the rich. It is consistent with Aristotle's statement that 'in this variety [of democracy] the law declares equality to mean that the poor are to count no more than the rich' (*Pol.* p. 167). This definition is similar to earlier definitions of democracy used in comparative politics, such as Lord Bryce's definition in his *Modern Democracies*, and used by Russell Fitzgibbon in his 'The Pathology of Democracy in Latin America'. The definition reads 'that form of government in which the ruling power of the state is legally vested ... in the members of the community as a whole'.[39]

Despite the vast differences between Aristotle's time and the historical situation in parts of the contemporary world, there is one key similarity that is worth noting. Aristotle wrote in times of political turbulence and tried to formulate a political theory in the context of this instability. Finley characterizes the typical politics of Aristotle's day as unstable. 'In city after city there was an oscillation between oligarchy and democracy, accompanied by civil war, wholesale killing, exile and confiscation. Sometimes tyrants intervened, adding another dimension.'[40] Political instability was prevalent during Aristotle's time, as it was in much of the world in the twentieth century, thus lending contemporary relevance to the questions inspired by ancient instability.

The theory

Instead of legitimacy, this approach provides a notion of purposes of the state. It is theorized that violence attacks the first level of rudimentary purposes of the state, preventing progress towards the second level. In addition, attacks of violence create fear and mistrust. Safety becomes a good in high demand. More and more people react by becoming less active politically and more isolated, further weakening the political community. As violence undermines the purposes of the state and as citizen confidence decreases, more opportunities for groups or individuals to act against the state emerge. And, as citizens become frustrated with the lack of fulfilment of the rudimentary purposes, they are more likely to support attacks against the state.

Terrorist and state violence are theorized to be causes of democratic breakdown. Resulting instability, however, is not automatic. Violence creates opportunities for others to act against the state. Whether or not those opportunities are realized is influenced by other factors. Before attempting to identify the consequences of violence, certain historical and contextual issues must be clarified. Acceptable levels of violence and forms of authority need to be determined to distinguish when levels have become critical and what other models of authority and governance are available. The military must be studied, since most attacks against democracy involve indirect or direct military support and action.

Acceptable form of authority

First, if the current state, and ultimately constitutional form, cannot fulfil its state purposes, people are likely to search for options to replace that state, and ultimately constitutional form, with some form that is capable of fulfilling its rudimentary purposes. After an erosion of citizen support, the possibility exists for people to attempt to destroy the constitution with popular support.[41] The available choices depend on each country's history and circumstance. If democratic leaders are perceived incapable of ending society's ills, then a different type of constitution, such as a military regime or rule by one, could be considered. Previous constitutional forms present themselves as handy, accessible options. Habits and norms inculcated during a previous constitutional form linger. However, it is worth noting that it is difficult to replace military rule if the military leadership is unwilling to relinquish power or if there is not a subgroup in the military that is willing to initiate a coup against the current leadership. It must be acknowledged that the military has the coercive capabilities to resist attempts to remove it from power, unlike civilian leaders who rely upon the military to obey them and who are vulnerable to military intervention.

Level of violence

Second, although it is ideal to have a political association that is free from all violence, many times that is not possible. In most countries, a certain level of violence is expected and almost impossible to eliminate within normal means. Throughout history, some countries have been afflicted more than others and some times are more turbulent than others. The reason behind different acceptable thresholds is not my concern. What appears to be salient is a marked increase in the violence or the reaching of a new plateau, beyond what is expected.

The military

Third, the military is especially important in areas plagued by political instability. Many times it is the only institution with a permanence extending past the last constitutional form. In every case of this study, those who successfully act against the state do so with the blessing of the military.

> **Hypothesis one**
>
> Terrorist violence threatens democratic stability by undermining both rudimentary purposes of the state, security, and integration. As the purposes of the state are unfulfilled, citizen confidence in the state declines. As citizen confidence decreases, democratic instability increases.
>
> **Hypothesis two**
>
> State repression and violence undermine the rudimentary purposes of the state, integration, and security. Decreases in citizen confidence should follow a decrease in the fulfilment of the rudimentary purposes. Finally, as citizen confidence in the state decreases, increases in democratic instability should be identifiable.

Security

In Aristotelian terms, both state and terrorist violence can create further instability. Specifically, violence creates fear and a desire for safety. If the state does not successfully respond to violence, fear and a lack of safety undermine the state, and possibly ultimately the constitutional form, at the rudimentary level of state purposes. Specifically, in situations with rampant violence, fear is a common emotion. Wrongdoers fear punishment and law abiding citizens fear victimization. Fear indicates a lack of safety, or at least a perception of a lack of safety. Fear of becoming a victim and contempt for those in power for their inability to deal with the problem provide potential support for people to attempt to overthrow the state. If a significant portion of the community believes it is the victim of injustice, then additional support for change could develop within the affected group. This can be seen with the emergence of violent groups on the right, in response to the groups on the left. Attitudes of superiority and concern for safety or honour can result in contempt for those in power, and ultimately support for change by the affected group.

Integration

Violence also undermines the second rudimentary purpose of the state: integration. It is expected that violence will encourage mutual suspicion and enmity and discourage people from attempting to achieve common goals, from deliberating in common affairs, and from actively engaging in politics. In healthy communities, in the Aristotelian sense, peers deliberate, participate, and act to further both individual and common goals. Violence encourages fear, creates intolerance, and becomes a hindrance to participation.

The treatment of justice is extremely complex in Aristotle's work. For the purpose of this study, only the type of justice applicable to exchange based societies is relevant. Exchange based societies are not bound by a common pursuit of the good and use a concept of reciprocal justice. Reciprocal justice is based on the idea of a proportionate return, somewhat like the idea of 'tit for tat'. Violence can undermine political stability by creating situations of unequal exchange (*NE* 1130a15-1132b20, pp. 110–116). The victims and those who feel they could be victims desire a response to restore balance to this exchange. But, in a situation where it is not always known who is responsible, it is not easy to restore the reciprocity. As Aristotle states, 'the well-being of every polis depends on each of its elements rendering to the others an amount equivalent to what it received from them' (*Pol.* p. 41). Random acts of violence, such as the detonation of bombs in crowded civilian areas or indiscriminate repression, begin to unravel the social ties. State sponsored repression isolates people, making mutual distrust common. Participation in politics becomes dangerous. The focus on indiscriminate repression and violence is essential to capture the concept of an uneven exchange. If the state uses limited violence targeted only at those who practise it, then it is acting to render an equivalent response. This would not be acting against reciprocal justice. Aristotle's discussion of tyrants provides a way of understanding repressive responses to political dissension, real or feared. A repressive response is one in which the state punishes in an indiscriminate manner. Indiscriminate repression is also an uneven exchange in terms of reciprocal justice. This way of understanding repressive responses helps one understand how they can undermine democratic stability. The effects of violence then spread. 'An offense against the laws destroys those possible relationships which make common pursuit of the good possible; defective character, while it may also render someone more liable to commit offenses, makes one unable to contribute to the achievement of that good without which the community's common life has no point.'[42] Violence, an uneven exchange in terms of reciprocal justice, can undermine the political association at the very first level of stability. The concept of the purposes of the state helps to illuminate the specific causality behind this. Indiscriminate repression might be effective in eliminating attacks on the state, but it is also very successful in eliminating the conditions necessary for a healthy community.

Both terrorist and state violence erode citizen confidence. If the state unsuccessfully deals with the initial violence, other factions within society start to believe they could handle the situation better. In many cases, the other faction is the military. Moreover, if the military is handed this role and succeeds, then there is the risk that this will change the composition of the state, and open up the possibility that some may act against the state. Aristotle warns that 'constitutions may also be changed . . . as a result of the growth in reputation or power of one of the magistracies, or of some other part of the state' (*Pol.* p. 213). This problem becomes especially salient during times of an internal conflict, in which the military may be called in to suppress a violent insurrection. Success of the military and growth of its prestige increases the possibility of the emergence of some military men to seize power. The rule of the military or one leader can be viewed as a more practicable form of constitution, if the existing form has demonstrated its inability to fulfil its two rudimentary purposes. This implies that it is conceivable that citizens would support the rule of the one or of the few over the rule by the many. The appeal to people in these cases is not whether or not the military will act democratically but whether or not the military will act effectively to fulfil the purposes of the state. Of course, the hopes of the people can be betrayed. The new constitutional form might turn out to be worse than an ineffective, enfeebled democracy.

Conclusion

The incorporation of certain Aristotelian concepts promises to illuminate the issues of violence and democratic instability in ways that other approaches to violence have not. Terrorist and state violence have effects more insidious and long lasting than previously thought. The Aristotelian approach can explain this by referring to the purposes of the state and to the importance of the political community.

To begin such a study, an assessment of the constitution is necessary. Upon what kind of authority is the state based? What is the end of the constitution: common or private benefit? Is the state well ordered? Aristotle provides two indicators for a well ordered state: general approval and stability. Stability is identifiable, but what about general approval? Understanding public opinion within the context of the political community and using the purposes of the state as guidelines allows a better understanding of seditious violence and its consequences.

How do terrorist and state repressive violence threaten the fulfilment of state purposes? How well a state is achieving its purposes provides a basis for this understanding and appraisal, rather than to what extent the state has achieved legitimacy as it is currently understood in most of social science. The concept of the purposes of the state illuminates the way in which terrorist and state repressive violence challenge the stability of democracy. The two levels of purposes of the state give insight into how an exclusively military and indiscriminate response to terrorist violence can succeed in eliminating terrorism and providing security, but at the expense of harming the integration of the community. Destruction of the first level makes progress towards the second level of achieving living well or the good impossible. In addition, this perspective allows us to understand why authoritarian regimes initially can enjoy popular support.

These concepts help us to understand the following events. In Uruguay, the military began assuming more power to respond, in a repressive manner, to the terrorist violence. Ultimately, it took power in 1973. In Peru, Fujimori, in 1992, responded repressively and consolidated control by dissolving Congress and suspending the judicial process, with the blessing of the military. In both these countries, a predominantly repressive response to terrorism was chosen. Subsequently, with their success in suppressing the terrorist violence came an initial growth of reputation for the military and contempt for the democratic form of rule. Ultimately, this led to democratic breakdown. Spain resisted the repressive response to terrorist violence and successfully consolidated its democracy. The application of the Aristotelian approach to the question of the consequences of terrorist and state repressive violence on democratic stability yields clarity for the cases of Uruguay, Peru, and Spain.

Notes

1 See the works of Stephen Salkever, Martha Nussbaum, Leo Strauss, Bernard Yack, and Alasdair MacIntyre, listed in the Select Bibliography. Unless otherwise noted, all citations from the *Politics* are from Ernest Barker's translation, *Politics* (London: Oxford University Press, 1958); and citations from the *Nicomachean Ethics* are from David Ross's translation (New York: Oxford University Press, 1992). The following abbreviations will be used in referring to works by Aristotle: Pol. = *Politics*; NE = *Nicomachean Ethics*.

2 Most studies of seditious violence, revolution, terrorism, and insurgency view violence primarily as a symptom of other problems. Correspondingly, much emphasis is given to the origins of violence. Typically, if terrorist violence is considered to be a strain on democratic stability in its own right, it is considered a threat to legitimacy.

3 Max Weber, 'Politics as a Vocation', in H. H. Gerth and C. Wright Mills (eds), *From Max Weber: Essays in Sociology* (New York: Oxford University Press, 1946), pp. 77–78.

4 Linz, 1978, p. 58.

5 Weber, p. 79.

6 David Easton, *A Systems Analysis of Political Life* (New York: John Wiley and Sons, 1965), pp. 289–310.

7 Robert A. Dahl, *A Preface to Democratic Theory* (Chicago: University of Chicago Press, 1960), 46n.

8 Geraldo Munck and J. Verkuilen, 'Conceptualizing and Measuring Democracy: Evaluating Alternative Ideas', *Comparative Political Studies* Vol. 35, No. 1, 2002, pp. 5–34; David Collier and Steven Levitsky, 'Democracy with Adjectives: Conceptual Innovation in Comparative Research', *World Politics* Vol. 49, No. 3, April 1997, pp. 430–451; Kenneth Bollen and Pamela Paxton, 'Subjective Measures of Liberal Democracy', *Comparative Political Studies* Vol. 13, No. 1, 2000, pp. 58–86.

9 Collier and Levitsy 1999, p. 433; O'Donnell et al., Giuseppe Di Palma, *To Craft Democracies: An Essay on Democratic Transitions* (Berkeley: University of California Press, 1990), p. 28; Samuel Huntington, *The Third Wave: Democratization in the Late 20th Century* (Norman, OK: University of Oklahoma Press, 1991), p. 9; Adam Przeworski, Michael Alvarez, José A. Cheibub, and Fernando Limongi, *Democracy and*

Development: Political Institutions and Material Well-Being in the World 1950–1990 (New York: Cambridge University Press, 2000).

10 Scott Mainwaring, D. Brinks, and A. Pérez-Liñán, 'Classifying Political Regimes in Latin America, 1945–1999', *Studies in Comparative International Development* Vol. 36, No. 1, 2001, pp. 37–65, pp. 41–43.

11 O'Donnell et al., p. 8.

12 Terry Karl, 'The Hybrid Regimes of Central America', *Journal of Democracy* Vol. 6, No. 3, 1995, pp. 72–86; Andres Schedler, 'Elections without Democracy: The Menu of Manipulation', *Journal of Democracy* Vol. 13, No. 2, 2002, pp. 36–50.

13 Linz, 1978, p. 16.

14 Linz, 1978, p. 18.

15 Linz, 1978, p. 20.

16 Jorge Nef and J. Vanderkop, 'The Spiral of Violence: Insurgency and Counter-insurgency in Peru', *Canadian Journal of Latin American and Caribbean Studies* Vol. 9, No. 17, 1988, pp. 53–72, p. 56.

17 Nef and Vanderkop, p. 59.

18 Huntington, p. 9.

19 Robert O. Keohane, 'Governance in a Partially Globalized World', *American Political Science Review* Vol. 95, No. 1, 2001, pp. 1–13, p. 1.

20 Latinobarómetro 2002. 'Informe de prensa'. Available online at www.latinobarometro.org/ano2002.htm.

21 Stephen Salkever, 'Aristotle's Social Science', *Political Theory* Vol. 9, No. 4, November 1981, pp. 479–508, p. 503. It should be noted that Salkever is using 'method' as in the different methods that are associated with specific disciplinary divisions, such as moral philosophy, specific social sciences, and political theory. Some scholars may insist that Aristotle used the method of dialectic in his own studies. Salkever is not referring to Aristotelian dialectic in this statement.

22 Salkever, 1990, p. 58.

23 Salkever, 1990, p. 7.

24 Salkever, 1990, p. 4.

25 It is not uncommon to find normative references such as Guillermo O'Donnell, Philippe Schmitter and Laurence Whitehead's statement that 'political democracy constitutes per se a desirable goal.' O'Donnell et al., p. 3.

26 The *polis*, like an individual, does not automatically progress towards its final end. Aristotle states, 'the polis belongs to the class of things that exist by nature, and that man is by nature an animal intended to live in the polis' (*Pol.* p. 5). The *polis* is not strictly natural, in the sense that its capacities will automatically be realized if nothing interferes with the realization, much like an acorn developing into a tree. The polis is natural in the sense that it exists in virtue of human beings whose natures require the polis to fully develop their capacities.

27 Alasdair MacIntyre, *After Virtue* (Notre Dame: University of Notre Dame Press, 1984), p. 215.

28 Bernard Yack, *The Problems of a Political Animal: Community, Justice and Conflict in Aristotelian Political Thought* (Berkeley: University of California Press, 1993), p. 10.
29 Salkever, 1981, p. 492.
30 Salkever, 1981, p. 492.
31 Leo Strauss, *The City and Man* (Chicago: University of Chicago Press, 1964), p. 6.
32 The component of attempting to achieve the good is inseparable from the Aristotelian approach. It would be inconsistent to call an approach Aristotelian that denied the value component. However, this does not mean that the approach needs to be disregarded by those who disagree with the incorporation of empirically unverifiable aspects. The orientation of the study is directed by the quest for the good; however, an empirical component remains, one that still may be examined according to those who may disagree with the approach in general.
33 Salkever, 1981, p. 492.
34 Martha Nussbaum, 'Human Functioning and Social Justice: In Defense of Aristotelian Essentialism', *Political Theory* Vol. 20, No. 2, May 1992, pp. 202–246, p. 231.
35 There are two additional criticisms that should be noted. Scholars such as John Wallach criticize the neo-Aristotelians as disingenuous in their use of Aristotle because of the separation of the 'essential' Aristotle from the aspects of his thought which are historically conditioned or unacceptable to them. Wallach characterizes 'Aristotelian' authors as using Aristotle as an authority and as a philosophical anchor instead of as an inspiration. It is true that these interpretations do differ from Aristotle's political thought in issues not considered essential to his political thought. Whether the application is relevant should be probed through application and theory testing.
36 Stephen Holmes, 'Aristippus In and Out of Athens', *APSA* Vol. 73, March 1979, pp. 113–128, p. 113.
37 Holmes, p. 126.
38 James H. Nichols, 'On the Proper Use of Ancient Political Philosophy: A Comment on Stephen Taylor Holmes's "Aristippus In and Out of Athens,"', *APSA* Vol. 73, March 1979, pp. 129–134, p. 129.
39 Russell Fitzgibbon, 'The Pathology of Democracy in Latin America: A Political Scientist's Point of View', *American Political Science Review* Vol. 44, 1950, pp. 118–129, p. 118.
40 M. I. Finley, *Politics in the Ancient World* (Cambridge: Cambridge University Press, 1983), p. 101.
41 Aristotle defines a constitution as 'the organization of the polis, in respect of its offices generally, but especially in respect of that particular office which is sovereign in all issues'; *Pol.* p. 110.
42 MacIntyre, p. 152.

3
A historical overview of Uruguay, Peru, and Spain

Introduction

This chapter presents a brief historical overview of the three cases. The presentation is organized to provide the necessary background to understand the consequences of state and terrorist violence for democratic stability. Specifically, acceptable forms of authority, historical precedent of violence, prior role of the military, and economic crisis are explored in the cases of Uruguay, Peru, and Spain.

Introduction to Uruguay

Although Uruguay was stable during the first fifty years of the twentieth century, nineteenth-century Uruguay was chaotic. Uruguay's independence was wrested from neighbouring Brazil and Argentina and the colonizing powers with the help of the gaucho chieftain José Gervasio Artigas and the group of thirty-three. After independence in 1828, Uruguay was embroiled in intrigue among Paraguay, Brazil, and Argentina. The intrigue culminated in a five year War of the Triple Alliance (Uruguay, Brazil, and Argentina) against Paraguay. With the end of the war, Uruguay was able to focus on domestic affairs. During the rest of the century, Uruguay experienced conflict between the church and state, civilians and military officers, and the two main political parties, the Blancos and the Colorados. The conflict between the two parties continued with intermittent struggles until they agreed in 1872 to a pact of cooperation that followed two years of intense conflict. This pact guaranteed the Blancos some of the advantages of office, through control over four of the country's departments. However, the peace between the parties was broken with the Blanco revolt of 1897 which was led by Aparacio Saravia. The revolt turned into a civil war. During the war, José Batlle y Ordóñez was elected president, serving from 1903–1907. The civil war ended with the death of Saravia at the battle of Masoller in 1904.

Since the end of the civil war in 1904, Uruguay had been peaceful. Elections were without violence, the military stayed out of politics, the parties shared power and cooperated, and labour relations were good.[1] Claude Williman succeeded Batlle as president (1907–1911) and continued with Batlle's basic policies. Batlle was reelected president and served from 1911 to 1915. Batlle's innovative policies included many reforms, including free primary and secondary education, the eight hour workday, pensions, and the rights to strike, to organize, and to vote.[2]

The spirit of participation in the 1872 agreement reemerged in the constitutional form of the *Colegiado*. During part of this century (1919–1933, 1952–1967), the Uruguayan executive was a *Colegiado*, an executive council formed of nine members. The nominal positions of president and vice-president were rotated among the members. Of the nine, six were from the majority party and three from the minority party. Administrative positions were also similarly divided between the two parties.[3]

In 1931, President Gabriel Terra broke the political calm. Terra faced strong opposition for his depression era economic and social policies from the National Assembly and the *Colegiado*. In 1931, Terra responded by dissolving both bodies, ruling by decree, and creating a new constitution. The 1934 constitution eliminated the *Colegiado* and returned Uruguay to a single executive. Martin Weinstein calls the coup a response by heavy-handed politicians, 'driven by personal vendetta and ambition' to an economic crisis. This period has been called a dictatorship, but it must be noted that freedom of speech and most individual rights were respected during the time. There were no torture, murder, or political prisoners. Moreover, the military was not involved.[4] Shortly after, in 1935, part of the army attempted a coup, but it failed.[5] In 1950, with the election of Andrés Martínez Trueba, a Colorado Batllista, the country returned to the executive council.

In 1954 scholar Russell Fitzgibbon described Uruguay as a 'staunch little democratic outpost'.[6] The small country was renowned for its high standard of living, democratic commitment, education, social services, and stability. Its experience was unique in Latin America. As Charles Gillespie points out, the military was not seething, waiting for democracy to fail. Instead, there was a strong, stable party system, a long history of avoidance of ideological polarization, the sharing of power among the major parties, and a high level of political learning.[7] The two traditional parties of Uruguay, the Blancos and the Colorados, are as old as modern Uruguay. The party system is one of the two oldest in Latin America (Chile's is the other). Its party system even predates many European party systems.[8] The Colorados are typically urban notables, Italian immigrant descendants, lawyers, intellectuals, and businessmen. The Blancos are usually traditional elites and large landowners.[9] In addition to a stable party system, Uruguay had an impressive public education system. Since the 1877 Lorenzo Latorre administration, public education has been free, secular, and compulsory. During much of the twentieth century, Uruguay had the largest expenditure for education in Latin America. The University of the Republic is free and all may enrol provided they finish secondary school.[10]

In the twentieth century, the Uruguayan military was known for its apolitical attitude, small budget and size, and strict civilian control over the organization.[11] The old attitude of military subservience to civilian authority was communicated as late as 1966. In 1966, the Inspector General of the army, Hugo Tirobochi, stated in response to uncertainty about the lawful change in the 1966 constitution:

> I am firmly disposed to respect and to make respected all electoral acts and pronouncements derived from those acts as the supreme expression of the will of the citizens and sovereign will of our nation recognized by the Constitution of the Republic. Nothing or no one can wrest us from the norms that guide us, we have contracted a commitment of honor and we will honor it to the end, giving anew an example to the world of the pride of the nation and to all of you to make us worthy of your respect and admiration.[12]

This attitude of subservience to civilian authority soon dissipated. Only seven years later, the military dissolved the National Assembly and took control.

As Uruguay moved into the 1970s, the Uruguayan constitution (in the broad Aristotelian sense) appeared to be less well ordered. Due to labour disputes, a state of siege (or medidas prontas de seguridad) was declared in 1965. The first four invocations of the state of siege were in response to labour disputes. This new strategy for dealing with strife was applied later to the disorder caused by the guerrilla group, the Tupamaros. By the 1970s, general approval of the Uruguayan government sagged and terrorism became more prevalent. The democratic principle of authority became overshadowed by recourse to a tyrannical style of governance with presidential decrees and the limitation of citizen participation. In response, fewer Uruguayans felt attached to the Uruguayan state and more began to view it as the enemy.

The military also began to issue policy demands to the civilian authorities. For example, in April 1972 the military demanded that President Bordaberry and the National Assembly decree a state of internal war with a cancellation of individual liberties, which they did.[13] One month later, in May 1972, the military demonstrated more independence. As the state of internal war was about to expire, the joint command of the armed forces and the police, both generals, demanded that it be extended. Rumours circulated that a coup may have resulted had Bordaberry not agreed. Bordaberry bolstered his support within the National Assembly by forming a coalition with the Blanco Echegoyen faction, a faction whose members fully approved of the state of internal war. This deal, however, fell apart with the pressure from some constitutionalist military officers who preferred a political solution to the problem. The constitutionalist faction of the military was concerned about the demoralization of some troops and the undisciplined behaviour of others, for example the use of torture and creation of some anti-terrorist groups.[14]

The military also began to defy orders from the civilian authorities. For instance, in April 1972 some in the National Assembly called for public exposure and punishment of those responsible for the most visible abuses in allegations of torture. Six hundred military officers responded with a resolution to prevent public censor.[15] The response demonstrates the increased politicization of the military. The military's growing independence and its defiance of civilian authority grew more serious in the autumn of 1972. In response to strikes, Bordaberry wanted to use the military to crack down on labour. The military refused and pushed for an increase in wages, siding with the workers. The military did not want to be implicated in an economic policy that they did not create.[16]

The military openly defied Bordaberry twice in October 1972. The colonel in charge of a base where four doctors were held prisoner refused to release them, despite court orders to do so. In response, Defence Minister Legnani directly ordered the colonel to release the men, but the colonel still refused. Minister Legnani resigned in frustration. The second incident occurred after an inquiry into an illegal financial dealing. The military had led an investigation that resulted in the arrest of over one hundred people. Senior officers and Bordaberry agreed that the findings and further inquiry should be turned over to a special committee. The investigating officers, many of them captains and their superior colonels, refused to hand over the documents or terminate their investigation.[17]

What had been known as Uruguayan exceptionalism came to an end in 1973, and with it one of the most stable and prosperous democracies in the Western hemisphere. Military intervention was carried out in what has become known as the 'slow coup'. The military assumed power in two steps. In February 1973, branches of the military revolted. On 7 February, Bordaberry had replaced Dr Armando Malet with retired General Francese as minister of defence. The commanders-in-chief refused to recognize Francese's authority. Bordaberry wanted a new minister of defence to break up the 'commands of the more independent minded military branches'. Instead, he faced a rebellion.[18] On the 8th, Minister of Defence Francese informed Bordaberry that the army and air force were to be confined to the barracks, as a precaution against disturbances. After the meeting, Bordaberry ordered the commander of the marines to confine marine troops to the barracks as well. The general command of the army, General Hugo Chiappe Posse, and air force commander General José Peréz announced their reasons for ignoring the orders of Francese. Shortly after, they demanded his resignation. Army General Esteban

Cristi directed the army to take control of some television stations. Francese offered his resignation to Bordaberry, who refused to accept it. That night, Bordaberry appealed to the public over radio and television to defend the institutions. Less than one hundred people showed up to protest the military defiance.

The army continued to occupy more and more radio and television stations. On the 9th, the army occupied the old city of Montevideo, isolating the other ministers and most of the judges, and assumed combat positions near the canal. The marines proclaimed themselves loyal to the president. Late on the 9th and early on the 10th, communiqués four and seven were released by the rebelling forces. Communiqué four demanded the elimination of unemployment, subversion, and calls for land reform. Communiqué seven called for the preservation of sovereignty and security, the pursuit of development and modernization, and further benefits for the citizens, such as better health care. The document denied any partisan affiliation.[19] On Sunday, the 11th, communiqué five was released. It announced control of the country by the police, the army, and the air force. The commanders of the army and air force demanded that Bordaberry remove the loyal commander of the marines. Bordaberry complied. On Monday the 12th, Bordaberry announced that he was essentially in agreement with the goals of the armed forces. On Tuesday the 13th, Bordaberry met with the military commanders at the Boiso Lanza air force base. The meeting concluded with a pact among them and a new defence minister, Dr Walter Ravenna, was announced. Bordaberry on 14 February, stated:

> The armed forces, who have repeatedly shown testimony of a great spirit, of a great capacity, could not stay away from national life, because of its anxieties and pains, its hopes and sacrifices ... Today I can announce that following this thought, the executive will create the appropriate institutional ways for the participation of the armed forces in the national task, within the framework of law and the constitution.[20]

The Boiso Lanza agreement between Bordaberry and the armed forces aimed to restructure foreign relations, public spending, development plans, subversion, services and organizations, social security, the relationship between the state and the military, the internal organization of the military, jail management, and unemployment. Part of this agreement was the establishment of the Consejo de Seguridad Nacional (COSENA). COSENA was composed of the president, his main ministers, and the commanders of the army, air force, and the navy. Other members serve in a consulting capacity. COSENA had an 'advisory' role for the president to help integrate all the aims of the state and military. In addition, a permanent secretary was established, Estado Mayor Conjunto (ESMACO), to advise the president and to help integrate the armed forces into the decision making process. The military claimed that it was indispensable that they participate in this task. The Junta de Comandantes en Jefe (the commanding military junta) was also formed.[21]

Those concessions did not permanently appease the military. In mid-June, the military attempted to rescind the immunity of two senators it suspected of subversive activity, Senator Vasconcellos and Senator Erro. The National Assembly refused the military's requests.[22] Undaunted, the military continued to pursue the leftist politicians. However, this time the head of the largest Blanco faction, Senator Dardo Ortiz, defended Erro and joined with the Frente Amplio against the military and attempted to refute the accusations. Ortiz claimed that the evidence against Erro was unreliable since it had been obtained by torture of a Tupamaro.[23] Finally, Generals Gregorio Alvarez and Esteban Cristi commanded the dissolution of the National Assembly on 27 June 1973.[24] Bordaberry nominally remained president. During the subsequent authoritarian rule, Uruguay had the highest number of political prisoners per capita in the world. What happened to the 'Switzerland of the South'?

Introduction to Peru

Peru is an ethnically diverse, poor country with a history of severe instability. Peru gained independence in 1821 with the help of legendary generals Bolívar and San Martín. Shortly thereafter, the country became embroiled in competition among chieftains for the presidency, resulting in many coups and counter-coups. This early instability continued into the twentieth century. Historically, Peru has excluded many popular groups from participation. APRA, the historically populist political party, established in 1930 by Haya de la Torre, was illegal until the government of Odria (1948–1956). The Communist Party was legal only under the governments of Bustamante y Rivero (1945–1948) and General Velasco Alvarado (1968–1975) before 1980.[25] The military intervened often to protect the 'political and economic prerogatives of the upper class against the growing challenge from the popular classes'.[26] From 1930–1968, the military ruled for eighteen of the thirty-eight years.

During the 1960s, Peru also was faced with guerrilla movements. In 1963, a group organized by Hugo Blanco operated in Cuzco. The police quickly quashed the movement. Later, in 1965, new groups, Movimiento de Izquierda Revolucionaria (Movement of the Revolutionary Left; MIR) and Ejercito de Liberación Popular (National Liberation Army; ELP) formed. MIR was founded by Luis de la Puente. ELP was founded by Héctor Béjar. MIR was active in the departments of Junín, Cuzco, and Piura. ELP was active in Ayacucho. The tenure of these groups was short-lived. Within six months both groups were destroyed by a massive army counterinsurgency campaign. In spite of the presence of these groups, guerrilla activity was not pervasive at the time.[27]

The aim of military interventions changed in 1968 with the Revolutionary Government of the Armed Forces led by General Velasco. In 1968, through their education in Centro de Altos Estudios Militares del Peru (CAEM), a group of officers became aware of the peasant grievances of inequitable land distribution, exclusion from politics, and persistent poverty. According to Victor Villanueva, 'since the end objective of the institution was to produce officers to direct and preserve the national defense, it was also necessary to prepare these officers for intervention in the general politics of the state where the roots of the problem of national defense were to be found'.[28] Military officers perceived military intervention to be a legitimate act of patriotism.

Velasco's land reform reduced the land disparity. Before his reform of the early 1970s, 69 per cent of privately held Peruvian land was composed of plots larger than 2471 acres or 1000 hectares. After his reform, only 42 per cent of privately held land was composed of plots larger than 1000 hectares.[29] Velasco's agrarian reform in 1973 created SINAMOS, or the National System of Support for Social

Mobilization, a national organization created to transform expectations of reform into reality by creating a network of state supported organizations.[30]

The military controlled Peru from 1968 until 1980. However, the military regime faced difficulties as protest increased. The revolutionary regime was unable to absorb the politically activated populations. Moreover, the national deficit reached high levels. For example, in 1974 45 per cent of the budget was financed by debt. In 1975, General Morales Bermúdez replaced General Velasco and slowed the pace of reform. Slowly, Morales Bermúdez began to liberalize the regime because of growing discord within the military, domestic opposition, and pressure from international banks. The military negotiated with APRA and eventually allowed elections to create a constitutional assembly. The transition to democracy was completed in 1980.[31]

Peru's experience with democratic governance has been limited. Although the constitution has been formally democratic, in the modern sense, until 1980 illiterates could not vote and many Peruvians rate the democratic leaders as authoritarian. Integration to the political community is also limited because of the extreme heterogeneity of the society and historical racism against indigenous peoples. Extreme income disparity also limits integration. According to Raúl González,

> we don't have a legitimate state. In this country, the state doesn't reach many zones, and in the zones where it is present, it is bad. To use a metaphor, this country never ceased to be colonized and it is a country because there are borders and we say we are a country. But this country never was a nation, but many nations together.[32]

Corruption and the treatment of indigenous people fed a cynicism and the belief that the state exists for the benefit of the few, as opposed to the common good. Indeed, many Peruvians rejected the notion that Peru was a real democracy. For example, Rodrigo Montoya charges that none of the democratically elected leaders really governed democratically.[33]

The newly democratic state faced many challenges. In spite of attempts at reform, Peru's most stubborn problems remained. Approximately 70 per cent of the people were impoverished. In 1990, life expectancy was less than fifty years. One out of every eight infants dies in the first year. Eighty per cent of Peruvian homes lack running water, sewerage, and electricity.[34] In addition to these fundamental problems, Peru also faces the challenges of severe economic crisis and rampant terrorist violence.

Was the Peruvian constitution well ordered, in Aristotelian terms? Approval ratings of the democratically elected presidents Belaúnde and García had sunk to extremely low levels by the end of their terms. The approval rating of Congress and the political parties hit a nadir before the coup. Only President Fujimori and the armed forces maintained support before the *autogolpe*. Moreover, during the twelve years of Peruvian democracy, rumours of possible coups were not uncommon. Coup rumours circulated at the end of Belaúnde's term and during numerous occasions after García's first year as president and rumours of a coup were common during the last year of his presidency.[35]

As president, Fujimori did not alienate the military. According to Enrique Obando, this can be done in one of two ways, by being an Aprista (an APRA member) or by being grossly ineffective. Fujimori was neither.[36] However, Fujimori did have to act to consolidate support in the military. He had difficulties with certain sectors of the military at the beginning of his term. For instance, in the 1990 election there were rumours that the navy would conduct a coup if Fujimori were elected. The navy at the time supported Vargas Llosa. After Fujimori's election, he promptly retired the navy's commander-in-chief.[37]

Whereas the military had become frustrated with a lack of state support to help them comply with their mandate to end the terrorist violence, Fujimori expanded their powers. Fujimori reorganized the system of national defence, expanding the military role. A 1991 law also allowed military involvement in areas not under a state of emergency, for example in prisons and universities. Within some universities, the military established permanent bases. The universities of San Marcos, Huamanga, and La Cantuta were notorious for Sendero activities.[38] Many students welcomed the increased presence. Senator Enrique Bernales stated: 'I am not a student, but I wonder what is happening in the universities to make the students be the first to ask for the tanks and the soldiers.'[39] The intent was to re-assert control over universities in which Sendero had established a presence. Fujimori also expanded military power by granting the military protection from charges of human rights violations.[40]

Fujimori acted to consolidate his control over the military and to curry their support. Fujimori forcibly retired officers who opposed him, like the previous navy commander-in-chief, and promoted those who supported him. Military officers who disagreed with Fujimori's policies were rooted out and retired. He involved the military in the decision making process of creating a strategy and granted them new powers and protections. Fujimori tightened his control of the armed forces with the help of his 'intelligence czar', Vladimiro Montesinos.[41] Montesinos kept files on all of Peru's influential military officers.[42] In 1991, Fujimori and Montesinos pushed for and received a law that changed the procedure for the selection of new commanders-in-chief. Previously, selection was made according to rank. Under Fujimori's reform, the president could pick his commanders from the top ranking officers and forcibly retire officers at will.[43] By September 1990, President Fujimori seemed to have consolidated support from the military. On this date, he received two important military decorations: the Peruvian Cross of Military Merit and the Francisco Bolognese Military Order in the grade of grand cross.[44]

By following a policy of eliminating officers he suspected of being disloyal, Fujimori succeeded in creating a military much more loyal to him than before.[45] By doing so he guaranteed himself military support for his coup. Fujimori committed his *autogolpe* or self-coup on 5 April 1992, one day before Congress was set to reconvene. All three branches of the military supported Fujimori and his coup.[46] Fujimori received the backing of the armed forces and the business community, in spite of the risk of jeopardizing international economic assistance in the short term.[47] On 6 April 1992, the armed forces joint command released communiqué one. It stated that the armed forces 'have unanimously agreed to give their most decided support and endorsement to the decision adopted on this date by the president of the republic and supreme commander of the armed forces and Peruvian national police'.[48]

Fujimori explained his reasons for his April 1992 *autogolpe*. 'What I have tried to apply are some pragmatic strategies and measures to gain good control of the country by confronting the three social diseases of corruption, inefficiency of the state and *Sendero Luminoso* violence.'[49] Fujimori stated his goals of amending the constitution, restoring morality to the judicial branch, modernizing public administration, pacifying the country, struggling with the drug problem, rooting out corruption, promoting a market economy, reorganizing the educational system, decentralizing the state, and increasing the standard of living. Fujimori stated that he was acting to rebuild democracy, not to destroy it. 'What I have been trying to do is reconstruct this weakened democracy so that it can stand up to the challenge of terrorist violence and to other challenges that may come in the future.'[50] According to Fujimori, he was acting to create a legal and effective democracy instead of what he characterized as a demagogic, obstructionist, inefficient, and corrupt system.[51]

Introduction to Spain

Spain's democratic tradition is as old as it is turbulent. This tradition began in 1812 with the drafting of the first constitution. It reemerged in the First Federal Republic of 1873–1874 and again in the Second Spanish Republic of 1931–1936.[52] In spite of this democratic tradition, nineteenth century Spain was violent and unstable. Between 1814 and 1886, there were forty-six military uprisings. From 1923–1936, there were another eight.[53] Stanley Payne characterizes nineteenth century Spain as a 'search for a viable structure of government'.[54] Factions of the Spanish army were involved in almost every constitutional change. The character of these pronunciamientos began to change in the early twentieth century. Pedro Vilanova characterizes the nineteenth century pronunciamientos as 'mostly liberal; that is anti-absolutist and in favor of a constitution'.[55] Moreover, none of these pronunciamientos led to a military dictatorship until Miguel Primo de Rivera in 1923. Primo de Rivera ruled until stepping down in 1930.

After Primo's rule ended, the Second Republic was proclaimed on 14 April 1931. The Second Republic was established 'through an unusual electoral and civil process that involved remarkably little disturbance'.[56] This calm beginning did not last. Shortly after the municipal elections in which the conservative and monarchist parties were defeated, King Alfonso XIII left Spain with the statement that 'we are out of fashion'.[57] The 1931 constitution was progressive, including provisions for universal suffrage, accommodation of some regional calls for autonomy, expanded state education, and a rejection of the special status of the Catholic Church within the state.[58] However, the process that created the 1931 constitution was not cooperative. The leftist coalition that dominated the process made little effort to appease those with other views.[59] Recovering from its electoral defeat in 1931, the right won the general elections in 1933. Two and a half years later, the Socialists, Communists and leftist Republicans created the Popular Front and regained control in the general elections on 16 February 1936.

In general, the period was marked by severe polarization and violence. During the short experiment of the Spanish Second Republic, more than two thousand lives were lost due to violence. Both the right and the left resorted to violence, although Payne notes that most of the violence can be attributed to the left.[60] By 1934, the political situation had become polarized and the number of deaths increased dramatically.[61] There were 2045 political killings from 1931–1936, with a peak in the violence in 1934 with 1525 political killings. According to Payne, the last straw was the assassination of rightist leader José Calvo Sotelo. Socialist activists and some leftist police were implicated.[62]

Many in the military and on the right could not tolerate the rule of the Popular Front. Instead, a military revolt was planned. The Nationalist military uprising of 17–18 July 1936, against the Republic, was conceived as a pronunciamiento. Instead, it escalated into a bloody three year civil war against the Republican forces.[63] In July 1936, General Franco[64] joined the Nationalist rebellion. The civil war years were bloody and chaotic. Franco was later chosen as commander-in-chief and head of the Nationalist state by his fellow Nationalist generals. The civil war ended with the Nationalist forces victorious. Franco retained command as Caudillo.[65]

General Franco's rule imposed stability onto Spain. Franco's rule, although brutal in the beginning, matured into a benign authoritarianism that most Spaniards came to accept, waiting for Franco's death for an opportunity for change. His rule was supported by the Catholic Church, the Falange, and the military. Most Spaniards did not want to return to the bloody chaos that characterized Spain before and during the civil war. After Franco, a 'broad consensus soon developed in a large part of political opinion, and ... all major and nearly all minor political groups have firmly rejected any tactic of violence'.[66] However, not everyone subscribed to the ideal of consensus. Violence was chosen as a means for some groups. For example, ETA, a Basque separatist group, assassinated Franco's most trusted prime minister, Admiral Carrero Blanco, by blowing up his car after mass on 20 December 1972.

On 20 November 1975, Francisco Franco, Generalisimo of Spain, died. Two days later, Juan Carlos was sworn in as King of Spain. Juan Carlos, grandson of King Alfonso XIII, had been named Franco's heir in 1969 and had been raised under Franco's supervision since his youth. Franco's plans for an orderly succession appeared to be working. The King re-appointed Franco's prime minister Carlos Arias Navarro. However, the King became frustrated with Arias and asked him to resign. On 1 July 1976 Arias resigned.[67] The King chose Adolfo Suárez as prime minister.[68] The selection of Suárez disappointed those who wished for reform. They were not disappointed for long.

The King and Suárez moved quickly. Less than one year after Franco's death, the *Cortés* passed the Law of Political Reform in November 1976, formally ending the dictatorship and creating a new elected bicameral legislature. A referendum was called in December to approve or disapprove of the Law of Political Reform. Seventy-eight per cent of the Spanish people affirmed the new law. The old Francoist *Cortés* approved the reform 425 to 59 with 13 abstentions. In February 1977, some political parties were legalized, in March free trade unions were allowed and the right to strike was granted.[69] In April 1977, the Communist Party was legalized.[70] Two months later, in June 1977, the first democratic elections since 1936 were held. One month later, the new *Cortés* opened.

Unlike the last round of elections, moderation and peace characterized this election. Participation was high. Almost 80 per cent of the electorate voted. Two parties, the UCD and PSOE, emerged as the dominant parties after the 1977 elections. The UCD was formed of a group of smaller centre parties in May 1977 just in time for the elections.[71] The UCD candidate was Adolfo Suárez. Many of the UCD members were former Francoist officials. The other major party, the PSOE, had defined itself as Marxist in its twenty-seventh party congress in 1977. However, before the first general elections, party leader Felipe González publicly retracted the statement of Marxist orientation.[72] In general, the political atmosphere was marked by cooperation. Most of the parties, even the PCE, supported the monarchy.[73] The conservative AP responded to its electoral defeat by revamping its image from the 'ogre of the country' to a more moderate law and order party that supported national unity.[74]

In addition to the main national parties, some Basque and Catalan regional parties won seats in the national *Cortés*. In the Basque country, the PNV had much support. The party, which was founded in 1895, emerged from the Franco period with immediate electoral success in the Basque country. Another party, Herri Batasuna (or People's Unity; HB), the political wing of ETA, did not do well enough to gain seats in the national *Cortés*. In Catalonia in 1977, the Unió Democrática de Catalunya (Catalan Democratic Union; UDC) and the Converéncia Democrática de Catalunya (Catalan Democratic Convergence Party; CDC) were the main regional parties. These two parties joined to create Convergencia i Unió (Catalan Convergence and Union; CiU) in 1979.[75]

The transition process, characterized by many as a process of pacts and agreements, has been called one of a negotiated break with the former regime.[76] In addition to the elections, the year of 1977 was marked by two grand events: the Moncloa pacts and the establishment of a new constitution. Representatives of political parties and the prime minister met in the Moncloa palace in October to craft an economic policy to respond to the economic crisis. All the major political parties were represented in the negotiations. The agreement among parties of the right, left, and centre specified reforms within the existing market economy:

wage ceilings, moderated union demands, a continued state intervention, and a tightening of the money supply. The pact dealt with potentially divisive issues in a conciliatory manner. Drafts of the constitution were completed in September 1977 and voted on by the *Cortés* on 31 October 1978. Eighty-seven per cent of the Spanish people ratified the constitution in a 6 December 1978 referendum.[77]

The nascent Spanish democracy was vastly different from the Spanish state under Franco. Although Franco's state was supported, or at least tolerated, by many Spaniards, at the end of his rule many Spaniards were ready for change. The desire for democracy was strong even before Franco's death. The new constitution appeared to be a good match for the Spaniards. It was based on a democratic principle of authority, with universal suffrage. The new constitution was well supported both formally in the plebiscite and informally in public opinion polls. The Spanish democracy enjoyed basic stability. However, dissension among the military and some violent groups existed.

In Spain, the newly democratic state faced an already politicized military. For forty years, the conservative, nationalist ideals of Franco had been supported by the military and taught in the military academies. Historically, the military was not uniformly conservative. However, the civil war of 1936–1939 forced a split within the Spanish armed forces. After the civil war, many of the leftist or liberal officers were simply eliminated by the victorious Nationalist forces. Approximately five thousand of them were either shot, imprisoned, or exiled. They were replaced with nearly eleven thousand Falangist and Carlist men who were admitted into the army as 'alféreces provisionales', or provisional lieutenants. Many of them remained in the military after the end of the war. The military became more conservative as it was incorporated into the new Franco state.[78] This trend towards conservatism continued even though many later officers did not fight in the civil war, because they were at least educated by those who did. They were taught that democracy was vulnerable to the chaos that erupted during the Second Republic. This military ideology resisted change because of the isolation and the distinct education of the military families.[79]

The transition to democracy troubled many in the military. Promises made to the military during the transition were broken. Not only was the Communist Party legalized in April 1977, but regional autonomy was granted.[80] In addition, certain aspects of military reform irked top officers. Reformist general Manuel Gutiérrez Mellado became minister of defence. He supported the creation of a civilian minister of defence, abolished the social investigation brigade, and reformed the military code of justice and the military ordinances. He changed the promotions and retirement procedures, replacing seniority with merit in promotions above the rank of major.[81] In February 1977, JUJEM, the joint chiefs of staff, was formed. JUJEM was subordinated to the minister of defence.[82] The military had lost many prerogatives. In an effort to appease the military, it was given one new role. In the new constitution, the military was granted the duty of defending the constitutional order.[83]

Suárez's UCD government had to act carefully in regard to reform. Many in the military had to be placated and reassured, especially in light of the challenges facing the new democracy. In the words of Carolyn Boyd and James Boyden,

> Terrorism, particularly but not exclusively in the Basque Provinces, made it difficult for the UCD to pursue further reforms with vigor. On the one hand, the party dared not offend officers already outraged by the frequent assaults on military personnel; on the other hand, the right wing of the party opposed the rapid and generous resolution of the autonomy question that might have undercut the terrorists.[84]

The new ruling coalition had to balance the pressures for reform with the reality of awakening sedition on the right or in the military. In addition, divisions within the military weakened its power.[85]

There were many conspiracies against the new democracy within the military. The first major rumble of trouble erupted in 1977. Rumours of a military coup followed the legalization of the Communist Party.[86] Months later some of this discontent developed further. In September 1977, the 'Játiva conspiracy' was formed. General Milans de Bosch and former ministers of the army and navy gathered to celebrate a wedding. At this gathering, they discussed what is widely believed to have been a conspiracy against the new democracy. Sentiments for a military intervention remained high.

In May 1978, the new chief of the high general staff, Lieutenant General Tomás de Liniers, publicly endorsed the legitimacy of the Argentine military dictatorship. A few months later, another conspiracy, 'Operation Galaxia', was discovered in November of 1978. Captain Ricardo Sáenz de Ynestrillas and Lieutenant Colonel Antonio Tejero Molina planned to seize Prime Minister Suárez and his cabinet while the King and Queen were in Mexico and other high officials were out of Madrid. The plot was foiled.[87] In the same month, General Atarés Peña was arrested for an act of indiscipline during the reunion of Defence Minister Gutiérrez with military leaders.[88] In January 1979, after the assassination of Madrid's military governor, General Ortín, more rumbles of trouble surfaced. At the general's funeral, high ranking officers paraded the coffin through the streets chanting 'power to the military'.[89]

In spite of the progress in elections, regional autonomy, and the new constitution, not all sectors were pleased with the reform. On 20 October 1979, the ultra-conservative publication *El Alcázar* published a letter by General Santiago, appealing for a military intervention.[90] In January 1981, another article appeared in *El Alcázar*, stating 'the constitution as it stands does not work. It causes the nation to be ungovernable.' The same publication warned on 8 February 1981 that Spain had reached the point of no return.[91] On 29 January 1981, Prime Minister Suárez resigned. He commented that he did not want 'the democratic system to be, once again, a parenthesis in Spain's history'.[92]

King Juan Carlos acted to rein in the potentially seditious military. The King was disturbed by the continued antidemocratic sentiments of the military. For example, King Juan Carlos called for discipline on the celebration of Pascua Military, an annual holiday.

> A soldier, an army that has lost discipline, cannot be saved. He is no longer a soldier, it is no longer an army. The spectacle of the undisciplined, disrespectful attitudes born in passing emotions which unleash passions that fully disregard the poise demanded of every military, is frankly shameful.[93]

The King's words were influential. He maintained good relations with all branches of the armed forces. Moreover, many officers, although reluctant to support the democracy, recognized the King as Franco's successor, and were more likely to support him.

The military discontent culminated in the attempted coup of 23 February 1981 when the entire *Cortés* was held hostage. After the resignation of Suárez, the *Cortés* had failed to approve the UCD's new candidate for prime minister, Leopoldo Calvo Sotelo y Bustelo. On the day of the second vote, 23 February 1981, Colonel Tejero and a company of the civil guardsmen invaded and held the *Cortés* captive. Simultaneously, General Milans de Bosch, in Valencia, rebelled and declared a state of emergency. The King and army chief of staff, General Gabeiras, contacted all eleven captains generals, and important commanders. Of the eleven, only one, Milans de Bosch, had openly rebelled. Only three, however, were unequivocally loyal to democracy. After successfully communicating to the military that the King would not support the attempted coup, Juan Carlos made a brief announcement on television. 'The Crown, symbol of the unity and permanence of the Fatherland, cannot in any way tolerate actions or attitudes of persons which attempt to interrupt by force the democratic process which the Constitution approved by the Spanish people determined in referendum.'[94] That night, thousands of Madrileños demonstrated in favour of the constitution. They encountered a small demonstration of pro-coup activists, who chanted 'Tejero shoot them all'.[95] Eventually, Tejero was convinced to surrender. In addition to the King's support for the democracy, a strong majority of Spaniards continued to support the democracy. In the following days, participation in pro-democracy marches and demonstrations filled the streets of major cities. The renegade military officers lacked support from the Spanish citizens, the King, and the politicians. In spite of a politicized military and a terrorist threat, Spain did not succumb to a return to authoritarianism. How did the new, fragile Spanish democracy survive?

Economic crisis

In addition to the presence of terrorist groups, each country was faced with a severe economic crisis. In all three cases, economic crisis preceded the coups or attempted coups. Moreover, citizens in each country recognized the economic problems as severe. The importance of economic problems is not discounted. However, economic crisis needs to be evaluated in a broader context and not viewed as a monocausal explanation for democratic breakdown.

Uruguayan economic crisis

After the Korean War, during which Uruguay benefited from the increased demand for its woollen goods, the Uruguayan economy began a long period of decline. This crisis was manifested in a decline in wages, in the standard of living, in the value of exports, and in the rate of investment. Some structural factors and the lack of innovation were to blame for the economic crisis. Henry Finch states:

> whether the form of technology incorporated was that of pedigree livestock, or wire fencing, or (most obviously) the refrigeration [of meat], the requirement on Uruguayan producers was to react to the availability of the new technology, rather than to modify or adapt it to local conditions. The pattern of production was thus broadly speaking imitative of practice elsewhere.[96]

According to Finch, this lack of innovation stalled further modernization. In addition, the level of investment was very low.[97] The ratio of gross fixed investment to GDP in Uruguay continued to decline from a high of 16 per cent in 1955–1959 to only 9.9 per cent in 1970–1974. By 1970, the investment in Uruguay was at half the rate of the rest of Latin America, which had a rate of 20.3 per cent. As investment slowed, growth and productivity stagnated. Moreover, most of the domestic industry was costly and inefficient. The rural exporting sector, based on cattle and sheep products, with its lack of investment and primitive husbandry techniques, was forced to subsidize the industrial sector with the transfer of some of its potential earnings.[98]

Economically, Uruguay struggled in the 1960s and 1970s as shown in table 3.1. The value of exports, in fixed dollars, fell 40 per cent from 1951 to 1961. Complicating the situation, the costs of imported goods and raw materials increased.[99] From 1956 to 1972 GNP fell 12 per cent.[100] In the 1960s, Uruguay had the worst growth rate in the Western hemisphere except for Haiti.[101] Wages declined while prices rose. For example, real wages for public employees fell 40

Table 3.1 Uruguayan economic indicators, 1965–1973

	1965	1966	1967	1968	1969	1970	1971	1972	1973
CPI changes %	56.6	72.7	89.1	125.4	20.9	16.4	23.9	76.5	96.8
GDP growth rate %	1	4	−4	1	6	5	−1	−4	1
Unemployment %	NA	NA	NA	8.4	NA	7.5	7.6	7.7	8.9

Sources: *Statistical Abstract of Latin America*, Vol. 20, p. 332, International Monetary Fund.
Note: CPI-Consumer Price Index.

per cent from 1957–1967.[102] After 1968, wages rebounded 16 per cent through 1971. However, 1972 and 1973 saw a significant decrease down to 94 per cent of 1968 wages. Inflation started increasing after 1970.[103]

Compounding these problems was the inability of the state to pare back social spending that it could no longer afford. Henry Finch believes that 'the country has grown accustomed to a relatively high standard of living in spite of a weak long-run economic performance, and deterioration in recent decades in that performance has found the country incapable of responding positively'.[104] Particularly unsustainable was the number of pensioners, guaranteed by the state, in the country. The number of pensioners rapidly increased by 44.9 per cent from 1958 to 1962.[105] By 1969 there were 213,000 people employed in the public administration sector with 346,000 pensioners, up from 66,400 public administration employees and 196,700 pensioners in 1955.[106] This situation became more difficult considering that Uruguay had an ageing population and that many of the youngest and most highly skilled workers had emigrated.

This problem of the increase in pensioners can be traced to the pact of *chinchulín* or pork barrel pact of 1931. This pact established that all *entes autónomos* (state run businesses) would be controlled by a seventeen member board of directors. Employment was determined by a proportion of Blanco or Colorado employees that reflected the latest election results. The resources of the state and public sector became a source of political patronage. The plan was incorporated into the 1952 constitution. Finch blames this agreement for the consequence of a 'state apparatus and public sector whose dominant contemporary characteristic is not its extent, but its grotesque financial – but more importantly, functional – inefficiency'.[107] By 1965, the *entes autónomos* paid 40 per cent of all salaries.[108] The political parties did not dare to reform this sector, since it was a lucrative source of patronage.

Peruvian economic crisis

In addition to the fierce guerrilla threat, Peru was faced with a severe and prolonged economic crisis, as demonstrated in table 3.2. Peru had declining growth from 1975–1992, with a 50 per cent decline between 1988 and 1992. Concurrently with the declines in growth, Peru suffered from hyperinflation. For example, Peru experienced hyperinflation of 7650 per cent in 1991. Although the economic situation was still bad at the time of the coup in 1992, the economy had stabilized almost two years before Fujimori's self-coup. Fujimori generally succeeded in controlling inflation and in resuming growth. The cost of this stabilization was an increase in poverty, however.

Alan García, who was elected president in 1985, attempted to implement a new type of economic policy, he called 'heterodox'. In his plan, he increased subsidies to business and labour, installed price controls, and used selective state intervention.[109] The unorthodox stabilization plan also included reduced foreign debt payments.

> The theory behind this reactivation program was that a sharp initial stimulus to consumer demand, particularly to that of small-scale farming peasants and shanty town entrepreneurs, would provide an impetus for growth while the modern mining and manufacturing sectors would produce import substitutes and exports, generating foreign exchange with which to recommence servicing the debt later.[110]

Initially, it seemed to work. In 1986 and 1987 GNP rose 8 per cent a year, wages increased, and inflation was acceptable. However, the heterodox experiment ended when García tried to nationalize the banks. He accused the bankers of refusing to reinvest the profits.[111] In addition, the policy provoked inflation and huge deficits. For example, in September 1988 the deficit was 16 per cent of GDP and reserves

Table 3.2 Peru: economic indicators, 1980–1992

	1980	1981	1982	1983	1984	1985	1986	1987	1988	1989	1990	1991	1992
Inflation rate (%)	60.8	72.7	72.9	125.1	111.5	158.3	62.9	114.5	1722.3	2775.3	7649.6	139.2	56.7
GDP growth rate (%)	5	5	−1	−12	6	2	10	8	−9	−12	−4	3	−2
Unemployment (%)	7.0	6.8	7.0	9.2	10.9	NA	5.3	4.8	NA	7.9	NA	5.8	9.4
Number of strikes	739	871	809	643	509	579	648	720	814	667	613	315	219
Man hrs lost (millions)	2.2	19.9	22.7	20.3	13.8	12.2	16.9	9.1	38.2	15.2	15.1	8.9	2.3

Sources: Instituto Nacional de Estadística e Informática, *Statistical Abstract of Latin America*, Volume 23. Edited by James W. Wilke (Los Angeles: UCLA Latin American Center Publications, 1984), p. 415, Volume 25, 1986, p. 251. Interamerican Development Bank, International Monetary Fund.

fell 60 per cent to $500,000,000 in one year.[112] As early as the end of 1987, García's chief financial advisor Carbonetto acknowledged that the state would have to cut spending. However, García delayed any implementation until September 1988, 'one of the most disastrous delays or pieces of political cowardice in Peruvian economic history'.[113] García's popularity suffered due to the dismal economic performance. On 24 October 1988, three out of four people rejected the president and two out of three blamed García, his government, and his party for the economic crisis, which was viewed as the worst in the twentieth century.[114]

The effects of García's eventual adjustment plan were harsh. The adjustment plan resulted in a 114 per cent increase in the Consumer Price Index. In 1987–1990, wages fell 75 per cent and production decreased by 20 per cent.[115] In 1980 wages were half of what they had been in 1970. By 1989, real wages were half of what they had been in 1980.[116] This drop followed an equally perilous drop. The worst performance of the Peruvian economy occurred in 1989 and 1990. The economic crisis may be a strong reason why APRA fared so poorly in the 1990 presidential elections. President Fujimori, after 1990, appeared to have stabilized the economy. The same trend can be seen in the national average of the price index and in strike data. In both cases, the worst occurred in the late 1980s, with a stabilization beginning in 1990.

When Fujimori became president in 1990, he inherited a significant difficulty with the international financial community. No payments on the national debt had been made since late 1987.[117] Fujimori normalized relations with the international financial community. In 1991, Peru negotiated a $2.1 billion financial package with the International Monetary Fund and World Bank.[118] Fujimori removed controls on foreign currency and introduced new bank laws in 1992.[119] Fujimori's economic plan, called the 'Fujishock', involved eliminating subsidies, reducing tariffs, reforming the tax structure, and slashing state employment.[120] The severe inflation was brought under control by Fujimori. Labour conflicts also became less common under Fujimori. The peak of labour troubles was in 1988, with a record number of man hours lost and the highest number of strikes since 1980.

Spanish economic crisis

Vivíamos mejor contra Franco.
We had it better against Franco.[121]

In addition to terrorist troubles, newly democratic Spain faced an economic crisis. Under Franco, Spain had achieved spectacular growth in the 1960s which has since come to be known as the 'economic miracle'. Franco's earlier economic policy had been based around state intervention and autarky. After a cabinet shuffle in 1957, the new cabinet, distinguished by the dominance of Opus Dei technocrats, marked the transition to a market economy and integration into the Western capitalist economy. The boom continued with expansions of industry, the service sector, and tourism. However, after the oil crisis of 1974, Spain began a period of economic difficulties. Growth was negative in 1975 and an anaemic 2 per cent in 1976, with rising unemployment, inflation, and a fiscal deficit.[122] Unemployment had reached over 10 per cent by 1979 and continued to climb. Correspondingly, the people faced high cost of living increases. Economic growth was sluggish and negative at times. After 1979, the increases in the cost of living stabilized. The unemployment rate, however, continued to increase.

Table 3.3 presents Spain's economic situation. In addition to rising unemployment levels, from under 5 per cent at the time of Franco's death to 15 per cent in 1981, Spain's economic growth slowed, due much in part to the oil crisis.[123] GNP growth was negative in 1979 and in 1981. During the year of the attempted coup, Spain faced negative growth and high unemployment. Approximately one out of six Spaniards was unemployed. However, concern about poor economic performance did not convince many citizens to support the attempted coup in 1981.

Conclusion

Uruguay, Peru, and Spain experienced similar national problems. Uruguay had a long history of cooperation between its main political parties. Its democracy had been stable for decades. Its military did not have a history of intervention. However, starting in the 1960s, the country was confronted

Table 3.3 Spanish economic indicators, 1974–1986

	1974	1975	1976	1977	1978
CPI increase (%)	15.4	17	17.7	24.6	19.8
Unemployment (%)	2.9	4.7	5.3	6.3	8.2
GDP growth (%)	6	4	3.3	3	1.4
Strikes	NA	NA	NA	NA	1356

Sources: Joseph Harrison, *The Spanish Economy in the Twentieth Century* (London: Croom Helm, 1985), pp. 175–177; José Feliz Tezanos, Ramón Cotarelo, and Andrés De Blas, *La Transicion Democrática Española* (Madrid: Editorial Sistema, 1989), p. 145; Omar Encarnacion, 'Social Concertation in Democratic and Market Transactions: Comparative Lessons from Spain', *Comparative Political Studies* Vol. 30, No. 4, August 1997, p. 387; Table 3, IMF.

with the emergence of terrorist groups. The Tupamaros, the group responsible for most of the violence, started their violent actions in a time when the country was already challenged by a severe and long lasting economic crisis. Uruguay's seemingly well established democracy was overthrown by the military with public support. Peru had a history of severe state instability and a strong tradition of military intervention. When the country was returned to democratic rule in 1980, the new democratic constitution was faced with a severe economic crisis and the emergence of terrorist groups. Peru's third elected president since the return to democracy in 1980, Alberto Fujimori, dissolved Congress in April 1992 with the support of the military to forcibly reform the state. Spain's new democracy was created after the death of General Franco. The military in the new democracy was considered a standing threat to the new state. While consolidating its democracy, Spain faced the challenges of the continuing activities of terrorist groups, an economic slowdown, and frequent rumours of possible military coups. In spite of the problems, Spain's democracy survived.

Each historical outcome is surprising in its own way. It is shocking that Uruguayan citizens, with their well developed democratic traditions, did not protest the military intervention. Although the Peruvian instability may not be surprising due to the history of extreme instability, the

1979	1980	1981	1982	1983	1984	1985	1986
15.7	15.5	14.6	14.4	12	11	9	9
10.1	12.6	15.4	17.1	NA	18.4	19.5	21.2
−0.1	1.2	−0.2	1.2	1.8	1.8	2.3	3.3
1789	1669	2556	2582	2714	3019	2026	2239

strong support Fujimori received puzzles many analysts. Spain, with the threat of Franco's military, economic crisis, and violent terrorist groups, managed to maintain the support of its citizens, in spite of the problems and the threats of a military coup. Why did the Uruguayans and Peruvians encourage and support coups and changes in constitutional form while the Spaniards rejected them? Chapter four explains these questions and presents the evidence to test the hypotheses.

Notes

1. Collier and Collier, p. 271.
2. Paolo Mieres, 'Elecciones de 1989 en Uruguay', *Sintesis* Vol. 13, April–June 1991, pp. 205–228, p. 211.
3. Kaufman, pp. 21–22.
4. Weinstein, p. 22.
5. William Davis, *Warnings from the Far South: Democracy versus Dictatorship in Uruguay, Argentina, and Chile* (Westport: Praeger, 1995), pp. 24–25.
6. Fitzgibbon, p. vii.
7. Gillespie, 1991, p. 247.
8. Mainwaring, p. 108.
9. Gillespie, 1991, p. 18.
10. Weinstein, pp. 11–12.
11. Originally, the Uruguayan military was linked to the rule of the Colorado party. Although the military was created to be opposed to military participation in politics, it was solidly Colorado. 'The armed forces were in fact not autonomous and linked as they were to a specific political family, did not regard themselves as situated above parties, with the right to set themselves up as the supreme authority and guarantor of the national interest'; Leslie Bethel (ed.), *The*

Cambridge History of Latin America Vol. VI, Latin America Since 1930 (Cambridge: Cambridge University Press, 1994), pp. 261–262.

12 Sergio Jellinek and Luis Ledesma, Uruguay: Del Consenso Democratico a la Militarismo Estatal Part 2, Paper No. 19, November (Stockholm: Institute of Latin American Studies, 1979b), p. 30.

13 Porzencanski, pp. 61–68.

14 Generals and Tupamaros: The Struggle for Power in Uruguay 1969–1973 (London: Latin American Review of Books, 1974). [No author listed], pp. 43–46.

15 Porzencanski, p. 69.

16 Generals and Tupamaros, p. 53.

17 Generals and Tupamaros, p. 55.

18 Servicio Paz y Justicia: Uruguay, Nunca Más: Human Rights Violations, 1972–1985 (Philadelphia: Temple University Press, 1986), p. 35.

19 Republica Oriental del Uruguay Junta de Comandantes en Jefe, Volumen 2. El Proceso Politico (Montevideo: Las Fuerzas Armadas al Pueblo Oriental, 1978), pp. 87–91.

20 Kaufman, p. 33.

21 Republica Oriental del Uruguay Junta de Comandantes en Jefe, 1978, pp. 100–118.

22 Senator Vasconcellos criticized the military, stating that 'a new political party has emerged; it consists of a group of generals'. Vasconcellos also criticized the state for torture and murder of prisoners. The military charged that Senator Erro was the leader of the Tupamaros. Generals and Tupamaros, pp. 68–70.

23 Kaufman, p. 29.

24 Kaufman, p. 59.

25 Eugenio Chang-Rodríguez, Opciones Políticas Peruanas (Trujillo, Peru: Editorial Normas Legales S.A., 1987), p. 217.

26 Victor Villanueva, 'Peru's New Military Professionalism: The Failure of the Technocratic Approach', in Peter Gorman (ed.), Post Revolutionary Peru (Boulder: Westview, 1982), pp. 157–159.

27 Collier and Collier, p. 717. See also Francois Bourricaud's Power and Society in Contemporary Peru (New York: Praeger Press, 1970); Julio Cotler's Clases, estado, y nación en el Perú (Lima: Instituto de Estudios Peruanso, 1978); Richard Gott's Guerrilla Movements in Latin America (New York: Anchor Books, 1972); and David Werlich's Peru: A Short History (Carbondale: Southern Illinois University Press, 1978).

28 Villanueva, p. 159.

29 Klaren, p. 29.

30 Later, as SINAMOS lost its influence, peasants organizations, as opposed to state led organizations, became more influential. For example, the Peruvian Peasant Confederation (CCP) from the 1970s became the main avenue for the pursuit of land reform. Deborah Poole (ed.), Unruly Order: Violence, Power and Cultural Identity in the High Provinces of Southern Peru (Boulder: Westview, 1994), pp. 225–227.

31 Susan C. Bourque and Kay B. Warren, 'Democracy Without Peace: The Cultural Politics of Terror in Peru', *Latin American Research Review* Vol. 24, No. 1, 1989, pp. 7–34, p. 9. See also Bethel (ed.), pp. 451–491.

32 'No teníamos un Estado legítimo. En este país el Estado no llegaba a muchas zonas; y en las zonas donde llegaba, llegaba mal. Para utilizar una metáfora, este país no terminó nunca de ser colonizado y es país porque existen unos límites que nos dicen que somos un país. Pero este país nunca fue una nación, sino muchas naciones juntas.' Author translation. Raúl González, 'Un País Violentado', in Rolando Forgues (ed.), *Perú: entre el desafío de la violencia y el sueño de lo posible* (Lima: Minerva, 1993), p. 127.

33 Rodrigo Montoya, 'Libertad, democracia y problema etnico en el Peru' in Alberto Adrianzén (ed.), *Democracia, etnicidad y violencia política en los países andinos* (Lima: Instituto de Estudios Peruanos, 1993), p. 105.

34 Americas Watch, *Peru Under Fire* (New Haven: Yale, 1992), p. 196, p. 2.

35 Werlich, 1978, p. 78.

36 Enrique Obando, 'The Power of Peru's Armed Forces', in Joseph Tulchin and Gary Bland (eds), *Peru in Crisis: Dictatorship or Democracy?* (Boulder: Lynne Rienner, 1994), p. 115.

37 Enrique Obando, 'Fujimori and the Military: A Marriage of Convenience', *NACLA* Vol. 30, No. 1, July/August 1996, pp. 31–37, p. 31.

38 María Escalante and Ana María Vidal, *Los Decretos de la Guerra* (Lima: IDS Minilibros, 1993), p. 28.

39 'Yo no soy estudiante, pero pregunto, ¿qué estará pasando en las universidades para que los estudiantes sean los primeros en pedir que los tanques, las tanquetas y los soldados no salgan de ellas?' Author translation. Enrique Bernales, 'Con la soga al cuello', in Rolando Foraues (ed.), *Perú: entre el desafío de la violencia y el sueño de lo posible* (Lima: Minerva, 1993), p. 39.

40 Obando, 1996, p. 36.

41 Montesinos has a dubious background. He was discharged from the army due to allegations that he had passed classified information to the US. In addition, in his civilian career as a lawyer, he defended drug traffickers in some high profile cases. Obando, 1996, p. 33.

42 Daniel W. Fitz-Simons, 'Sendero Luminoso: Case Study in Insurgency', *Parameters* Vol. 23, No. 2, Summer 1993, pp. 64–73, p. 70.

43 In spite of Fujimori's efforts at consolidating control over the military, two dissident groups formed within the military after the *autogolpe*. COMACA (Commanders, Majors, and Captains) and 'Sleeping Lion' were groups opposed to Fujimori's manipulation of the military, including promotions and retirements, the low budget of the military, and the low salaries. Plans for a coup against Fujimori were frustrated after the capture of Sendero leader Guzmán. Two months later, the groups were infiltrated by the Servicio de Inteligencia Naciona. Obando, 1996, p. 33.

44 'Poll Reveals Opinion on Market Economy', Lima, *El Comercio* 25 July 90, 19 FBIS LAT 90 174, p. A6.

45 Obando, 1996, p. 32.
46 Joseph Tulchin and Gary Bland (eds), *Peru in Crisis: Dictatorship or Democracy?* (Boulder: Lynne Rienner, 1994), p. 7.
47 Cameron, 1995, p. 145.
48 'Armed Forces Support Fujimori', Lima Radio Programas del Peru, 6 April 1992, FBIS LAT 92 066, p. 31.
49 'Saving the State in Peru', *New Perspectives Quarterly* Fall 1993, pp. 10–12, p. 10.
50 'Saving the State in Peru', p. 12.
51 'Addresses Message to Natian', Lima Panamericana Television Network, 6 April 1992, FBIS LAT 92 066, pp. 28–31.
52 Newton with Donaghy, p. 1.
53 Miguel Angel Aguilar, 'The Spanish Military: Force for Stability or Insecurity?', in Joyce Lasky Shub and Raymond Carr (eds), *Spain: Studies in Political Security* (New York: Praeger, 1985), p. 49.
54 Stanley Payne, *Politics and the Military in Modern Spain* (Stanford: Stanford University Press, 1967), p. 1.
55 Pedro Vilanova, 'Spain: The Army and the Transition', in David Bell (ed.), *Democratic Politics in Spain* (New York: St. Martin's Press, 1983), pp. 148–149.
56 Stanley Payne, 'Political Violence During the Spanish Second Republic', *Journal of Contemporary History* Vol. 25, 1990, pp. 269–288, p. 271.
57 Carr and Fusi, p. 2.
58 Newton with Donaghy, p. 1.
59 Bonime-Blanc, p. 124.
60 Payne, 1990, p. 269.
61 For an excellent analysis of the violence of this time, see Luis Romero's *Por qué y cómo mataron a Calvo Sotelo* (Barcelona: Planeta, 1982) and Ramiro Cibrián's 'Violencia política y crisis democrática: España en 1936', *Revista de Estudios Políticos* 6 November–December 1978, pp. 81–115.
62 Payne, 1990, p. 284.
63 Juan Linz, 'Church and State in Spain from the Civil War to the Return of Democracy', *Daedalus* Vol. 120, No. 2, Summer 1991, pp. 159–179, p. 161.
64 In 1926, Franco became the youngest brigadier general in Europe because of his service in the pacification of Morocco.
65 Carr and Fusi, p. 6.
66 Payne, 1990, p. 285.
67 Arango, pp. 102–103.
68 However, it should be noted that the King could not directly choose a replacement prime minister. The King and Fernández Miranda, his former tutor, presiding chief of the *Cortés* and president of the Council of the Realm, arranged that Adolfo Suárez would be among the three

names presented to the King as possible candidates from the Council of the Realm.

69 Arango, pp. 102–111.
70 Carolyn Boyd and James Boyden, 'Armed Forces and the Transition to Democracy in Spain', in Thomas D. Lancaster and Gary Prevost (eds), *Politics and Change in Spain* (New York: Praeger, 1985), p. 102.
71 Share, p. 156.
72 Julia Santos, 'The Ideological Conversion of the Leaders of the PSOE', in Frances Lannon and Paul Preston (eds), *Elites and Power in Twentieth-Century Spain: Essays in Honour of Sir Raymond Carr* (Oxford: Clarendon Press, 1990), p. 270.
73 Carr and Fusi, p. 233.
74 Richard Gunther, Giancomo Sani, and Goldie Shabad, *Spain After Franco* (Berkeley: University of California Press, 1988), pp. 170–175.
75 Chris Ross, 'Nationalism and Party Competition in the Basque Country and Catalonia', *West European Politics* Vol. 19, No. 3, July 1996, pp. 488–506, pp. 489–491.
76 Maravall, p. 11.
77 Arango, pp. 116–120.
78 Christopher Abel and Nisso Torrents, *Spain: Conditional Democracy* (New York: St. Martin's Press, 1984), p. 165.
79 Julio Buaquets, Miguel Angel Aguilar, and Ignacio Puche, *El Golpe* (Barcelona: Editorial Ariel, 1981), pp. 14–15.
80 Share, p. 170.
81 Arango, p. 137.
82 Thomas D. Lancaster and Gary Prevost (eds), *Politics and Change in Spain* (New York: Praeger, 1985), p. 103.
83 Joyce Lasky Shub and Raymond Carr (eds), *Spain: Studies in Political Security* (New York: Praeger, 1985), p. 53.
84 Boyd and Boyden, 1985, p. 108.
85 Some scholars, such as Felipe Aguero, argue that the potential power of the military was squandered by internal divisions in the military. For example, in May 1979 the high army council was unable to decide on a chief of staff. Instead, Defence Minister Gutiérrez Mellado appointed someone. See Aguero, 1995, p. 140.
86 Lancaster and Prevost, p. 103.
87 Lancaster and Prevost, p. 109.
88 Paloma Roma Marugan, 'Cronología', in José Félix Tezanos, Ramón Cotarelo, and Andrés de Blas Guerrero (eds), *La transición democrática española* (Madrid: Editorial Sistema, 1989), p. 893.
89 Aguero, 1995, p. 141.
90 Abel and Torrents, p. 181.
91 Abel and Torrents, p. 35.
92 Share, p. 168.

93 Aguero, 1995, p. 146.
94 Aguero, 1995, p. 165.
95 Krasikov, p. 162.
96 Henry Finch, *Contemporary Uruguay* (University of Liverpool, Institute of LA Studies, Working Paper No. 9, 1989), p. 14.
97 Finch, 1989, p. 16.
98 Finch, 1989, p. 17.
99 Ronald McDonald, 'Confrontation and Transition in Uruguay', *Current History* Vol. 84, February 1985, p. 57.
100 US Government, Library of Congress, *Uruguay: A Country Study* (Washington, DC, Federal Research Division Library of Congress, 1990), p. 37.
101 Weinstein, p. xv.
102 US Governments Library of Congress, p. 37.
103 Weinstein, p. 69.
104 Finch, 1989, p. 12.
105 Aguiar, p. 38.
106 Kaufman, p. 25.
107 Finch, 1989, p. 23.
108 Weinstein, pp. 21–35.
109 Philip Mauceri, *State Under Siege: Development and Policy Making in Peru* (Boulder: Westview, 1996), p. 62.
110 Paul Glewwe and Gillette Hall, 'Poverty, Inequality, and Living Standards During Unorthodox Adjustment: The Case of Peru, 1985–1990', *Economic Development and Cultural Change* Vol. 42, No. 4, July 1994, pp. 689–718, p. 691.
111 Mauceri, 1996, pp. 62–65.
112 Glewwe and Hall, pp. 691–692.
113 R. F. Watters, *Poverty and Peasantry in Peru's Southern Andes, 1963–1990* (Pittsburgh: University of Pittsburgh Press, 1994), p. 291.
114 '2 Polls: 3 out of 4 "Reject" President Garcia', Madrid EFE, 25 October 1988, FBIS LAT 88-207 p. 40.
115 Glewwe and Hall, p. 692.
116 Mauceri, 1996, p. 86.
117 David Scott Palmer, '"Fujipopulism" and Peru's Progress', *Current History* February 1996, p. 70.
118 David Scott Palmer, 1992, p. 67.
119 Manuel Castillo Ochoa, 'Fujimori and the Business Class', *NACLA* Vol. 30, No. 1, July/August 1996, pp. 25–30, p. 27.
120 Palmer, 1996, p. 71.
121 Arango, p. 134.
122 Carr and Fusi, pp. 49–79.
123 See Geoffrey Pridham (ed.), *The New Mediterranean Democracies* (London: Frank Cass, 1984), p. 160.

4
Terrorist violence

Introduction

Chapter four is the first of three chapters to provide evidence to test the two hypotheses. Chapter four examines the consequences of terrorism on democratic stability. The three cases of Uruguay, Peru, and Spain are similar in the first stage. Although there are many differences among the countries, they all share the presence of violent, terrorist groups. With the activity of violent groups, it is expected that citizens will become disenchanted with state performance, and ultimately with the constitution, if peace is not promptly restored. Specifically, according to hypothesis one, as terrorist violence increases or reaches a critical level, the state's fulfilment of its purposes of integration and stability should decrease. As the state fails to comply with its purposes, then levels of citizen confidence in the state should decrease. As the citizens have less confidence in their state, and ultimately the constitutional form, then there should be an increase in democratic instability. Up to this point, the three cases are similar. Chapter five discusses crucial differences among the state responses.

Terrorist groups

In all three cases, the countries were challenged by well organized and active guerrilla groups. In these cases, the terrorist groups challenged the appropriateness of the existing form of constitution, advocating change. The actions of these groups were sufficiently influential that the citizens in the countries viewed the violence and disorder as a significant challenge to the state. In addition, the presence of the groups was cited as a reason for coups and attempted coups in the three countries.

Uruguayan terrorist groups

'O bailan todos or no baila nadie'
Everyone dances, or no one does
        (Tupamaro slogan painted on a raided nightclub)

The most dominant and powerful terrorist group in Uruguay was the Tupamaros, or the MLN-T. The Tupamaros were established by a small group of intellectuals led by Raúl Sendic, Julio Marenales, and Jorge Maner Lluveras in 1962.[1] In 1967, the Tupamaros released a bulletin announcing that they had placed themselves outside of the law.[2] A Tupamaro message, broadcast on Radio Sarandi, on 15 May 1969 charged that the state benefited only an oligarchy. 'Anyone is a Tupamaro if he does not merely make demands but disobeys the laws, decrees and ordinances made by an oligarchy to their interests.'[3] Until 1969, the group concentrated most of its energy on organization and ideology.[4] The Tupamaros organized their action around four principles: the exhaustion of peaceful means for change, the necessity of armed struggle, action to promote unity, and defining politics by action, not ideology. Their actions were astutely designed to increase mass support.[5] The Tupamaros were a very effective group. They were self-sufficient, effective, and astutely handled public relations. In an interview in 1970, Tupamaro Urbano explained the Tupamaro position:

> if there isn't a homeland for all, there won't be one for anyone. At present, the actions the dictatorship is now undertaking are in furtherance and defense of an established order. That order means hundreds of workers fired, hundreds of teachers without a job, the government meddling in educational matters, the senior high school closed, and a steady worsening of poverty – the result of the drastic freezing of wages and a far from drastic freezing of the prices of staple goods.[6]

The Tupamaros did not believe the state to be a representative of the common interest. They viewed the state as a representative of purely private interests.

The Tupamaros were completely of Uruguayan origin. Arturo Porzencanski in *Uruguay's Tupamaros* stated, 'no evidence has been found that the Tupamaros ever received either money or arms from other countries or from social movements abroad'.[7] The Tupamaros were self-sufficient. They funded and stocked their organization through robberies, kidnapping, and theft. The Tupamaros explained their tactics:

> We do not go outside the country to seek financing for our revolution, but seize from our enemies the money to mount the necessary revolutionary campaign ... We must make a clear distinction between what the bourgeoisie's property and the worker's property really is. The former is, beyond a doubt, the outcome of workers' exploitation; the latter is a result of work and individual effort. Therefore, the bourgeoisie's property is our natural fountain of resources and we have the right to expropriate it without compensation.[8]

Some of the more infamous Tupamaro actions include the theft of six million dollars worth of jewellry from a branch of the Banco de la República on 12 November 1970 and the theft of four hundred thousand dollars worth of gold from the Mailhos family mansion on 4 April 1970. The Tupamaros stole 450 arms and a supply of ammunition from an army garrison on 29 May 1970. In addition, the Tupamaros raided industry to obtain chemical and explosive supplies. These strategies were very effective in maintaining and supplying the Tupamaro organization.

The Tupamaros were also effective in spreading their propaganda to the Uruguayan public. Before strict censorship was imposed on the reporting of terrorist actions, the Tupamaros regularly sent communiqués to the media. Later they used other strategies of communication, including the distribution of leaflets and posters. Later, the Tupamaros even temporarily took over businesses to give speeches to their captive audiences. Radio stations were also stormed, including the Tupamaro interruption of a soccer match on 15 May 1969 and the takeover of a radio station that provided background music for all Montevidean department stores on 24 May 1969.

The Tupamaros also used kidnapping of state officials, foreign diplomats, businessmen, and landowners for both political and financial gain. Notable kidnapping victims include U. Pereyra Reverbel, head of the state electricity and telephone corporations, G. Pellegrini Giampietro, a banker, D. Pereyra Manellie, a judge involved in the prosecution of Tupamaros, Dan Mitrione, an Agency for International Development expert and advisor to the Uruguayan police force, Geoffrey Jackson, Ambassador of the United Kingdom to Uruguay, and H. G. Ruíz, president of the Uruguayan House of Representatives. The kidnap victims were held for up to eighteen months in the 'people's jail' of the Tupamaros. Only Mitrione was killed.[9]

The Tupamaros projected themselves as a shadow government. After the March kidnapping of prosecutor general Dr. Guidi Berro Oribe, the Tupamaros tried him in a mock trial for his irregularities in office. The Tupamaros attempted to portray the image of an alternate state; a state which did what the real state should have been doing, but was unable to. In addition, tape recordings of the trial were released to the press, all in a deliberate attempt to appear as a viable alternative to the existing state. Once released, Oribe stated that the Tupamaros seemed to be extremely well briefed lawyers, perhaps with access to secret files. His comments started a concern that many state officials or functionaries were secretly Tupamaros.[10]

The Tupamaros also succeeded in discrediting the Uruguayan police. Not only did the police have difficulty in arresting Tupamaros, but if they did manage to arrest some, they usually were released shortly thereafter or escaped from prison. There were four mass prison breaks. Through the use of police disguises, thirteen women were freed from the women's prison on 9 March 1970. Later, on 20 July 1971, thirty-eight more were freed from the same prison. At the maximum security prison called Punta Carretas, 106 prisoners were freed on 6 September 1971 and 15 on 12 April 1972. In addition to bribing and intimidating prison workers, the Tupamaros constructed tunnels to escape.[11] The Tupamaros freed approximately 108 of their own members from prison.

Although most Uruguayans disagreed with Tupamaro tactics, many agreed with their aims. For example, in April 1971 Alberto Heber, a possible Blanco presidential candidate, announced that the state should negotiate with the Tupamaros on questions of national policy.[12] Others, including senators and representatives, agreed with some of the Tupamaro policy proposals, although they disagreed with their means of achieving them.

Although the Tupamaros were the best organized and most influential terrorist group in Uruguay, there were also other groups. Other small leftist, urban guerrilla groups include FARO, the Fuerzas Armadas Revolucionarios, and OPR-33, the Organización Popular Treinta y Tres. In addition, there were other groups such as the Frente Revolucionario de Trabajadores (FRT), the Movimiento XXII de Diciembre (a splinter group of the Tupamaros), La Guerrilla, Grupo de Acción Unificadora (the alleged illegal counterpart to its legal faction of the Frente Amplio), the Comandos de Autodefensa del Pueblo (CAP, formed of medical students), students groups 'Alcides' and 'Franco,' Agrupaciones Rojas and the Frente Armado Popular (FAP).[13]

Peruvian terrorist groups

The party has a thousand eyes and a thousand ears.
(Sendero slogan)

The Communist Party of Peru in the Shining Path of José Carlos Mariátegui (PCP-SL), is a splinter group of the Peruvian Communist Party.[14] It was founded by Abimael Guzmán in 1970, after he had returned from a year in China. The split was caused by the Communist Party's rejection of clandestine organization and armed struggle that Guzmán advocated.[15] The early base of the new Sendero organization was urban and based in Ayacucho, according to Deborah Poole and Gerardo Renique. 'The principal early base of popular support for the PCP-SL was a broad-based urban defense front which held large, public and extremely visible assemblies and marches in the Plaza de Armas of Ayacucho.'[16] In 1980, Sendero's first acts were the hanging of dogs in Lima and ballot burning in Chuschi.[17] Bombings of private companies and public buildings started in late 1980. In 1982, Sendero sent a message to Lima by blowing up five high tension electrical towers in Lima, leaving the city without power or lights.[18] Sendero had a grand plan for its actions: to turn the backwards areas into bases of revolutionary support, to attack the state and revisionist elements, to develop guerrilla war and spread violence, to expand the bases of support, to seize the cities, and to cause the collapse of the state.[19]

At first, Sendero was not considered a threat. State officials thought Senderistas were common criminals or a product of an international subversive movement. For example, Peruvian president Belaúnde stated: 'it was a conspiracy against Peru within a universal strategy . . . This is totally demonstrated with the discovered archives in democratic Germany and now with some notices in Moscow: the support that was given to the subversive movements for the exportation of revolutions.'[20] The left thought they were part of a CIA plot to discredit them. The right believed that Sendero was merely a covert arm of the left.[21] However, Sendero was not a covert arm of the legal left, was not a group of common criminals, and was not a product of international subversion. Sendero was a violent group of domestic origin that viewed everyone who did not cooperate with them as an enemy, whether on the right, the left, or without affiliation. Sendero was estimated to have approximately 10,000 active members with 50,000 to 100,000 supporters in the early 1990s. [22]

In addition to Sendero, another group, MRTA, or Movimiento Revolucionario Tupac Amaro, emerged. MRTA started its violent actions in January 1984, with an assassination and an attack on a police station in Villa El Salvador, a neighbourhood of Lima. MRTA viewed itself as a movement modelled in the style of Che Guevara and pursued a socialist revolution.[23] MRTA publicly revealed its name in July 1984. Later, it spread beyond Lima to the province of Paucartambo in the department of Cusco. Soon after, MRTA suffered a blow in Paucartambo on 26 November 1984 when the police captured a dozen activists and confiscated rifles, uniforms, and ammunition. MRTA responded with the kidnapping of a reporter and her cameraman to document charges of torture and mistreatment of suspected terrorists in Cusco.[24] MRTA's presence continued to grow in Lima. In October 1987, MRTA began activity in the department of San Martín.

MRTA attempted to gain a reputation of being the 'good guerrillas'. For example, when MRTA took command of the city of Juanjuí, in the department of San Martín, they announced that 'they don't come to sentence any public official or local person to death, but on the contrary, they come to have a frank discussion with the local population'.[25] In the beginning of García's term as president, MRTA temporarily suspended actions against the state, in hopes that García would comply with his campaign promises. Two MRTA leaders, Luis Varesse and Víctor Polay Campos, demanded that the state break with the International Monetary Fund and declare a moratorium on debt payments, raise the minimum wage to reflect the cost of living, declare an amnesty for all political prisoners, and end the 'dirty war'.[26]

Spanish terrorist groups

Euskadi ala hil.
Basque Country or death.[27]

ETA originated in a small group of students who created a journal called *Ekin* (Action) in 1953–1954.[28] In 1959, some Basque youths, frustrated with a lack of action, formed ETA. Although the history of ETA as an organization is complex, significant splits can be identified. In the early 1970s, ETA split into two groups: ETA-militar (ETA-m) and ETA-político-militar (ETA-pm). ETA-m is more committed to violence whereas ETA-pm was more inclined to negotiate.[29] Another group, EIA (Euskao Iraultzale Alderdia, the Basque Revolutionary Party), was formed as a splinter group of ETA, although it is committed to nonviolent action.[30] Two political groups emerged from within the rebel organizations. ETA-pm, which disbanded in 1981, transformed itself into the Euskadiko Eskerra (EE). ETA-m, which remains an active violent group, is represented by Herri Batasuna.[31]

ETA's main goals are self-determination and the reunification of *Euskadi*. *Euskadi* was the name given to the desired Basque state by Basque nationalist and founder of the PNV, Sabino de Arana, in 1865. The claimed region consists of the Spanish northwestern provinces of Alava, Navarra, Guipuzcoa, and Vizcaya in addition to three French southern provinces.[32] An ETA 1964 pamphlet called 'Insurrection in the Basque Country' compared the Basque country to a Spanish colony as in Franz Fanon's *Wretched of the Earth*, and called for rebellion against the Spanish national state.[33] Herri Batasuna proposed a five point programme which included Basque independence, the inclusion of Navarra into the region, amnesty for all political prisoners, improved working conditions, and the withdrawal of Spanish security forces.[34]

ETA continued its activities even after the democratization, calling the new democracy a 'pseudo-democracy'. The referendum of the constitution was not well supported in the Basque country by either the citizens or the main parties. The PNV recommended abstention and both HB and EE advocated a no vote in the referendum. In the final tally only 45 per cent of eligible voters participated, compared with 68 per cent nationally. Of those who voted, only 31 per cent approved of the constitution and 24 per cent rejected it.[35] ETA has been responsible for the vast majority of terrorist violence since the return to democracy.

Initially, ETA targeted symbols of the Franco regime and later the Spanish nation state, including the military, the police, and the civil guard. ETA assassinated Franco's prime minister, Admiral Carrero Blanco, by detonating eighty kilos of explosives under his car after he returned from mass in 1972.[36] Later, the targets included Basque industrialists and banks.[37] ETA continued to target prominent military officers. From 1976 to 1986, ETA killed thirteen generals. Many times, assassination of high ranking officials coincided with symbolic occasions. For instance, on 21 July 1978, the day the constitution was approved by the *Cortés*, ETA killed an army general. ETA assassinated Madrid's military governor General Ortín in January 1979, shortly after the constitutional referendum. On the eve of the Armed Forces Day on 25 May 1979, ETA assassinated the army chief of personnel and two colonels.[38] Another symbolic assassination occurred in November 1982, when ETA assassinated the commander of the elite Brunete military division, General Lago Roman. The assassination took place five days before the new socialist prime minister Felipe Gonzalez was to assume power.[39]

The activities of ETA have been varied and extensive. ETA mainly operates in the Basque area and in the cities of Barcelona, Madrid, and Zaragosa.[40] In addition to bombings and armed attacks, ETA also conducts kidnappings and extortion.[41] One estimate cites that ETA has been responsible for over five hundred assassinations, over a thousand people maimed, more than sixty kidnappings, and countless armed assaults, robberies, and bombings. Its extortion, presented to the 'contributors' as 'revolutionary taxation,' has been substantial, with thousands of Basque industrialists and professionals being 'taxed'.[42]

Who participates in ETA? Most ETA members are young, single men. Instead of being full time rebels, most hold regular jobs and then participate in ETA as a part time activity.[43] One study conducted by R. P. Clark characterized ETA members as typically young men between the ages of twenty-five and thirty. He found that most were of working class or lower middle class origin with either one or two native Basque parents.[44] In addition to the part time rebels, there are full time leaders, whose identities, but not whereabouts, are usually known to the police.[45]

In the mid-1980s two things began to change the environment in which ETA operated. First, both the PNV and the EE were less supportive of the violence used by ETA. In fact, the parties condemned ETA violence. In addition, the Spanish state began to gain the cooperation of French authorities in combating ETA, both within Spain and in France.[46]

In addition to ETA, two other groups practised violent dissension. GRAPO, or Grupos de Resistencia Antifascista Primero de Octubre/the Antifascist Resistance Groups of the First of October, emerged on 1 October 1975, after a shooting in which four Madrid police officers were killed.[47] The aim of GRAPO was to create a revolutionary vanguard.[48] GRAPO never had more than thirty militants as members.[49] A few attacks attributed to GRAPO occurred in 1990.[50] The other small group was Frente Revolucionario Antifascista y Patriótico (FRAP). The group emerged in the 1970s from the Communist Party. It aimed to overthrow Franco's Spain and establish a people's republic instead.[51]

In addition, Basques were targeted by other violent groups. These groups became active in 1975. For example, the Batallón Vasco-Español or BVE killed five, wounded thirty-four, and kidnapped two between 1975 and 1977. There were also urban riots started by groups of rightists who attacked Basques. These groups, called *incontrolados*, committed at least twenty attacks, killing one and wounding twenty-four, in the last half of 1977.[52]

Uruguay: terrorist violence

Uruguay was fairly peaceful until the late 1960s. An average of ten or fewer incidents occurred yearly until 1968. Despite Uruguay's well established democracy, the Tupamaros emerged. In Uruguay, terrorist violence can be measured by tallying the number of bombings, assassinations, robberies, instances of forced propaganda, armed attacks, and kidnappings.

In 1968, the number of incidents increased tenfold, as shown in figure 4.1. The amount of violence continued to increase until the election year of 1971. During this year, the major group, the Tupamaros, had declared a unilateral cease-fire to participate in the presidential elections, favouring the Frente Amplio. After the 1971 elections and the inauguration of President Bordaberry, the Tupamaros launched more attacks. The year 1972 showed an increase of over 300 per cent in violent incidences. The eruption of violence was short-lived, however. The following year, only two incidents were reported.

Figure 4.2 breaks down the incidents into the type of action. Overall, bombings were most common, followed by robberies. Armed attacks and assassinations occurred, but were less frequent than other incidents. The spreading of propaganda by creating captive audiences was a common, bloodless action of the Tupamaros. The vigorous fundraising by kidnapping and robbery is also apparent. The peak of kidnappings occurred in 1971. There were more robberies in 1972.

Figure 4.3 shows how explosive the growth in terrorist violence was in 1972. The first half of 1972 saw prolific action by the Tupamaros and by others. Although the year

---

Hypothesis one: terrorist violence

Terrorist violence threatens democratic stability by undermining both rudimentary purposes of the state, security, and integration. As the purposes of the state are unfulfilled, citizen confidence in the state declines. As citizen confidence decreases, democratic instability increases.

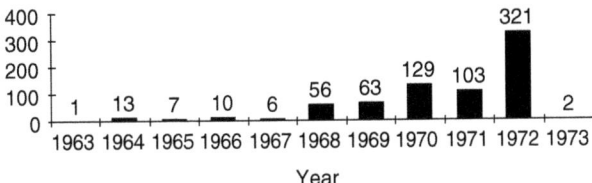

Figure 4.1 Uruguay: total incidents of terrorist violence, 1963–1973
Source: Republica Oriental del Uruguay Junta de Comandantes en Jefe, *La Subversion* (Montevideo: Las Fuerzas Armadas al Pueblo Oriental, 1977).

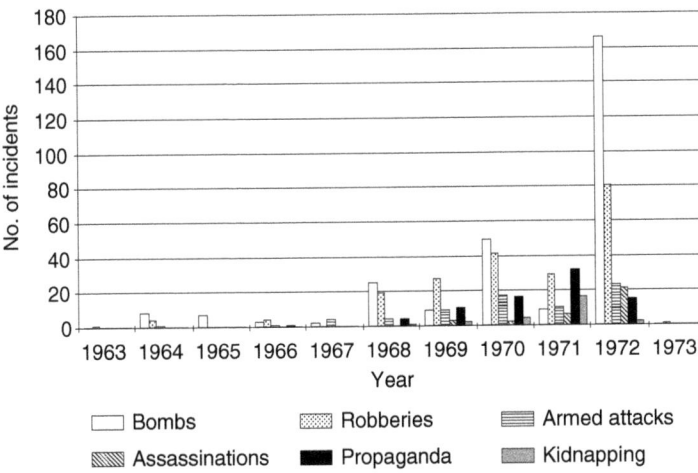

Figure 4.2 Uruguay: terrorist incidents by category, 1963–1973
Source: Republica Oriental del Uruguay Junta de Comandantes en Jefe, *La Subversion* (Montevideo: Las Fuerzas Armadas al Pueblo Oriental, 1977).
Note: In this chart, bombs are counted one per location, and unspecified pluralities are counted as two. Robberies are armed assaults with the gain of some material as the aim of the action (this includes money, supplies, automobiles, evidence, etc.). Propaganda is material publicly released by subversive groups. This includes numerous incidents of the Tupamaros holding a captive audience to make announcements. Armed assaults are armed attacks by seditious groups on the military, the police, or other people affiliated with the government. Assassinations are deaths of people caused by seditious action. (Note: if an armed assault resulted in a death, it is counted both as an assassination and as an armed assault.)

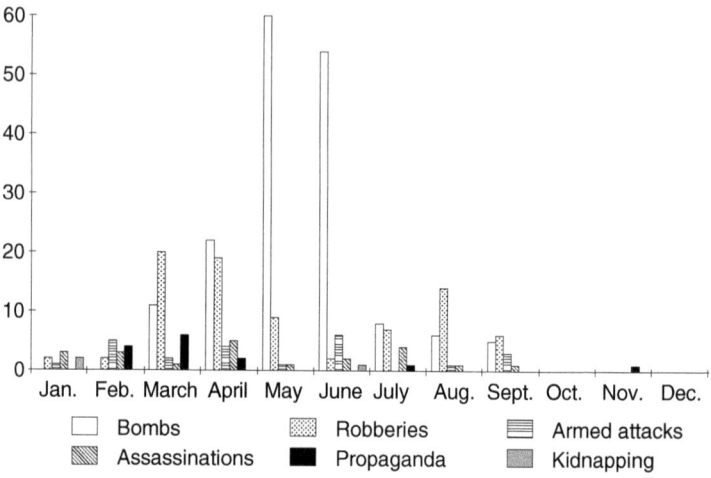

Figure 4.3 Uruguay: monthly terrorist incidents by category, 1972
Source: Republica Oriental del Uruguay Junta de Comandantes en Jefe, *La Subversion* (Montevideo: Las Fuerzas Armadas al Pueblo Oriental, 1977).

had over three times as many incidents, most of them occurred in the first half of the year. To Uruguayans, it appeared that there were more than six times the incidents than the year before.

On 14 April 1972 the Tupamaros started a new offensive against the armed forces. After Bordaberry assumed the presidency, the Tupamaros kidnapped a policeman named Nelson Bardesio. Bardesio confessed to the Tupamaros that he had participated in extreme right anti-Tupamaro groups, although he claimed he had been forced to participate. He produced evidence for his claims that the Tupamaros forwarded to the press. Shortly after, the Tupamaros issued a communiqué condemning to death officials who had participated in the anti-Tupamaro commando group, Caza Tupamaros. Four were assassinated within hours of the announcement. In May, there was a significant increase in the number of bombings, from twenty-two in April to sixty in May. However, this rabid increase in violence did not last. After the military's takeover of the fight against subversion, rapid gains were made in quelling the terrorist violent

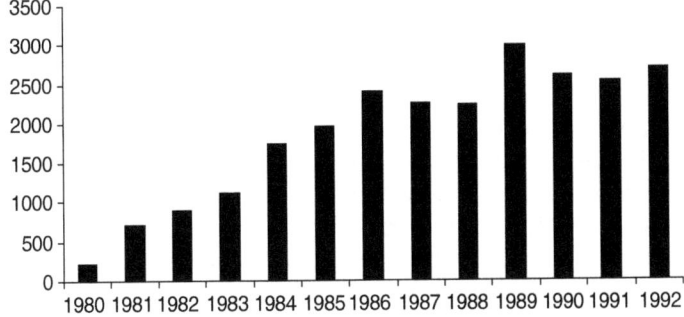

Figure 4.4 Peru: non-state terrorist violent incidents, 1980–1992
Source: Ministry of the Interior.

activity. As of September 1972, for all practical purposes, the threat from the terrorist groups had ended.

Peru: terrorist violence

The amplitude of the threat of guerrilla groups[53] to Peruvian democracy exceeded that of any other country examined in this study. Violent rebellion greatly increased despite the return to democratic governance in 1980. In the case of Peru, threats from Sendero were credible and deadly. Both citizens and leaders were afraid and targeted. In Peru, terrorist violence can be measured by tallying the number of bombings, armed attacks, and assassinations.

From the restoration of democracy in 1980 to the *autogolpe* of Fujimori in 1992, the number of terrorist violent incidents increased tenfold, as demonstrated in figure 4.4. During the last three years of democracy, the level of violence stabilized, but at an alarmingly high level.

The most striking increases of violence occurred during Belaúnde's presidency of 1980–1985. The frequency of incidences increased 795 per cent. During García's term (1985–1990), violence increased an additional 33 per cent. In the two constitutional years of Fujimori's rule (1990–1992) violence increased an additional 3 per cent.

Sendero also asserted its power by depriving Lima and Peruvian industry of electricity. This type of attack had grave consequences for the economic activity of the country. A total of 1409 electrical towers were toppled from 1980–1991, with a peak of 276 towers toppled in 1989. The Senate

Commission of National Pacification estimated the total cost to be US $19,440,984,000 from mid-May 1980 to December 1991.[54]

The influence of the terrorist violent groups, Sendero and MRTA, can also be measured by the rankings of their respective leaders, Abimael Gúzman and Victor Polay, as powerful Peruvians. Gúzman emerged on the survey of Peruvian power in 1982, in twenty-eighth place. After 1983 and before his arrest, however, Gúzman had been consistently rated in the top ten. For example, in 1991 Gúzman ranked fourth. Polay, however, did not appear until 1989. In that year, he ranked twenty-fifth. In 1990, he ranked seventeenth and tenth in 1991.[55] In 1992, Gúzman ranked third and Polay ranked twenty-fourth.[56] In that year, only Fujimori and one of his top ministers ranked higher than Gúzman. Gúzman evidently was considered a very powerful man as a result of his leadership of Sendero.

Spain: terrorist violence

It is interesting to note that the main terrorist group emerged while the authoritarian Franco still ruled. Despite the origin of these groups under Franco's non-democratic regime, the new democracy inherited the challenge of responding to their threats. As democratic consolidation progressed, it continued to be challenged by violent groups. Table 4.1 provides trends of the different types of violence. ETA violence in particular increased after the death of Franco until 1980, when the violence peaked. Grapo violence peaked in 1979. However, the ETA violence proved to be resilient, continuing at a modest level of activity until 1986.

In response to ETA, violent groups emerged from the right. There is some disparity in accounts tallying the number of people killed by the extreme right. In table 4.1, different accounts of the number of those killed by the extreme right are represented. Some of the groups of the far right were Antiterrorísmo ETA, Alianza Apostólica Anticomunista (AAA), and the Acción Nacional España. These groups targeted suspected members of ETA in Spain and in France. Sometimes leftist activists were targeted. For example, in 1977 AAA killed four lawyers who represented illegal workers' organizations.[57] Depending on the source, extreme right violence peaked either in 1976 or in 1980.

Table 4.1 Spain: non-state terrorist incidents with attributions of responsibility, 1976–1986

	ETA series 1	ETA series 2	ETA kidnappings	Violent right	Extreme right	Violent left	GRAPO	Other separatist	Unknown
1976	7	11	4	10	3	12	1	0	7
1977	14	10	1	3	4	14	5	85	8
1978	33	58	6	2	1	3	6	3	13
1979	56	63	13	2	5	9	23	0	1
1980	28	72	13	3	13	4	4	0	4
1981	20	27	10	5	1	1	4	0	3
1982	8	31	8	0	0	0	2	0	0
1983	6	35	5	0	0	3	2	0	0
1984	10	26	0	0	0	4	4	5	1
1985	21	31	3	0	0	0	0	0	0
1986	17	19	3	0	0	0	0	5	2

Sources: ETA series 1, violent right, violent left, other separatist, and unknown come from TWEED. TWEED data are based on the coding of Keesings World News Archive. The data are discussed in Jan Oskar Engene, 'Five Decades of Terrorism in Europe: The TWEED Dataset', *Journal of Peace Research*, Vol. 44, No. 1, 2007, pp. 109–121. The data are also available online at www.uib.no/people/sspje/tweed.htm. ETA kidnapping data are from the Spanish Ministry of the Interior www.mir.es/oris/infoeta/esp/p12-esp.htm. Estimates of ETA series 2, Grapo and extreme right incidents are from Salustiano del Campo (ed.), *Tendencias Sociales en España Volumen II* (Bilbao: Fundación BBV, 1993), p. 70.

Notes: For 1977 Other separatist, includes incidents from Movimiento para la Autodeterminación e Independencia del Archipiélago de las Canarias (MPAIAC) and other pro-Canary Islands activists. ETA tallies include ETA-pm and ETA-m. Incidents of domestic terrorism that are covered by the international press are reported here.

Table 4.2 Spain: non-state terrorist incidents by type, 1976–1986

	Bombings	Armed attacks	Kidnapping	Victim profile	ETA	Violent right	Violent left	Other separatist
1976	22	5	5	Military	29	0	6	1
1977	16	16	2	Police	126	0	17	2
1978	25	26	1	Senior civil servants	6	0	1	0
1979	31	30	3	Politicians	7	0	0	2
1980	11	17	0	Business Executives	4	0	3	0
1981	3	7	6	Union leader	0	5	0	0
1982	0	6	2	Clergy	0	0	0	0
1983	3	3	2	Other militants	0	1	0	0
1984	5	9	0	Civilians	88	8	10	0
1985	5	13	1					
1986	7	9	2					

Source: TWEED data.

Terrorist violence can be measured by the number of bombings, armed attacks, and kidnappings, shown in Table 4.2.

The number of kidnappings by ETA follows a similar pattern to right-wing violence, with a peak of ETA kidnappings occurring in 1981. The main mode of terrorist activity was either a bombing or an armed attack. The targets of ETA and violence tended to be predominantly directed towards the police or the military. The violent right, on the other hand, targeted union leaders and civilians, exclusively.

Part one summary

In all three countries, a significant amount of terrorist violence existed. In Uruguay, the terrorist violence peaked in 1972. In Peru, the amount of violence continued to increase until 1989, when it stabilized at a high level. In Spain, the violence hit its highest point in 1980. The consequences of the terrorist violence for the fulfilment of the rudimentary purposes of the state, on citizen confidence, and on democratic stability are examined in part three.

Notes

1 *Generals and Tupamaros*, p. ii.
2 Marvin Alisky, *Latin American Media: Guidance and Censorship* (Ames: Iowa State University, 1981), p. 196.
3 Alain Labrousse, *The Tupamaros: Urban Guerrillas in Uruguay* (Harmondsworth: Penguin Books, 1970), p. 149.
4 Porzencanski, p. 52.
5 *Generals and Tupamaros*, p. ii.
6 'Interview with Urbano' by Leopoldo Madruga; James Kohl and John Litt, *Urban Guerrilla Warfare in Latin America* (Cambridge: MIT Press, 1974), p. 275.
7 Porzencanski, p. 41.
8 Porzencanski, p. 40.
9 Porzencanski, pp. 40–44.
10 *Generals and Tupamaros*, pp. 22–23.

11 Porzencanski, p. 41.
12 *Generals and Tupamaros*, p. 23.
13 Republica Oriental del Uruguay Junta de Comandantes en Jefe, *La Subversion* (Montevideo: Las Fuerzas Armadas al Pueblo Oriental, 1977), pp. 349–353.
14 José Carlos Mariátegui, *Seven Interpretive Essays*, translated by Marjory Urquidi (Austin: University of Texas Press, 1971). Mariátegui founded the Socialist Party of Peru in 1928 and broke with APRA. Mariátegui believed in a national, democratic revolution as a step towards socialism. See Julio Cotler, 'Democracy and National Integration in Peru', in Cynthia McClintock and Abraham F. Lowenthal (eds), *The Peruvian Experiment Reconsidered* (Princeton: Princeton University Press, 1983), p. 8.
15 Deborah Poole and Gerardo Renique, 'The New Chroniclers of Peru: US Scholars and their "Shining Path" of Peasant Revolution,' *Bulletin of Latin American Research* Vol. 10, No. 2, 1991, pp. 133–191, p. 141.
16 Poole and Renique, p. 157.
17 Palmer, 1986, p. 129.
18 'El gran apagon de los luminosos,' *Equis X* (Lima) No. 305, 23 August 1982, pp. 8–10, p. 8.
19 *Caretas* on 20 September 1982. The early literature on Sendero has been severely criticized by two scholars, Deborah Poole and Gerardo Renique (see n. 15).
20 Fernando Belaunde Terry, 'El Destino Reparador', in Rolando Forgues (ed.), *Perú: entre el desafío de la violencia y el sueño de lo posible* (Lima: Minerra, 1993), p. 28.
21 Philip Mauceri, 'Military Politics and Counter-insurgency in Peru,' *Journal of Interamerican Studies and World Affairs* Vol. 33, No. 4, Winter 1991, pp. 83–109, p. 90. See also Gustavo Ellenbogen Gorriti, *Sendero: historia de la guerra milenaria en el Perú* (Lima: Editorial Apoyo, 1990).
22 McClintock, Cynthia, *Revolutionary Movements in Latin America: El Salvador's FMLN and Peru's Shining Path* (Washington, DC: United States Institute of Peace, 1998), pp. 74–75.
23 Yehude Simon Munaro, *Estado y Guerrillas en el Peru de los '80* (Lima: EES Asociación Instituto de los Estudios Estratégicos y Sociales, 1988), p. 120.
24 Munaro, pp. 108–110.
25 *QueHacer*, March/April 1988, p. 32.
26 *QueHacer*, March/April 1988, p. 40.
27 William Douglass and Joseba Zulaika, 'On the Interpretation of Terrorist Violence: ETA and the Basque Political Process,' *Comparative Studies in Society and History* Vol. 32, No. 2, April 1990, pp. 238–257, p. 252.
28 Stanley Payne, *Basque Nationalism* (Reno: University of Nevada Press, 1975), p. 242.
29 Arango, p. 225.

30 For a complete history of the numerous splits and conflicts within the organization, see Cyrus Zirakzadeh, *A Rebellious People: Basques, Protests and Politics* (Reno: University of Nevada Press, 1991).
31 Douglass and Zulaika, p. 246.
32 H. H. Tucker (ed.), *Combating the Terrorists: Democratic Responses to Political Violence* (New York: Facts on File, 1988), pp. 155–156.
33 Douglass and Zulaika, p. 244.
34 Goldie Shabad, 'After Autonomy: The Dynamics of Regionalism in Spain', in Stanley Payne (ed.), *The Politics of Democratic Spain* (Chicago: Chicago Council on Foreign Relations, 1986), p. 149.
35 Goldie Shabad and Francisco José Llera Ramo, 'Political Violence in a Democratic State: Basque Terrorism in Spain,' in Martha Crenshaw (ed.), *Terrorism in Context* (University Park: Pennsylvania State University Press, 1991), p. 452.
36 Peter Janke, *Spanish Separatism: ETA's Threat to Basque Democracy* (London: Institute for the Study of Conflict, 1980), p. 3.
37 Shabad and Llera Ramo, p. 443.
38 Aguero, 1995, p. 142.
39 Edward Moxon-Browne and Peter Janke, 'Terrorism and the Spanish State', in H. H. Tucker (ed.), *Combating the Terrorists: Democratic Responses to Political Violence* (New York. Facts on File, 1988), p. 161.
40 Douglass and Zulaika, p. 246.
41 Arango, p. 226.
42 Shabad and Llera Ramo, p. 441.
43 Douglass and Zulaika, p. 245.
44 Moxon-Browne and Janke, p. 159. See also R. P. Clark, 'Patterns in the Lives of ETA Members', in P. Merkl (ed.), *Political Violence and Terror* (Berkeley: University of California Press, 1986), pp. 283–307.
45 Shabad and Llera Ramo, p. 438.
46 Shabad and Llera Ramo, p. 462.
47 Robert Clark, *The Basques: The Franco Years and Beyond* (Reno: University of Nevada Press, 1979), p. 282, p. 58.
48 José Feliz Tezanos, Ramón Cotarelo, and Andrés De Blas, *La Transición Democrática Española* (Madrid: Editorial Sistema, 1989), p. 625.
49 Luis Alonso and Fernando Reinares, 'Conflictividad', in Salustiano del Campo (ed.), *Tendencias Sociales en España Volumen I* (Bilbao: Fundacion BBV, 1993), p. 23.
50 Arango, p. 223.
51 Alonso and Reinares, p. 22.
52 Robert P. Clark, *Negotiating with ETA: Obstacles to Peace in the Basque Country, 1975–1988* (Reno: University of Nevada Press, 1990), p. 39. See also Miguel Castells Arteche, *Radiografía de un model represivo* (San Sebastián: Ediciones Vascas, 1982) and Robert P. Clark, *The Basque Insurgents: ETA, 1952–1980* (Madison: University of Wisconsin Press, 1984).

53 Edward Muller, Henry Dietz, and Steven Finkel examine the reasons for participation in the insurgent groups in Peru. They find that alienation from the political system is the most relevant to explain participation. Edward Muller, Henry Dietz, and Steven Finkel, 'Discontent and the Unexpected Utility of Rebellion: The Case of Peru,' *American Political Science Review* Vol. 85, No. 4, December 1991, pp. 1261–1283.

54 Comisión Especial de Investigación y Estudio sobre la Violencia y Alternativas de Pacificación, 1992, pp. 70–72.

55 'Results Published', p. 33, Lima Debate in Spanish, July–September 1991, FBIS LAT 91 180, pp. 32–36.

56 '"Power of Peru" Evaluated in Annual Survey', Lima Debate in Spanish, June-August 1992, pp. 28–43, FBIS LAT 92 179, p. 38.

57 Peter Janke, *Guerrilla and Terrorist Organizations* (New York: Macmillan, 1981), pp. 76–86.

5
State repression and violence

Chapter five examines state repression and violence in the context of democratic stability. To fully understand the consequences of terrorism, both the terrorism and the state response to it must be examined. It is theorized that state repression and violence, like terrorism, undermines the rudimentary purposes of the state. Consequently, declines in citizen confidence in the state and an increase in democratic stability are expected.

> **Hypothesis two: state repression and violence**
>
> State repression and violence undermine the rudimentary purposes of the state, integration, and security. Decreases in citizen confidence should follow a decrease in the fulfilment of the rudimentary purposes. Finally, as citizen confidence in the state decreases, increases in democratic instability should be identifiable.

Uruguay

How did Uruguay respond to Tupamaro violence? In general, the government began to shift resources from social spending to military and police spending. From 1968–1973 education spending went from 24 per cent of the budget to only 16 per cent of the budget. At the same time, military spending rose from 13.9 per cent to 26.2 per cent of the budget.[1]

When faced with guerrilla groups and economic unrest, the Uruguayan state turned to indiscriminate, repressive means. Instead of due process for suspected criminals, the state invoked security measures that suspended individual rights of all citizens. The police began to torture those in its custody. Striking workers were drafted. The media was censored. The military was put in charge of anti-terrorist operations and the prisons.

Repressive state actions and policies

When Jorge Pacheco Areco became president after the death of President Oscar Gestido on 6 December 1967, Pacheco was faced with severe national problems: deep economic trouble, strikes, student unrest, and violent rebellion. Pacheco responded by ruling by executive decree and suspending rights. Within a week of taking office, Pacheco banned five small leftist parties for their alleged support of armed conflict. These actions were taken despite the lack of a legal statute allowing the executive branch to close newspapers or outlaw political associations.[2] The five parties banned by executive resolution 1788/967 were the Partido Socialista del Uruguay (Socialist Party), the Federación Anarquista (Uruguayan Anarchist Federation), the Uruguaya Movimiento Revolucionario Oriental (Oriental Revolutionary Movement), Movimiento de Acción Proletario Unitario (United Proletarian Action Movement), and the Movimiento de Izquierda Revolucionario (Movement of the Revolutionary Left).[3] Also in response to worker and student unrest, President Pacheco declared the establishment of prompt security measures (medidas prontas de seguridad, or MPS) on 13 June 1968.[4] These security measures were implemented numerous times until the dissolution of the National Assembly.

Furthermore, to prevent workers from striking, Pacheco militarized the workers, forcibly drafting them into service. Consequently, the workers could be court-martialled for striking. In July 1968, Pacheco drafted 15,000 striking workers from the National Telephone Company, 11,500 from the National Fuel, Alcohol, and Cement Administration, 1600 from the State Telecommunications Agency and 4000 from the State Sanitation Department.[5] Faced with more labour unrest, Pacheco militarized the police force on

7 July 1969. Later, in response to a bank strike, Pacheco militarized the workers and ordered them back to work.[6] In general, 1969 was not a good year for labour. During that year, hundreds of labour leaders were arrested and allegedly beaten. In response to the repression, in July 1969, the labour union the National Confederation of Workers was operating clandestinely.[7]

Pacheco also responded forcibly to student protest. In August 1968, police raided the central university and the Colleges of Agriculture, Architecture, Fine Arts, and Medicine. On 14 August 1968 a student, Liber Arce, was killed in a student protest. Two more were killed on 20 September and forty were wounded.[8] In general, Pacheco did not hesitate to use his powers, constitutional or otherwise, to suppress unrest.

Starting in late 1967, the closure of news agencies became a common occurrence in Uruguay. Pacheco's government also instituted press censorship on 24 September 1968. The InterAmerican Press Society declared that in 1968, 1969, and 1970 freedom of the press did not exist. For example, the words 'Tupamaros', 'seditious', and 'subversive' were banned. Censorship of private mail was allowed.[9] Starting in November 1970, the newspapers were only able to publish items and pictures of the Tupamaros provided by the state.[10] From 1967 to 1972, thirty-six papers and radio stations were temporarily closed and ten were permanently closed.[11] Censorship, previously practically unknown in Uruguay, was thorough and pervasive. Pacheco also moved beyond standard censorship in controlling the press, by instituting news blackouts. On 12 April 1971, he decreed that only state supplied news about guerrilla activities could be reported. This was expanded on 11 August 1971 to include labour strikes, union meetings and decisions, and anything else the state considered subversive. A few days later, on 16 August 1971, another decree was issued prohibiting any printed material dealing with armed protest or with an origin in 'nondemocratic', 'totalitarian', or 'subversive' countries. On 4 September 1971, Pacheco temporarily closed all opposition newspapers after the assassination of two national guardsmen.[12]

After 1970, the police and the armed forces conducted numerous house searches. For example, in August 1970 the police searched approximately 20,000 houses, attempting to uncover Tupamaro hideouts and rescue kidnapped victims. Often these searches occurred at night and without proper warrants. Instead of finding Tupamaros, these searches 'created great resentment among Montevideo's population'.[13]

In June 1971, Interior Minister Santiago de Brum Carbajal declared the country to be in a state of war. He also announced that a registry to track every Uruguayan residence, occupation, and place of work was almost complete. He said it was necessary to know 'what every Uruguayan was doing all the time'.[14] On 9 September 1971, after the jailbreak of 106 Tupamaros, Pacheco reassigned jurisdiction of the prisons to the military. On the same day he placed the military in charge of the anti-Tupamaro campaign.

President Pacheco also suspended the right of habeas corpus. On 25 October 1971 the Uruguayan Supreme Court challenged the legality of the decree. The court ruled that the 'recourse to habeas corpus is the indispensable remedy that keeps the security measures from losing their existence of that same Rule of Law, in moments of unexpected disturbance'.[15] In spite of the court challenge, Pacheco continued with the policy. The president replied that habeas corpus no longer applied under MPS or prompt security measures.

The universities also were affected by the repression. In December 1972, the system of public education lost its long held autonomy and was placed under the authority of the Consejo Nacional de Educación (National Council on Education; CONAE). According to Article 25 of the Law of General Education, CONAE

> is authorized to apply or see to the application, individual or collective, of restrictive disciplinary and eliminatory measures, including transfer, change to open scheduling or whatever measure is considered appropriate to the gravity of the situation.

It also allowed prison terms for professors who 'attack the sovereignty of the state'.[16] In addition, the law required that all meetings be authorized. The law was followed with protests.

The recourse to repressive state actions that became habitual under President Pacheco was continued by

President Bordaberry. A state of internal war was declared in April 1972. It was imposed 'for the sole purpose of authorizing the measures necessary to suppress the activities of individuals or groups that in any way conspire against the nation, in the terms set forth in the constitution'.[17] That same month and despite opposition in the National Assembly, in April 1972, Bordaberry gained passage of his 'Law of State Security'. The new law institutionalized many of the decrees that Bordaberry and Pacheco instituted in their attempts to curb subversion. The new law increased penalties to thirty years for revolutionary activity, to eighteen years for association with a subversive group, and to two years in jail for journalists who commit press crimes.

Security measures, suspension of liberties, and the militarization of society became common. From October 1965 to June 1973, there were twenty suspensions of individual liberties and imposition of the MPS. In addition, a state of internal war was declared three times, on 15 April 1972, extended on 12 May 1972, and again extended on 30 June 1972. On 10 July 1972, military courts were established for civilians.[18] The stern policies continued in 1972 and resulted in the elimination of Tupamaro activity. For example, in June 1972 the 'people's jail' of the Tupamaros was discovered. In July 1972, civil rights were suspended for another ninety days and the state of internal war was extended.[19] Law 14068 also placed civilians under military control.[20] The events during the month of July 1972 included massive and indiscriminate arrests of leftist politicians and supporters. Estimates of those detained range from 1600 to 4000 for the month.[21] By the end of 1972, over 5000 people had been arrested by the military and the Tupamaro organization was virtually destroyed.[22]

Were these repressive policies legal? Some of Pacheco's actions had a basis in Uruguayan law. According to the constitution, Article 29 allowed the judiciary to interfere with the press and impose a penalty of a three to twelve month imprisonment. However, there was no statute allowing the suppression of the press.[23] The MPS were to be used in times of extraordinary internal disturbance.[24] However, they were applied in ways that were not originally intended. According to *Violations of Human Rights in Uruguay (1972–1976)*, 'in principle, the basis for instituting these measures was the fight against subversion, but they were applied in a much broader sense. Thus striking workers and employees were put into military service; churches, hospitals, high schools, and universities were raided.'[25]

Uruguayan state violence

The use of state violence began in 1970. The police and the military began to use torture, extrajudicial executions, and other unconstitutional means in police activities. Originally, the Uruguayan National Police were responsible for combating the Tupamaros. Specifically, the Information and Intelligence Directorate, composed of eight departments, and the Metropolitan Guard, a paramilitary organization headed by army officers, were in charge. The Tupamaros accused the Metropolitan Guard of mistreating, torturing, and killing guerrillas who had surrendered. The beginning of the violent state policy is marked by the resignation of the head of the Department of Intelligence and Liaison, Alejandro Otero, over the introduction of state violence in police work in January 1970. Porzencanski reports Otero was replaced

> Since his superior officers reportedly were impatient for more arrests and disagreed with his practice of being 'soft' on captured guerrillas. On the other hand, Mr. Otero was supposedly upset by his superiors' lack of support for detailed and patient police laboratory work as well as by the introduction and extensive application of torture.[26]

After his dismissal, Otero reported to the *Jornal de Brasil* that the wave of Tupamaro violence was a result of repressive methods.[27] Evidence of torture was corroborated. In addition, in July 1970 it was alleged that some detained Tupamaros were executed even though they had surrendered to police.[28] In June 1970, dissident Colorado senator Vasconcellos headed a commission of inquiry, which unanimously concluded that 'inhuman torture, including electric shocks, cigarette burns and psychological pressure, was used by police as a "normal, frequent, and habitual" matter on Tupamaros, common criminals and innocents alike'. The committee called for further inquiry.[29]

The military was placed in charge of the effort to end the violence of the Tupamaros in 1971. After the initiation of the Tupamaro campaign of assassinations in April 1972, the

Tupamaros discovered that the military had used the cease-fire to organize an effective counter-campaign. The military killed nineteen within four days in clashes with the Tupamaros. Under a state of internal war, the armed forces were free to engage in a counterinsurgency war, 'without regard for judicial accountability or individual rights'.[30] By 2 June, thirty Tupamaros, soldiers, policemen, and innocents had been killed and more were wounded. More than five hundred suspected Tupamaro members and collaborators were held by the military. This counterinsurgency policy included the use of truth drugs and torture in the interrogation of those arrested, including leftist politicians and their supporters.[31]

As well as state violence carried out by official state institutions, additional groups emerged and operated with the approval of officials. These groups formed to counter the leftist groups, such as the Tupamaros. The Juventud Uruguaya de Pie (JUP) and Comando Caza Tupamaros were allegedly established with the blessing of the Ministry of the Interior and other law enforcement officials. In the spring and summer of 1971, the JUP began a series of disturbances in Montevideo high schools. JUP members beat leftist teenagers who were accused of collaborating with the Tupamaros. One third of Montevideo high schools had to be closed because of the violent clashes between students. The JUP also harassed families of captured Tupamaros and others who had been released. Comando Caza Tupamaros killed at least two suspected Tupamaros. Nelson Bardesio, who began as the driver for CIA officer Cantrell, became part of a secret team under the control of the Minister of the Interior. This team, composed of three traffic police and two police institute members, was sent to Argentina's SIDE (the Argentine Information Service). This group was later implicated in the bombing of the houses of lawyers and teachers sympathetic to the Tupamaros.[32] Other senior officials were also implicated in right-wing death squads. In July 1970, a senior official in the Pacheco administration was rumoured to have said 'They too have families', implying extrajudicial reprisals.[33] In addition, there were other violent groups with ties to the state such as the Defensa Armada Nacionalista, Comando Armando Leses; Movimiento Armado Nacional Oriental (MANO), Brigadas Nacionales, and a Brazilian style death squad.[34] Many of the counter-guerrillas targeted members and supporters of Frente Amplio and the traditional left.[35] The violence became prevalent such that it created the fear of 'an expanding civil war situation'.[36]

As the number of terrorist actions decreased, the state anti-subversive actions increased, as seen in figure 5.1. July, August, and September of 1972 were marked by the increasing eradication of the seditious movements by the military and the increase in actions by state groups.

According to the standard of eradicating the Tupamaros, the military was very successful. From 28 November 1972 to 15 February 1973 a total of 2228 cases were tried in the military courts with only 55 cases remaining and 321 outstanding arrests.[37] In fact, the military campaign was so successful that it was difficult for the government to justify the continued security policies. Moreover, at the same time it was lobbying for an extension of the suspension of individual liberties, the government attempted to take credit for the elimination of the Tupamaros, the threat upon which

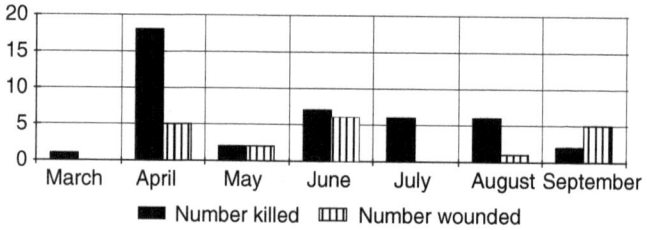

Figure 5.1 Uruguay: state violence, spring and summer 1973
Source: Servicio Paz y Justicia: Uruguay, *Nunca Más: Human Rights Violations 1972–1985* (Philadelphia: Temple University Press, 1986), p. 337; Uruguay Ministro del Interior, *Siete Meses de la lucha antisubversiva* (Montericleo: Ministro del Interior, 1972), pp. 88, 357.
Note: Deaths include people killed as a result of operations carried out by the joint forces, or assumed to have been, and prison deaths. An additional three deaths were attributed to the government between October and June. The figures for arrests, confiscations, hideouts discovered, wounded, and wanted come from *Siete*, pp. 88, 357. 'During 1970–71 at least 15 innocent people were accidentally killed by policemen or soldiers while engaged in searches, arrests, and patrol operations'; Porzencanski, p. 61.

the suspension of liberties was justified. Later Colonel Bolentini announced the discovery of new terrorist movements, in an attempt to avoid any contradiction.[38] By September, what had been called one of the most successful guerrilla movements in Latin America had been eliminated. However, democracy and the regular police force did not receive credit for the eradication. The military received credit for the successful, but highly repressive, campaign against the Tupamaros.

Peru

> The great virtuality, not virtue, of Sendero, was to touch the skin of our institutionalization and immediately provoke a vomit of bitterness that generated an official terrorism more cruel, more harsh and more morally forbidden than the insurrection.
> (Javier Valle Riestra, Diputado and Senator, APRA)[39]

The Peruvian state's policy towards violent groups was inconsistent but it persistently included repressive and violent elements. During the terms of Belaúnde and García, it could be said that a guiding policy was absent. Instead, these governments largely abdicated responsibility for the containment of terrorism to the military. The only policy or oversight given to the military was a directive to eliminate terrorism. A mixture of states of emergency, military control over civilian areas, forced participation in armed peasant groups, and some incentives for cooperating with the state against terrorists was used to combat the violent groups. Under President García, paramilitary groups with ties to the governing APRA party emerged.

Peruvian state repressive policies

All three democratically elected presidents pursued repressive policies. The first democratically elected president since the military coup in 1968, President Fernando Belaúnde, was largely unaware of the threat posed by Sendero. At first, he relied on the ill-equipped 'Sinchis', a special police battalion, to combat Sendero. As the threat continued to grow, Belaúnde resorted to involving the military and to using his constitutional powers to fight terrorism. Article 231 of the Peruvian constitution of 1979 recognizes two levels of states of exception: a state of emergency and a state of siege. Both states of exception involve the suspension of liberties. The constitution allows a state of emergency when there are 'disturbances of peace and internal order, catastrophes or grave circumstances affecting the life of the nation'.[40] A state of emergency lasts sixty days.[41] A state of emergency allows security forces to enter houses and make arrests without warrants. The freedom of movement and right to assemble are also suspended. Americas Watch notes that although the accused's rights to know his accusers and the charges against him are not legally suspended in these states of exception, in practice they were.[42] In December 1982, Belaúnde formally involved the military. Invoking Articles 231 and 276 of the 1979 constitution,[43] he placed the military in control of the counterinsurgency campaign. Belaúnde also transferred control of areas under a state of emergency to political military commanders, reducing the power of civilian authorities in those areas.[44]

Belaúnde declared a state of emergency fifty-six times during his presidency. Of those, forty-six were related to Sendero, with the remaining ten used as a response to social or labour unrest. Laws of counterinsurgency were written and re-written in the 1980s to allow the police and the military more control of the counterinsurgency efforts. Belaúnde also decreed Anti-Terrorist Law 46, which allowed police to hold suspects for fifteen days without court interference and also dictated stiff penalties for terrorists and their accessories.[45] Under this law, many opposition political activists, peasant leaders, and labour officials were prosecuted.[46] In 1983, the executive attempted to define terrorism as treason, so that it would meet constitutional standards for capital punishment.[47]

Alan García, the leader of APRA, was elected president in 1985. In the beginning of his administration, García tried to change the state's policy and better coordinate the counterinsurgency effort. He forcibly retired some military commanders who were implicated in human rights violations. In addition, he announced a limited amnesty and the establishment of a peace commission. However, by February

1986 Lima was under a curfew and a state of emergency due to the escalation of bombings. García attempted another amnesty aimed at MRTA, but the group responded by assassinating a police sergeant. García, in response, mobilized the army and sent counterinsurgency troops into the area. García continued with more repressive policies. One year later, in 1987, the García administration amended law 24,700, which had established procedures for the investigation, prosecution, and trial of alleged terrorists. The changes limited the ability of provincial prosecutors and human rights organizations to intervene in cases. A new law (NO. 25,031) granted police control of investigations and expanded allowable circumstances of an incommunicado detention.[48] García continued Belaúnde's practice of imposing states of emergency and increasing military involvement. There was little judicial presence in these areas.[49] By 1989, further progress had been made in crafting a more sophisticated counterinsurgency strategy which prioritized winning the support of the population as opposed to conquering territory. Both military analysts and the Comisión de la Verdad y Reconciliación (CRV) commission[50] note its success in reducing human rights violations, increasing intelligence, isolating Sendero, and bolstering government support in areas of conflict. According to Major George Franco (US Special Forces), 'the [Ucayali Front] developed a strategy that relied on civic action and development programs, psychological operations, intelligence activities, the aggressive deployment of security forces in rural outposts, and the formation of civilian self-defence militias. It was essentially an indirect strategy: its primary aim was not to kill the insurgents, but to create conditions that made it increasingly difficult for the guerrillas to continue their campaign and that constrained their operating space.'[51] Moreover, 250 rondas were established in the Ucayali.

Fujimori was elected president in 1990. Upon taking office Fujimori began to expand and consolidate the state's policies with the cooperation of the military. For the first time since the return to democracy in 1980, Fujimori appointed a general as minister of the interior. In decree law 171–90, Fujimori granted all military members in emergency zones protection from civilian charges. Military courts would handle all charges. The decree also guaranteed their anonymity.[52] As the policies became more coherent, opposition to them increased. These acts were repealed in February 1991 by Congress.[53] In November 1991, after receiving expanded power from Congress, Fujimori decreed 120 laws ranging from land reform to an expansion of the power of the armed forces. One law allowed civilians to be drafted and their property expropriated to assist the fight against subversion.[54] The decrees expanded the power of the military in areas not under a state of emergency. The law also restructured the Servicio de Inteligencia Nacional (SIN), the National Mobilization and National Defence System.

In general, there was a constant increase in areas under a state of emergency in Peru. In 1980, at the beginning of the restoration of democracy, no provinces were under a state of emergency. The percentage of provinces under a state of emergency increased to 18 per cent in 1984. In addition, the entire country was under a state of emergency in 1983 from 30 May to 9 September, in 1984 from 20 March to 3 September and from 27 November to 30 November. By 1990, 63 per cent of the provinces were under a state of emergency. After 1990, the number fell to approximately 43 per cent for 1991 and 1992.[55] However, under Fujimori, even though there was a decrease in the percentage of provinces under a state of emergency, the broad powers given to the military gave the institution the ability to operate freely in areas not under a state of emergency.

Critics complained that Fujimori only further militarized the state's response to the terrorism.[56] The opposition in the Senate, in December 1991, released a statement that the presidency was in effect vacant because the chief executive was morally incapable.[57] Manuel Dammert, sociologist and senator of the Revolutionary Communist Party, described Peruvian democracy in February 1992: 'What we have now is an authoritarian regime that we hope will not become a civil military regime or unconstitutional.'[58] In February 1992, Congress reconvened and rescinded many of Fujimori's decrees.[59] For example, Congress passed law 25397 to restrict the legislative power of the president.[60] Congress also stipulated that states of exception specify the territory included, the time of exception, and which constitutional rights would be suspended.[61] Congress was preparing to fully examine the counterinsurgency strategy at the next session, which was to begin on 6 April 1992, when Fujimori committed his *autogolpe*.

Peruvian state violence

In Peru, state violence had numerous sources. The military used violent means to achieve its goals. In addition, the state set up armed groups of civilians, called rondas, to defend against terrorist violent groups. In addition to official groups, there were also covert state sponsored violent groups. The military, placed in control of the fight against terrorist violence in December 1982, gained new powers in July 1984, when Belaúnde placed the military in control of the entire country's counterinsurgency policy. Military action was no longer limited to areas under a state of emergency.[62] The state gave the military one objective: 'to defeat Sendero, to make it disappear'.[63]

Under Belaúnde, no oversight was established. Massive human rights violations followed.[64] Initially, President García did not establish much more oversight than Belaúnde. His commitment to human rights was viewed as hypocritical after a June 1986 Sendero prison mutiny in which García gave the military permission to do whatever was necessary to retake the prisons. Over 250 prisoners died in the shelling of one prison and another hundred were shot and killed after surrendering to the authorities.[65] According to Americas Watch, the repressive policies of García were ineffective at curbing the violence. In 1987, the organization determined that the invocation of the state of emergency was ineffective and harmful. 'Unfortunately, the imposition of a state of emergency also has tended to correspond to an increase in human rights abuses.'[66]

In Peru, state forces killed many people under the pretext that they were subversives. Raúl González cites a widely accepted belief that the military and police forces execute all who belong to Sendero. According to González, the army and intelligence services require 90 per cent certainty of an individual's complicity in guerrilla groups before execution while the marine infantry only requires 5 per cent probability to pull the trigger.[67] This quotation is from the early time period, in which many rural peasants were indiscriminately targeted by counterinsurgency forces.

Another source of state violence was the rondas campesinas. Rondas campesinas, or peasant groups, were armed by the state.[68] The rondas campesinas organized by the state were mainly of two types.[69] The first type of ronda was a civil defence committee that was organized in the emergency zones. Membership in this group was not voluntary. Refusal to participate resulted in suspicion of being a subversive. These rondas were under military jurisdiction. The military used both coercion and rewards for villagers to participate in the rondas. Orin Starn reports a meeting of ronda leaders in which the military leaders provided tools, medicine, guns, trucks, and food as rewards for cooperation.[70] Sometimes participation was effective. Many local residents learned that by volunteering for a ronda, it was possible to ameliorate military repression and to repel Sendero. The second type was a civil defence patrol. These groups participated with the military in operations against Sendero and MRTA.[71] Instead of living scattered about the countryside, the political/military commander would transplant them into 'strategic hamlets'. Some have charged that these patrols had a 'licence to kill'. Indeed, there have been many reports of disappearances and executions in areas with these patrols. *QueHacer* reports that a doctor from an international organization, who travelled the Peruvian countryside on a vaccination campaign, felt more threatened in areas controlled by the committees of civil defence than in areas controlled by Sendero.[72] Indeed, many reports of disappearances and executions have been made in areas with these committees.[73] In addition to threatening other citizens, the creation of the rondas campesinas had other effects. According to Americas Watch, it was a 'tactic that converted civilians into targets for insurgent reprisals'.[74] In 1989, García added the rondas as a new component to the counterinsurgency policy. Fujimori also placed more emphasis on the rondas. They were expanded, armed, and empowered. Fujimori had armed 526 peasant communities by the end of 1992.[75] More than 10,000 shotguns were distributed to the rondas. By 1993, almost every village had a ronda.[76]

In addition to the military and the rondas campesinas, state violence also took the form of groups with unofficial ties to the state. Many of these groups emerged during the presidency of García. García seemed to encourage violence.

For example, at a youth APRA rally in 1988 he stated that he admired the dedication of the Senderistas.[77] He also condoned some violence within the party. For example, in 1987 Rodrigo Franco, a friend of García, was assassinated by Sendero.[78] After the assassination, García called human rights groups 'accomplices of subversion' and alluded to the need of APRA's right to protect itself. Shortly after, Comando Rodrigo Franco (CRF) began its attacks on leftist politicians and supporters. The military did not pursue CRF.[79] Javier Valle Riestra, a high ranking APRA senator, admitted 'of course everyone knew that the party had búfalos [APRA affiliated violent groups that first gained notoriety in the 1940s[80]] but maintained that the party had a right to protect itself'.[81] The spread of violence to state led violence increased the threats to the political community.

A special senate commission examined the costs of the violence in 1991. In this year, it was reported that ronderos had killed 1 student and 84 Sendero members. Other local organizations had killed 3 peasants, 3 residents, 1 student, and 23 Sendero members. The majority of the state violence came from either the military or the police. The police killed 3 businessmen and professionals, 3 workers, 12 peasants, 11 residents, 4 students, 1 military member, 248 Sendero members, 42 MRTA members, and 22 drug traffickers. The military killed 2 businessmen, 2 workers, 14 peasants, 2 residents, 13 police, 720 Sendero members, and 296 MRTA members.[82] The senate commission's report explains that the deaths listed under the subversive category are defined as such by the military or specific ministries in charge of the counterinsurgency effort and should be interpreted as alleged subversives. In addition, the commission also stated that the number of MRTA and Sendero deaths is probably underreported because of the hesitance, due to fear of reprisal, of family members to report deaths to the state. Overall, the 1991 senate report estimated that its numbers could reasonably be increased by 10 per cent.

Table 5.1 presents demographic characteristics of the victims of state violence. This includes victims of the police, the military, rondas, and paramilitary forces.

Similar to the cost of non-state terrorist violence, the disproportionate majority of the victims were Quechua speakers and the peasants were targeted, reflecting the

Table 5.1 Peru: victim profiles of state violence with attributions of responsibility, 1980–2000

Characteristics	Torture (%)	Deaths and disappearances (%)
Education	(3293)	(4709)
None	12.09	19.07
Some	0.39	0.49
Primary	42.64	44.79
Secondary	26.54	24.10
Superior	18.34	11.55
Maternal language	(3370)	(5003)
Quechua	65.34	75.00
Spanish	34.01	24.59
Other native language	0.65	0.42
Occupation	(2596)	(4300)
Peasant	45.03	53.09
Local authorities	17.33	11.37
Housewives	4.47	6.07
Sales and business people	7.63	7.02
Independent workers	5.82	6.00
Teachers	5.12	3.93
University students	5.35	4.56
Employees	3.43	2.63
Military and police	0.31	0.72
Workers	2.31	2.16
Professionals and intellectuals	0.50	0.40
Others	2.70	2.05

Source: Comisión de la Verdad y Reconciliación, Informe Final, Anexo Estadístico (Lima: Comisión de la Verdad y Reconciliación August 2003), pp. 86, 327.
Note: Number in parentheses represent the numbers on which the percentages are based.

indiscriminate nature of the conflict, especially in the early 1980s. The mayor of Tambo, Rubén Rojas, described the situation as 'caught between the wall and the sword'.[83] Additionally, many local authorities, students, and teachers were also targeted because they were suspected of collaborating with rebels. However, in general, a greater proportion of victims of state violence were less educated than the general population, of which approximately 40 per cent did not have a secondary education. Of those killed or disappeared, almost 65 per cent had not been educated to the secondary level.

Spain

Spain, unlike Peru and Uruguay, did not engage in widely applied indiscriminate or excessive force to combat its terrorist threat. In general, democratic Spain reacted to the terrorism within its own constitutional bounds. Violence caused significant disturbance in Spain. People were afraid. However, the state attempted to remove the incentives to join violent groups. Compared with the Franco regime, the citizens had full political liberties. In addition, the previous restrictions on regional languages and cultures were abolished. For example, under Franco Basque cultural activity was severely limited and the language outlawed.[84] Eventually the violence became less frequent, especially after 1980. The state's attempts at reinforcing the political community seemed to be working, as violent actions became less frequent in the 1980s.

Spanish state reaction

Soon after the death of Franco, King Juan Carlos initiated a national reconciliation. Part of this included the commutation of death sentences to life in prison and reduction for other sentences. In July 1976, the state announced an amnesty for all political and ideological crimes and allowed many exiles to return. However, those convicted of terrorist acts were not pardoned. Many Basques called for a complete amnesty for political prisoners. Another amnesty in March 1977 left only about twenty people jailed. Support for another amnesty was high among Basques. These actions were widely supported. In a September 1977 poll, only 12 per cent of Spaniards believed the previous amnesties had been excessive. Another 16 per cent thought they were sufficient. However, a third of Spaniards and almost one half of the Basques thought that it was not enough.[85] Finally, in October 1977 the state freed the remaining prisoners, on the condition that they leave the country.[86] In 1984, the Spanish state began to offer another form of amnesty called 'social reintegration' to ETA members who were ready to publicly renounce future acts of violence. Incarcerated ETA members and exiled ETA members were allowed to participate.[87]

In 1977, another tough issue was tackled: regional separatist demands. The new constitution allowed two procedures for each region in Spain to gain the status of an autonomous community within Spain. The historical communities of Galicia, Catalonia, and the Basque country were offered fast routes to autonomy, while the other regions were allowed a slower route to autonomy.[88] In addition, the autonomy agreement for the Basque country granted the region more autonomy than ever before. The 1979 statute, 'Estatuto de Guernica' delegated to the Basque community the administration of justice, some control over economic policy, and the creation of a Basque public television channel. The statute also established the Basque language as joint official language, established a Basque government, and gave the community the option of later joining with Navarra.[89] The control over economic policy included restoration of the 1876 economic agreements. These agreements allow the Basque government to collect taxes, but only require the Basque government to give the national state about one third of the proceeds.

Political liberties were also restored by the new democracy. By the end of 1976, the King had abolished Franco's special courts for trying terrorists.[90] By 1978, press censorship had been greatly reduced from the policies under Franco.[91] It was generally considered a free press by 1979.[92] Overall, the state did not implement indiscriminate repression, although charges of torture are occasionally raised, most often in the Basque region. However, the Spanish state has cooperated with human rights organizations such as Amnesty International.[93] In 1983, the Spanish Human Rights Association received 120 complaints of torture or mistreatment. Of those, 30 cases were actively investigated. The conclusion of Amnesty International was that the incidents were the results of individual transgressions, as opposed to an officially sponsored policy.[94]

The state did institute some anti-terrorist legislation. In 1978, Law 21/1978 was passed, giving the police new powers of arrest and detention. Suspects could be held for up to seventy-two hours without charge. Judicial oversight of this practice was also established, but rarely invoked. Police could also intercept mail and telephone messages by suspected terrorists. This law was supplemented by Law 56/1978, 'Special Measures toward Crimes of Terrorism Committed by Armed Groups Act', which allowed detention of up to ten days and the holding of suspects incommunicado. Also, the decree law called 'On the Protection of Citizen Security' was instituted in January 1979 which increased penalties for terrorist crimes, restricted the rights of prisoners to seek provisional release from prison, and criminalized statements that could be interpreted as defending terrorist acts or groups.[95] A 1980 law passed by the National Assembly allowed an extension of preventive detention, searching of homes without a warrant, and the violation of privacy of mail and telephone communications. This suspension of the rights could be applied to people suspected of complicity in or participation in terrorist acts. Preventive detention and the observation had to be ordered by a magistrate.

During the transition after Franco, the existing security forces were being reformed and new ones created. In 1981, the new five hundred strong Basque police force, Ertzaintza, started traffic duties, while the old Civil Guard (Guardia Civil) maintained control of security. By 1986, the Ertzaintza was under full control of the regional government[96] and by 1999 it had grown to more than 7000 agents.[97] The new force helped to abate the tension that had previously existed between the forces of the national police and Guardia Civil and the general Basque public. For example, in the last half of 1977 police broke up 30 demonstrations, killing 3 and wounding 87 in the process.[98]

It should also be noted that the Spanish military did not have a role in internal security, other than limited involvement in surveillance and some protection duties.[99] Searches were conducted, arrests were made, and ETA infiltrated by new police forces. A new anti-terrorist police force of 50 men based in Bilbao, led by Roberto Conesa, was formed in 1978. In February 1980, two counterterrorist police forces were formed: the 120 member Special Operations Group dealt with urban terrorism and the 450 member Rural Anti-terrorist Groups of the Guardia Civil operated in other areas. These forces were supplemented by 12,000 regular Guardia

Civil troops and 6,000 national policemen. The increase in arrests resulting from these forces undoubtedly created resentment in the Basque country.[100] In 1980, the number of arrests increased from only 561 in 1979 to 2140. Previously the peak of arrests had occurred in the year of Franco's death, 1975, with over 4600 arrests. By 1983, the numbers had dropped to under 1200 a year.[101] Because of the slow pace of reform, some indiscriminate repression occurred while security forces were conducting counterterrorism operations. However, many of those arrested during this time were never formally prosecuted. For example, between 1977 and 1987, only about one third of the approximate 5700 people arrested for ETA related terrorism were prosecuted.[102]

In May 1981, a new law called Law for the Defence of the Constitution was passed. The definition of terrorism now included nonviolent efforts to secure independence from the Spanish nation. The state also had the power to close media that communicated any apology for terrorism.[103] After the coup attempt in 1981, further legislation was passed, generally intensifying Spanish anti-terrorism policy. In May 1983, a new security initiative called Operation Zen was instituted in the Basque region. The Civil Guard was given extra training to introduce them to the special circumstances of the Basque region, a public affairs initiative was launched to engender cooperation between the public and the police, more cooperation was established between the Civil Guard and the Basque police, and, finally, judges were allowed to shut down associations and publications that advocated terrorism.[104] The Basque government, however, refused to cooperate with the Spanish state in implementing the plan. In 1984, a new law (8/1984) was passed that reaffirmed many earlier police powers included in prior laws. In addition, judges were now allowed to ban political parties and groups headed by convicted terrorists and to order the detention of suspected terrorists for up to two and a half years. Not surprisingly, Basque political leaders resisted the law. For example, HB leader Miguel Castells described it as a 'Nazi law more regressive than the Francoists in many respects'. Spain's highest court deemed part of the law unconstitutional and, in December 1987, the Spanish state repealed the remainder.[105]

Spanish state violence

Despite the efforts of the state in restoring liberties, declaring amnesties, and granting autonomy, the actions of the state were not entirely nonviolent. The police and Civil Guard killed many in violent clashes. For example, between February 1976 and December 1979 in the Basque provinces, forty people were killed in demonstrations, by police.[106] In March 1981, in response to a flood of ETA attacks and the attempted military coup, the state deployed army and navy troops to the Basque provinces for the first time since the return to democracy.[107] From 1976 to 1979, eighty people were killed by the police or Civil Guard. In 1980, only six were killed. In 1981, sixteen were killed. In 1982, only seven were.[108]

In addition, a clandestine group Grupo Antiterrorista de Liberación (the Anti-Terrorist Groups of Liberation; GAL), with ties to the state, became active in 1983, killing suspected terrorists. GAL used illegal means, including assassination and kidnapping, to fight terrorism. GAL assassinated at least twenty-seven people, nine of whom did not have ties to ETA, and wounded thirty-one. GAL was also active abroad and is attributed with the deaths of twenty ETA members in France.[109] Most of the deaths occurred in France or very near the border. However, the actions of GAL were not widely known until later. Reports and investigations of its activities began only after February 1986.[110] Most importantly, GAL was not active before the attempted coup in 1981. Because of the small number of dead, the delay until the actions became known, and the location of the occurrences, the Spanish state did not lose citizen support before the events became known. Many scholars attribute the loss of the Socialists in the 1990s partly to the emergence of evidence linking the Spanish government to GAL. Overall, in spite of the deaths, GAL, and the March 1981 military deployment, the Spanish state did not appear to be pursuing an indiscriminate repressive state response that would undermine support prior to the 1981 attempted coup.

Table 5.2 provides an overview of domestic Spanish counterterrorism actions from 1976–1986. More civilians were killed in 1976 than in the rest of the years combined. The number of accused killed was also quite low each year, with

Table 5.2 Spain: state counterterror/internal security actions, 1976–1986

	Accused killed	Civilians killed	Civilians injured	Arrests	Convictions	GAL activities
1976	0	14	2	43	17	NA
1977	0	4	1	68	0	NA
1978	2	4	3	0	2	NA
1979	2	2	4	75	21	NA
1980	9	0	0	13	40	NA
1981	3	4	0	121	21	NA
1982	1	0	0	0	19	NA
1983	0	0	0	5	21	5
1984	6	0	0	3	0	14
1985	0	0	0	19	10	17
1986	0	0	0	14	0	6

Source: Tweed, GAL activities from Paddy Woodworth, *Dirty War, Clean Hands* (Crosses Green Cork: Cork University Press, 2001). There was one additional GAL attack in 1987.

relative peaks in 1980 (nine killed) and 1984 (six killed). 1981 saw the most arrests for terrorism, followed by none the following year. Arrests, if any, were fewer than twenty each year from 1982 to 1986. The number of convictions was steady at approximately twenty a year from 1979 to 1983, with the exception of forty in 1980. GAL activities, which were by and large later discovered, peaked in 1985.

Part two summary

Whereas in the first stage of analysis, all three countries are faced with a similar violent challenge, this second stage of analysis uncovers an important difference. Both Uruguay and Peru responded to the terrorist violence with extensive state violence and indiscriminate repression. Spain, on the contrary, did not implement either policy. GAL activities did not start until after the attempted coup. It is expected that this difference will account for the consolidation of the Spanish democracy and the demise of the Uruguayan and Peruvian democracies in part three.

Notes

1. Weinstein, p. 44.
2. Porzencanski, p. 57.
3. Inter-Church Committee on Human Rights in Latin America, p. 2.
4. MPS emergency powers are granted to the president by the constitution in Article 168 'in case of serious and unforeseen events, foreign attack or internal upheavals'; Labrousse, p. 53. However, the executive must consult parliament within twenty-four hours. Sergio Jellinek and Luis Ledesma, *Uruguay: Del Consenso Democratico a la Militarismo Estatal* Part 1, Paper #19, November 1979 (Stockholm: Institute of Latin American Studies, 1979a), See also Porzencanski, p. 57.
5. Inter-Church Committee on Human Rights in Latin America, p. 3. According to Article 27 of law 9943, a State of Emergency entitles the president to break trade unions. 'Under a state of emergency the citizens may be placed under martial law and jurisdiction.... so that services indisputable to the life of the country may be maintained'. See also Labrousse, p. 56.
6. Porzencanski, p. 57. This strike took place from 2 July–15 October 1969.
7. Weinstein, p. 46.
8. Labrousse, p. 63.
9. Servicio Paz y Justicia, p. 11.
10. Labrousse, p. 54.
11. Porzencanski, pp. 58, 64.
12. Porzencanski, pp. 62–63.
13. Porzencanski, p. 56.
14. *Generals and Tupamaros*, p. 26.
15. Servicio Paz y Justicia, p. 17.
16. Inter-Church Committee on Human Rights in Latin America, p. 19.
17. Decree 277/972, Inter-Church Committee on Human Rights in Latin America, p. 11.
18. The preceding list is compiled with data from Inter-Church Committee on Human Rights in Latin America, and Republica Oriental del Uruguay Junta de Comandantes en Jefe, 1977. Republica Oriental del Uruguay Junta de Comandantes en Jefe. Tomo 1, 1977.
19. *Generals and Tupamaros*, pp. 44–46.
20. Inter-Church Committee on Human Rights in Latin America, p. 17.
21. *Generals and Tupamaros*, p. 47.
22. Porzencanski, pp. 62–68.
23. Labrousse, p. 53.
24. *Uruguay: A Country Study*. p. 40.
25. Inter-Church Committee on Human Rights in Latin America, p. 5.
26. Porzencanski, pp. 53–55.

27 *Generals and Tupamaros*, p. 17.
28 *Generals and Tupamaros*, pp. 13, 24.
29 *Generals and Tupamaros*, pp. 10–12.
30 Porzencanski, pp. 61–68.
31 *Generals and Tupamaros*, p. 47.
32 Langguth, p. 246.
33 *Generals and Tupamaros*, p. 15.
34 Porzencanski, p. 61.
35 Kaufman, p. 38.
36 Kaufman, p. 38.
37 Inter-Church Committee on Human Rights in Latin America, p. 21.
38 *Generals and Tupamaros*, p. 70.
39 Chang-Rodríguez, p. 164.
40 Americas Watch, *A Certain Passivity: Failing to Curb Human Rights Abuses in Peru* (New Haven: Yale University Press, 1987), p. 5.
41 Comisión Especial de Investigación y Estudio sobre la Violencia y Alternativas de Pacificación en el Perú, *Violencia y Pacificación* (Lima: Senado de la República, 1989), p. 298.
42 Americas Watch, 1992, p. 6.
43 Article 276 of the Peruvian constitution gives the armed forces the fundamental aim of protecting the independence, sovereignty, and territorial integrity of the republic. Under Article 231, they may assume control of the country. Comisión Especial de Investigación y Estudio sobre la Violencia y Alternativas de Pacificación, 1992, p. 27.
44 Mauceri, 1991, pp. 90–91.
45 David Werlich, 'Peru: The Shadow of the Shining Path', *Current History* Vol. 83, February 1984, pp. 78–84, p. 81.
46 Americas Watch, 1992, p. 7.
47 Javier Diez Canseco, *Democracia, militarización y derechos humanos en el Perú 1980–1984* (Lima: Asociación Pro Derechas Humanos: Servicios Populares, 1985), p. 48.
48 Americas Watch, 1992, p. 22.
49 Americas Watch, 1992, p. 22.
50 Comisión de la Verdad y General Conclusions, point 60; www.cverdad.org.pe/ingles/ifinal/conclusiones.php.
51 George Franco. 'Battling Narcoterrorism: The Peruvian Experience in the Ucayali', *Orbis: A Journal of World Affairs* Vol. 48, No. 3, Summer 2004, pp. 505–514, p. 508.
52 'Impunidad Oficial', *Caretas* No. 1141, 7 January, 1991, p. 31.
53 Americas Watch, 1992, p. 27.
54 Mauceri, 1991, p. 100.
55 David Scott Palmer, 'The Revolutionary Terrorism of Peru's Shining Path', in Martha Crenshaw *Terrorism in Context* (ed.), (University Park, Pa: Pennsylvania University Press, 1995), Table 7.7, p. 299.

56 Amnesty International, *Peru: Human Rights During the Government of Alberto Fujimori* (New York: Amnesty International, 1992), pp. 7–8.

57 María Escalante and Ana María Vidal, *Los decretos de la guerra: dos año de políticas antisubersivas y una propuesta de paz* (Lima: IDS, 1993), p. 50.

58 'Y lo que tenemos ahora es un régimen autoritario del cual esperamos que no sea un régimen cívico militar e inconstitucional'; author translation. Forgues, p. 59.

59 Cameron, 1995, p. 149.

60 Cameron, 1995, p. 149.

61 Escalante and Vidal, p. 78.

62 'FFAA asumen control', *Equis X* No. 400, 23–30 July 1984, pp. 16–18, p. 16.

63 Raúl González, 'Y ahora qué, especial sobre Sendero', *QueHacer* No. 30, August 1984, pp. 7–29, p. 9.

64 Mauceri, 1991, p. 91.

65 Susan C. Bourque, and Kay B. Warren, 'Democracy Without Peace: The Cultural Politics of Terror in Peru', *Latin American Research Review* Vol. 24, No. 1, 1989, pp. 18–24.

66 Americas Watch, 1987, p. 24.

67 González, 1984, p. 15.

68 Mauceri, 1991, p. 101.

69 These rondas should not be confused with an earlier type of Peruvian ronda. In Peru, there are numerous types of rondas. For a complete discussion of rondas, see Raúl González, 'Sendero vs. MRTA', *QueHacer* No. 46, April–May 1987, p. 72 and Orin Starn, 'Noches de ronda', *QueHacer* No. 69, Jan.–Feb. 1991, pp. 76–92.

70 Orin Starn, 'To Revolt Against the Revolution: War and Resistance in Peru's Andes'. *Cultural Anthropology* Vol. 10, No. 4, November 1995, pp. 547–581, p. 562.

71 González, 1987, p. 78.

72 *QueHacer* No. 58, April-May 1989, p. 29.

73 *QueHacer* No. 58, April-May 1989, p. 29.

74 Americas Watch, 1992, p. 9.

75 Daniel Masterson, 'In the Shining Path of Mariategui, Mao Zedong or President Gonzalo? Peru's Sendero Luminoso in Historical Perspective', *Journal of Third World Studies*, Vol. 11, No. 1, Spring 1994, pp. 154–179, p. 169.

76 Starn, 1995, p. 553.

77 Graham, pp. 132–139.

78 Bourque and Warren, p. 17.

79 Mauceri, 1991, p. 97.

80 Bourque and Warren, p. 11.

81 Graham, p. 164.

82 Comisión Especial de Investigación y Estudio sobre la Violencia y Alternativas de Pacificación. *Violencia y Pacificación en 1991* (Lima: Senado de la República, 1992), pp. 195–199.

83 Mario Fumerton, 'Rondas Campesinas in the Peruvian Civil War: Peasant Self-Defence Organizations in Ayacucho', *Bulletin of Latin American Research* Vol. 20, No. 4, 2001, pp. 470–497, p. 483.

84 Shub and Carr, p. 122.

85 Centro de Investigaciones Sociológicas, 'Encuesta y sondeos del Centrol de Investigaciones Sociológicas', *Revista Española de la Opinion Publica*, Vol. 50, 1977, pp. 243–290, p. 266.

86 Janke, p. 10. See also Clark, 1979, p. 299.

87 Janke and Moxon-Browne, p. 167.

88 Arango, p. 139.

89 Juan Díez Medrano, *Divided Nations: Class, Politics, and Nationalism in the Basque Country and Catalonia* (Ithaca: Cornell University Press, 1995), p. 146.

90 Clark, 1990, p. 38.

91 The Department of State, *Report Submitted to the Committee on International Relations. U.S. House of Representatives and Committee on Foreign Relations. U.S. Senate* (Washington, DC: Government Printing Office, 1978), p. 310.

92 The Department of State, *Report Submitted to the Committee on International Relations. U.S. House of Representatives and Committee on Foreign Relations. U.S. Senate* (Washington, DC: Government Printing Office, 1979), p. 659.

93 The Department of State, *Report Submitted to the Committee on International Relations. U.S. House of Representatives and Committee on Foreign Relations. U.S. Senate* (Washington, DC: Government Printing Office, 1980), p. 875.

94 The Department of State, *Report Submitted to the Committee on International Relations. U.S. House of Representatives and Committee on Foreign Relations. U.S. Senate* (Washington, DC: Government Printing Office, 1983), p. 1089.

95 Clark, 1990, p. 41.

96 Rogelio Alonso and Fernando Reinares, 'Terrorism, Human Rights, and Law Enforcement in Spain', *Terrorism and Political Violence* Vol. 17, Nos. 1–2, (2005), pp. 265–278, p. 271.

97 Spanish Ministry of the Interior, www.mir.es/oris/infoeta/esp/p06-esp.htm.

98 Clark, 1990, p. 39. See also Miguel Castells Arteche.

99 Alonso and Reinares, p. 273.

100 Clark, 1990, pp. 42–43.

101 Francisco J. Llera, José M. Mata, and Cynthia L. Irvin, 'ETA: From Secret Army to Social Movement – the Post Franco Schism of the Basque National Movement', *Terrorism and Political Violence* Vol. 5, No. 3, Fall 1993, pp. 106–134.

102 Alonso and Reinares, p. 274. (Citing Florencio Dominguez Iribarren *De la negotiacion a la tregua: El Final de Eta?* (Madrid: Taurus, 1998), pp. 201-221.
103 Clark, 1990, p. 49.
104 Tucker, pp. 165-166.
105 Clark, 1990, p. 65.
106 Carr and Fusi, p. 237.
107 Lancaster and Prevost, p. 77.
108 Tezanos, et al., p. 215.
109 Salustiano del Campo (ed.), *Tendencias Sociales en España Volumen I* (Bilbao: Fundocion BBV, 1993), p. 39.
110 Paddy Woodworth, *Dirty War, Clean Hands* (Crosses Green, Cork: Cork University Press, 2001).

6
Testing of hypotheses one and two

Introduction: the hypotheses

> **Hypothesis one**
>
> Terrorist violence threatens democratic stability by undermining both rudimentary purposes of the state, security, and integration. As the purposes of the state are unfulfilled, citizen confidence in the state declines. As citizen confidence decreases, democratic instability increases.
>
> **Hypothesis two**
>
> State repression and violence undermine the rudimentary purposes of the state, integration, and security. Decreases in citizen confidence should follow a decrease in the fulfilment of the rudimentary purposes. Finally, as citizen confidence in the state decreases, increases in democratic instability should be identifiable.

According to these hypotheses, the cases of Uruguay and Peru, countries that suffered both increasingly high levels of terrorist violence and state repressive policies and violence, should offer evidence of a lack of fulfilment of the rudimentary purposes of the state and decreased citizen confidence. In addition, as these measures decline, it is expected that there should be an increase in democratic instability. In the case of Spain, a country that faced terrorist violence but not extensive state repressive policies or state violence, some declines in measures of security due to terrorist violence are expected but not from the state reaction.

Purposes of the state

Uruguayan rudimentary purpose of the state: security

How did the state and terrorist violence affect the fulfilment of a rudimentary purpose of the state, security, in Uruguay? Four measures of the rudimentary purpose of the state, security, can be used. Public opinion data provide the first three measures. Specifically, questions about fear, disorder, and the Tupamaros are available. Finally, the death toll due to violence also serves as an indicator of a failure to maintain security.

Clear evidence exists documenting concern about terrorist violence. Concern about the disorder was evident as early as 1968. Gallup Uruguay, in a random selection of Uruguayan adults over the age of eighteen, asked the respondents to describe the current social situation. Uruguayans perceived an increase in disorder as the incidents of terrorist violence increased from six in 1967 to fifty-six in 1968 and to sixty-three in 1969. In October 1968, 46 per cent thought there was major disorder and 35 per cent thought there was minor disorder. By June 1969, 54 per cent thought there was major disorder and 37 per cent thought there was minor disorder. Uruguayans believed their social situation to be more disorderly in 1969 than in 1968. At the same time, there was an increase of 13 per cent in the number of terrorist actions in the same period. Uruguayans found the late 1960s to be particularly turbulent for a society that was previously peaceful.[1]

The main group responsible for most of the terrorist violence, the Tupamaros, was viewed as dangerous by the citizens, reflecting a concern for security. Gallup asked some specific questions about the Tupamaros in the late 1960s and early 1970s. With an increase in the frequency of violence in 1969, the group was increasingly viewed as dangerous. The respondents were asked to fill in the blank to the question 'How would you describe the [Tupamaros]? ... It [The Tupamaros] is an organization that is ...'. In 1969, almost half, 48 per cent, of the respondents believed the Tupamaros to be highly dangerous, up from 40 per cent in 1968. Only 10 per cent believed them to be harmless, down from 18 per cent in 1968. These numbers are significant since the threat was realized even before the higher levels of violence were reached in 1972.[2]

Another measure of security is the number killed by the terrorist actions. Although the method of choice for the terrorist groups was not assassination, on occasion assassination was used. The political killings began in 1969 with three killed. In the following year, only two were killed, followed by six in 1971. A relative eruption of political killings occurred in 1972, when twenty-one people were killed. In 1973, there were no political killings by the terrorist groups.[3]

Adding to the insecurity caused by the Tupamaros was violence from groups originating from the far right. For example, MANO was formed in July 1970. MANO threatened to 'terminate five "useless lives" for every policeman, soldier or other citizen killed by left wing terrorists. The "useless lives" would be selected from a list of known left-wingers and common criminals.'[4] Not only were those targeted by the Tupamaros afraid, but also many on the legal left who were targeted by far right groups.

One of the scholars who studied Uruguay at the time, Howard Handelman, conducted polling and interviews of industrial leaders. Handelman concluded that industrial leaders feared for their safety in the early 1970s. They were the targets of Tupamaro bombings and kidnappings. These industrial leaders increased their ties to the state and to the military.[5]

The effects of state violence are harder to document due to a lack of data. In spite of this, it is probable that the suspension of individual liberties, including habeas corpus and the practice of torture in interrogations, resulted in some citizens viewing the state as a threat to their security. Moreover, with the appearance of clandestine violent state sanctioned groups such as the JUP and the Comando Caza Tupamaro, it seems reasonable to infer damage to security due to state repression and violence.

Peruvian rudimentary purpose of the state: security

How did the state and terrorist violence affect the fulfilment of the rudimentary purpose of the state, security? Evidence of a decrease in the fulfilment of the rudimentary purpose of security can be measured in public opinion data and in the death toll. Through an examination of public opinion, the main concerns of the citizens can be tracked. Not surprisingly, the people viewed violence as a severe problem. Public opinion data also document fear of both state and terrorist groups. Finally, the death toll supports that the citizens' perception of insecurity was based on a bloody reality.

The brutality of Sendero is evident. The CRV figures reported in table 6.1 do not reflect a complete estimate of violence, but represent the number of cases reported to the commission. The true numbers, which can be extrapolated from these figures, are estimated to be much higher. In 1984 alone, Sendero was reported to have killed 1061 people and tortured another 142. Although the violence decreased by half or two thirds in the following years, by 1989 the conflict was returning to the earlier level of intensities. Table 6.1 details the number of reported victims of terrorism from 1980–1992. In addition to deaths and disappearances, torture was reported. Similar to killings, the relative bloodiness of Sendero is also clear compared with the other group of guerrillas, MRTA. The peaks of Sendero torture are in 1984 and 1989. In the final report, the CVR estimated that 69,280 individuals died in the conflict from 1980–2000, with Sendero responsible for 54 per cent of the deaths and MRTA responsible for 1.5 per cent.[6] In general, the death toll due to terrorism is especially high in 1983 and 1984 and the period of 1989–1992.

In 1991, a Peruvian Senate Commission examined terrorist violence in that year. Sendero attacked and killed people from all parts of society. Peasants, residents, MRTA members, ronderos and members of the military were all frequently targeted by Sendero. In this report, it is documented that, in 1991, Sendero killed 366 suspected MRTA members, 420 peasants, 172 ronderos, 100 professionals and businessmen, 58 workers, 227 residents, 44 authorities, 6 foreigners, and 133 military and police. Their strategy was

Table 6.1 Peru: victims of non-state terrorism with attributions of responsibility, 1980–1992

	Torture			Deaths and disappearances			Deaths due to terrorism		
	Sendero	MRTA	Others	Sendero	MRTA	Unknown	Police & armed forces	Civilians	Presumed subversives
1980	9	0	1	24	0	7	0	2	9
1981	21	0	3	41	0	6	6	5	71
1982	50	1	5	231	0	25	32	52	109
1983	117	0	3	614	0	48	61	682	1226
1984	142	0	8	1061	0	82	82	1785	1721
1985	57	0	5	348	2	27	76	731	630
1986	90	0	8	305	2	22	129	504	781
1987	69	0	8	388	1	49	192	603	341
1988	126	0	8	490	7	36	280	825	404
1989	249	17	12	847	29	94	338	1365	1175
1990	170	8	16	851	21	74	298	1531	1879
1991	83	5	8	492	24	56	387	1282	1375
1992	123	4	12	536	24	63	397	1301	934

Sources: The data for torture and deaths and disappearances come from the Comisión de la Verdad y Reconciliación, *Informe Final Anexo Estadístico*, (Lima: Comisión de la Verdad y Reconciliación August 2003), pp. 84, 324. The data on deaths due to terrorism are from Table 7.1, David Scott Palmer, 'The Revolutionary Terrorism of Peru's Shining Path', in Martha Crenshaw (ed.), *Terrorism in Context* (University Park: Pennsylvania University Press, 1995), p. 271.

that if you were not a supporter, then you were an enemy. MRTA tended to target members of the police, the military, and Sendero, although it did target civilians as well. MRTA killed 4 businessmen, 8 workers, 13 residents, 2 authorities, and 77 military and police.[7]

Table 6.2 provides a complete victim profile of Sendero Luminoso, MRTA, and those whose perpetrators are unknown, based on reports given to the CRV.

The CRV notes that the vast majority of victims spoke either Quechua or another native language. This contrasts with the 1993 census, which estimated that only 16 per cent of the population spoke a native language. Especially in terms of Sendero victims, the individuals were overwhelmingly undereducated, with almost three quarters of the victims finishing at most primary school, compared with the general population of 40 per cent. This violence against the traditionally marginalized population of indigenous peasants aggravated a historical divide among the population, further undermining integration. In general, peasants and local authorities were frequent targets for attacks. Additionally, targeting prominent civil society leaders or local authorities was the goal – to scour the countryside of all competing authorities. MRTA's victim profile was different, tending to be Spanish speaking and more educated. The brutality of Sendero militants prevented them from being able to recruit among peasants, because of their lack of respect and knowledge of indigenous cultures.[8] Moreover, Sendero's first act of hanging black dogs also alienated people of traditional beliefs, who believe black dogs to be guides to the afterworld.[9]

According to public opinion data, the violence of Sendero, MRTA, and other terrorist groups was viewed as threatening. The National Questionnaire about Violence, commissioned by the Bernales senate commission in 1988, reported that 64.3 per cent of the people viewed terrorist violence as the predominant type of violence in the country.[10] The population clearly viewed the terrorist violence as more of a threat than police or military violence in 1988. In general, terrorism was consistently ranked among the most critical problems of Peru. Table 6.3 charts the perception of inflation, unemployment, terrorism, and nutrition. Respondents were asked, 'In your opinion, what are the three principal

Table 6.2 Peru: victim profiles of non-state terrorism with attributions of responsibility, 1980–2000

Characteristics	Torture			Deaths and disappearances		
	SL (%)	MRTA (%)	Others/Unknown (%)	SL (%)	MRTA (%)	Unknown/Others (%)
Education	(1064)	(31)	(81)	(8022)	(245)	(1143)
None	16.17	6.45	6.17	22.86	6.53	13.65
Some	0.56	0.00	1.23	1.47	0.00	0.00
Primary	54.70	51.61	48.15	50.54	50.61	41.03
Secondary	21.80	41.94	22.22	19.76	33.47	27.38
Superior	6.77	0.00	22.22	6.51	9.39	17.94
Maternal language	(1110)	(37)	(87)	(8693)	(266)	(1215)
Quechua	79.46	29.73	64.37	78.09	26.69	62.96
Spanish	20.45	64.86	34.48	19.95	71.43	36.13
Other native language	0.09	5.41	1.15	1.97	1.88	0.91
Occupation	(929)	(29)	(64)	(7854)	(231)	(1085)
Peasant	45.32	51.72	35.94	51.32	46.75	43.78
Local authorities	29.17	13.79	25.00	21.40	17.75	13.64
Housewives	5.60	6.90	4.69	7.75	3.03	3.04
Sales and business people	5.71	6.90	12.50	6.06	10.39	8.94
Independent workers	3.77	10.34	6.25	3.62	6.06	6.36
Teachers	2.91	0.00	1.56	2.16	2.16	3.41
University students	0.86	0.00	3.13	0.79	2.60	5.53
Employees	2.80	10.34	4.69	2.01	5.19	3.59
Military and police	0.65	0.00	0.00	1.72	1.30	4.42
Workers	1.08	0.00	0.00	1.02	2.16	1.38
Professionals and intellectuals	0.54	0.00	1.56	0.50	0.43	1.94
Others	1.61	0.00	4.69	1.64	2.16	3.96

Sources: Comisión de la Verdad y Reconciliación, *Informe Final*, Anexo Estadístico Lima: Comisión de la Verdad y Reconciliación, (August 2003), pp. 86, 327.
Note: The numbers in parentheses represent the numbers upon which the percentages are based.

Table 6.3 Peru: four principal problems, 1988–1992

	Inflation (%)	Terrorism (%)	Unemployment (%)	Nutrition (%)
January 1988	51	67	32	22
April 1989	61	59	49	23
February 1990	59	62	58	46
October 1990	46	35	50	34
January 1991	27	53	31	36
July 1991	34	43	34	41
October 1991		43	31	35
April 1992	14	49	39	16

Sources: APOYO, *Informe de Opinion*, January 1991; APOYO, *Informe de Opinion*, July 1991; APOYO, *Informe de Opinion*, October 1991; APOYO, *Informe de Opinion*, April 1992.
Note: Figures are the percentage of respondents that named the category as one of the top three problems facing Peru.

problems facing the country?' The table includes the top four problems chosen most frequently as among the top three. January 1988 showed the highest concern about terrorism. However, in April 1992, the month of the coup, terrorism was still considered one of the most severe problems facing the nation, with 49 per cent of those questioned choosing it. Unemployment, nutrition, and inflation followed as severe problems. The violence was perceived to be so severe that some considered the country to be in a state of civil war. In a poll conducted on 25 July 1989, 56 per cent of Peruvians feared that their country was on the brink of a civil war and that in some parts of the country, subversive forces were in control. Nineteen per cent of the people believed that a civil war already existed.[11] The importance of violence as a concern to the Peruvians is even more impressive given the context of the prolonged and severe economic crisis that Peru was facing.

The violence instilled a sense of fear in the vast majority of the population. The 1988 Bernales commission documents the fear of terrorist groups. It reported that 72.6 per cent of Peruvians admitted that the terrorist acts had made them afraid, 15 per cent said they were somewhat afraid, and only 6.5 per cent said the acts had not succeeded in frightening them.[12] In 1991, *Perú Económico* reported an

APOYO survey of Lima residents on terrorism. Of those questioned, 78 per cent admitted that terrorist attacks and blackouts had created an environment of fear and anxiety.[13]

In addition, the citizens were not only afraid of terrorist groups, such as Sendero, they were also afraid of state forces. APOYO asked, 'What does a policeman inspire – security or fear?' The National Police inspired more fear than security in three out of four surveys. In November 1990, only 34 per cent reported feeling secure and 41 per cent reported fear of the National Police. There was improvement in February 1991, when 48 per cent reported feeling secure and only 36 per cent being fearful. However, beginning in July 1991, there was a steady decline in the amount of security (31 per cent) that the National Police inspired. Instead, most people reported being fearful (52 per cent). By October, 61 per cent of those questioned replied that the police made them feel fearful instead of secure (26 per cent).[14]

The general fear that three out of four Peruvians felt reflected the bloody reality of Peruvian life. Thousands of non-combatant civilians had been killed by both state and terrorist groups. Hundreds of officials had been assassinated. Many of the deaths in 1983 and 1984 were due to the actions of the military in emergency zones. According to Starn,

> General Noel's counteroffensive of 1983–4 displayed the most brutal and imperial side of the military. Torture, rape and murder of suspected rebels remained a mainstay of the counterinsurgency in subsequent years, leaving Peru with the world's highest number of 'disappeared' from 1988 to 1991.[15]

The increasing numbers of dead starting in 1989 reflect the recovery of Sendero from the June 1986 prison massacre and their advancement into their phase of 'strategic equilibrium' where Sendero tried to match the strength of the state.

Peruvians from all parts of the ideological and economic spectrums were victims of violence. In an examination of the total death toll, it can be seen that civilians and alleged subversives make up the overwhelming majority of victims. However, some groups have questioned the number of subversive deaths, believing many of the dead who were labelled subversives to be non-combatant citizens instead. Of the 24,250 killed from January 1980 to July 1992, approximately

1 per cent were drug traffickers, 42 per cent civilians, 49 per cent alleged subversives, and 8 per cent security forces.[16] Non-combatant civilians have paid a high price for the conflict, with a minimum of 10,000 deaths in 12 years. This conflict was also economically costly. In the 15 years from 1980–1995, economic losses due to the violence were estimated to total approximately $25 billion US dollars.[17] Raúl González described a frightening situation in Ayacucho:

> No one knows where it is safe, no one: neither the police who expect an attack at any time, nor the citizen, who fears if not the detention, the exceptional authority used in the search of his house by the police who are looking for terrorists and who believe that all are terrorists.[18]

Sendero and other terrorist groups targeted victims. State human rights violations threatened the safety of the citizens. Forced participation in rondas transformed citizens into targets. In Peru, it seemed difficult not to be perceived as the enemy of either the terrorists or of the state.

Spanish rudimentary purpose of the state: security

How did the terrorist violence affect the fulfilment of the rudimentary purpose of the state, security, in Spain? Available evidence of the Spanish case, presented in table 6.4, is limited to data documenting the biggest problems facing the nation and death tolls from violence. During the transition to democracy, two main problems dominated public opinion: economic troubles and public order. A series of Gallup polls traced the public concern for different problems. In 1977, inflation and public order consistently ranked among the highest concerns. The numbers for the problem of public order are broken down according to party affiliation for the December data. Not surprisingly, members of the conservative Popular Alliance and the centre right Union of the Democratic Centre were more concerned about order. Over half of the members of the Popular Alliance, 57 per cent, were most concerned with order. Forty-four per cent of the Union of the Democratic Centre were most concerned about order. Order remained important for other party members also. Over 20 per cent of those affiliated with the regional and the leftist parties listed it as a top problem.[19] In 1978 and 1979, public order and economic

Table 6.4 Spain: top problems facing the country, 1977–1986

	Dec. 77	Nov. 78	June 79	Mar. 80	July 80	Feb. 81	July 82	April 84	July 86
Unemployment	66	91	88	84	88	91	88	91	85
Crime			72	35	33	30	23	38	63
Drug trafficking									53
Terrorism	32*	51*	72*	49	60	61	68	63	28
Cost of living	70	82	72	40	40	35	39	30	19

Sources: Gallup, Spain, IG-600/085; Gallup, Spain, IG-600/129; Gallup, Spain, IG-600/067; Gallup, Spain, IG-600/081; Gallup, Spain, IG-600/147; Foreign Broadcast Information Service; *El País*.

issues were the first two concerns but, starting in 1979, more than 70 per cent of those questioned chose order as a top problem. The increase in concern about public order corresponds to the increase in deaths due to terrorist violence, which increased from 28 in 1977 to 85 in 1978 and to 108 in 1979. A follow-up poll in March 1980 by Gallup found that unemployment and terrorism were the top concerns for the year.[20] Concern about terrorism continued to increase as the number of deaths continued to increase that year. Concern about terrorism remained high through out 1985.

The responses for 1977 to 1979, marked with an asterisk, instead of asking about terrorism, asked about public order. Economic troubles and terrorism dominate citizen concerns throughout the first years of democracy. The concern about terrorism peaked in July 1982. By July 1986, only 28 per cent listed it within the top three problems facing the nation.

Finally, the death toll from terrorist violence measures the fulfilment of the rudimentary purpose of the state, security, as shown in table 6.5. The return to democracy resulted in an intensification of violence. The bloodiest year was 1980. In that year ninety-two people were killed by ETA alone. The number of deaths from terrorist violence dropped after 1980 and began to stabilize at a lower level. By 1981, the number of dead had dropped to one quarter of the number of victims of the year before.

Table 6.5 Spain: deaths due to terrorism, 1976–1986

	ETA	GRAPO	Extreme right (Ministry of the Interior)	Others
1976	17	1	3	0
1977	10	7	8	1
1978	66	6	1	13
1979	76	21	6	3
1980	92	6	20	2
1981	30	5	1	2
1982	37	2		2
1983	32	2		2
1984	32	5		3
1985	37	0		21
1986	43	0		1

Sources: The figures for GRAPO and Others come from Salustiano del Campo (ed.), *Tendencias Sociales en España Volumen II* (Bilbao: Fundacion BBV, 1993), p. 70. Figures for ETA violence come from the Ministry of the Interior.

Approximately half of those killed between 1976 and 1986 were either affiliated with the professional military or with the police. Almost 90 per cent of the police and professional military fatalities were caused by ETA. In the same 10 years, 289 civilians and non-professional military personnel were killed. (Spain has a mandatory military service for young men. Non-professional military personnel include young men serving their compulsory service.) Of the civilian and non-professional military casualties, 58.5 per cent were caused by ETA. Of all those killed, ETA was responsible for almost 75 per cent of the deaths.[21]

A relationship between the number of dead and the amount of concern about terrorism or public order can be seen. Unfortunately, there was a change in the wording of the Gallup questions from questions of public order to terrorism during the critical year of 1980. However, we can still establish that as the number of deaths increased from 1977 to 1979, the percentage of people choosing public order as a main problem increased from 32 per cent to 72 per cent. Similarly, as violence increased in 1980, the percentage of people listing terrorism as a main concern increased from

49 per cent to 60 per cent. After 1981, the number of deaths declined. Public concern with terrorism did not begin to decline until 1984, however.

Uruguayan rudimentary purpose of the state: integration

How did the state and terrorist violence affect the rudimentary purpose of the state, integration in Uruguay? Specific questions of tolerance towards citizens of opposing views are unavailable. The available anecdotal evidence is compelling. Reaction to the state policies appeared to undermine integration. For example, in June 1970 Generals Borda and Francese, as police chief and minister of the interior, insisted that the state decree that attacks against military establishments or personnel would be tried by court marshal. Penalties for 'spreading subversive ideas and undermining public order' were also greatly increased. The punishment for those who 'aid, organize, direct or participate in association tending to arouse hate or violent class struggle, or upset the political and social order of the state, as well as those who diffuse ideas of this kind' would be up to fifteen years.[22] This broadly defined law did not make an exception for the Communist Party. The Communists objected to the law, noting that it would possibly implicate them, given their belief in the class struggle as a law of history. For instance, after an incident at a Communist club in April 1972 in which seven people were killed, one officer involved in the incident commented 'so long as my comrades are being killed [four officials had been shot dead by the Tupamaros three days earlier on 14 April] I am not making fancy distinctions between leftists'.[23] This statement definitely indicates a lack of tolerance for citizens who ascribed to a leftist view of politics.

In addition to anecdotal evidence, expectations about the consequences of terrorist and state violence are supported by the work of other scholars in the existing literature. Charles Gillespie, in his study of the eventual redemocratization of Uruguay based on interviews with leading politicians and businessmen in Uruguay, concludes that the Tupamaros 'had a corrosive effect on the Uruguayan political system, eroding tolerance for opponents and creating a polarized ideological climate. Traditional politicians became more and more convinced that guerrillas represented a threat to democracy.'[24] Howard Handelman, in a study conducted in the late 1970s and based on interviews with leading businessmen, concluded that there was a 'conspiratorial view of the left which failed to distinguish between differing (and often hostile) leftist factions or divisions within the labor movement'. Of three hundred people surveyed,[25] one half believed the labour strife and guerrilla movement to be part of a leftist conspiracy. Ultimately, Handelman believed that this conflict and decrease in tolerance led to instability. A majority of the 'industrial elite felt that the dissolution of Congress and the elimination of democratic processes in 1973 [were] necessary for the nation's political and economic survival... Questions regarding unions and labor relations prior to 1973 often elicited highly emotional, at times hysterical responses.'[26] Carina Perelli, in her study of the Uruguayan military in the 1970s, concludes that the attitude of the business class was shared by others. Within the circle of politicians, the same distrust and intolerance of opposing views became prevalent. According to Perelli,

> To make things worse, the new breed of Leftist politicians was not particularly accommodating. Opposition was understood as adversarial politics, which meant, among other things, that the rules of courtesy stemming from the feeling of belonging to the same 'club' or political class no longer applied. This, in turn, made it more and more difficult to maintain the old division between private vices and public virtues, even as a pretense... Confrontational politics, hostility, and polarization began to dominate the political arena, reducing the possibilities of dialogue and negotiation to nil. Little by little the more polarized sectors of society started to equate difference and diversity with enmity. The breakdown of consensus had an immediate paralyzing effect on state bureaucracies heavily dependent on the guarantees given by the political and party systems.[27]

The long tradition of cooperation among politicians appeared to have disappeared. The limited available evidence suggests that the violence of the Tupamaros did undermine integration. However, the evidence also suggests that state action also undermined integration by polarizing the political community and reducing tolerance. The fear and mistrust led to a situation in spring 1972, according to Langguth, in which 'families were reduced to whispering to each other in their own homes. Everyone was taken for being a spy.'[28]

Peruvian rudimentary purpose of the state: integration

How did the state and terrorist violence affect the rudimentary purpose of the state, integration in Peru? Historically, the political community in Peru was weak even before the outbreak of violence. For instance, when asked about the possibility of national integration, Senator Enrique Bernales replied that

> it will be very difficult, because of the past stigma and because of the deep and strong ethnic and cultural divisions. This is a racist country. The apartheid doesn't exist in the laws, but it functions in everyday life and I don't know how much time it will take to combat it.[29]

It is expected that the stresses of state and terrorist violence further undermined integration. In Peru, integration can be measured by examining electoral and public opinion data. Elections were interrupted, as candidates were assassinated and election boycotts enforced by Sendero violence. Tolerance for opposing viewpoints decreased. Many young people reported being suspected of being terrorists. Finally, many citizens declined to cooperate with the state's antisubversive campaign.

Electoral participation was hindered due to the violence. In an already poorly performing state, death threats from Sendero drove many from office and prevented others from replacing them. For example, at the end of 1984 224 council members and 104 mayors had resigned because of death threats.[30] In 1988, dozens of mayors resigned because of lack of protection from death threats.[31] In 1989, 10 governors and lieutenant governors, 6 engineers and officials of development projects, 7 judicial officials and 19 other state officials were killed. From January to October, 46 mayors were killed and 263 received death threats. Sendero's attacks had the effect of leaving 123 out of 435 districts without registered candidates in that year's elections.[32] From 1986 to August 1989, 99 mayors and 350 town councillors either resigned or abandoned their posts, and 17 mayors and 2 town councillors were killed.[33] The result of this intimidation was less state presence. For example, in August 1989 80 districts and 4 provinces had no municipal authority due to the assassination of 92 public officials.[34] In addition, many more local authorities resigned due to threats. For example, in the department of Huánuco, more than 70 officials resigned.[35] Although these data could be reasonably viewed as an indicator of security, they are a more salient indicator of integration. Death threats and assassinations of community leaders and officials are an extreme example of the undermining of integration by preventing political participation.

In addition to creating vacancies in official offices, Sendero also influenced the ability of many citizens to vote. Voting is universal and mandatory in Peru, with the exception of active duty military and police, who are barred from voting.[36] In spite of mandatory voting, many people did not participate in elections. Not all abstentions, nulls, and blank votes can be attributed to Sendero's boycotts of elections, but the forced boycotts and the threatened retaliation against voting did affect many areas. Nationally, votes varied from seven to nineteen percentage of null votes, from 3 to 6 per cent blank, and from 16 to 30 per cent absenteeism.[37] At the department level, there were wide variations. In areas with a strong Sendero presence, such as in Ayacucho, elections were strongly affected. For example, in the 1983 municipal elections, 75 per cent of eligible voters either abstained or cast blank votes. Of the votes cast, 56 per cent were blank or spoiled.[38] In addition, elections could not be held in the four rural Ayacucho provinces of Cangallo, Victor Fajardo, La Mar, and Huanta in 1983. In the 1989 municipal elections in Ayacucho, absentee rates approached 56 per cent with the null and blank votes totalling 73 per cent.[39] In the areas under state of emergency, many elections were annulled because of low turnout or too many invalid votes.[40] In addition to problems with excessive blank and null votes or absenteeism, some districts did not have candidates to fill the open positions because of Sendero intimidation. For example, of all districts holding elections in 1991, 123 districts, or 25 per cent, did not have candidates to fill the positions for election.[41]

In addition to electoral disturbances, the violence affected tolerance for people of opposing views and increased suspicion of others. Sendero's threat was recognized by those on the legal left. Many on the left rejected the violence of Sendero. For example, an *Equis X* editorial states, 'the socialist left has to sincerely and consciously opt for representative democracy and reject the road of violence, which would lead to the left being the first victim'.[42] José María Salcedo, in *QueHacer*, commented that Sendero is the principal enemy of the left and that the left has the most to lose because of Sendero. 'Sooner than later, militarized repression will be unable to coexist with democratic spaces. This is something which would not affect Sendero, but which is vital to the left.'[43] The legal left feared that they would pay for the actions of Sendero in the form of repression and intolerance.

In addition to a lack of tolerance, many Peruvians reported being suspected of being terrorists by other Peruvians and by the state authorities. *QueHacer* reports that young people, especially students, report being harassed and suspected of being terrorists. According to one student: 'We university students are suspected of being terrorists, all of us, especially those who attend state universities.'[44] Peruvians living in areas with a Sendero presence were assumed to be Senderistas. For example, a general in charge of one emergency zone stated of the success of Sendero's attacks: 'It is possible thanks to the support which the inhabitants many times lend ... [and because] many times they can easily blend in with the villagers.'[45] Moreover, people who fled the violence plagued interior were assumed to be Senderistas either spreading violence to new areas or fleeing prosecution. In general, Peru became very dangerous for everyone. For instance, Enrique Mayer characterizes contemporary Peru as a country in which 'security employees, narco-traffickers, arms dealers, grave robbers, and police all operate underground. Terrorists dress up as police, while police don Sendero guise to carry out acts of unauthorized violence. Is it any wonder that no one can trust anyone in Peru?'[46]

The undermining of integration is also indicated by the unwillingness of Peruvian citizens to cooperate with the state to apprehend known terrorists. In spite of the broad fear that the terrorist violence inspired, the state could not rely on citizens' collaboration to fight the subversion. When asked whether or not they would collaborate with the state against terrorism, 30.2 per cent said they would collaborate, 48.7 per cent said they would not, and 18.7 per cent did not know what they would do.[47] More specifically, when asked what they would do if they witnessed a terrorist act, 41.1 per cent said they would 'forget it,' 10.0 per cent said they would report it without reservation, 39.5 per cent said they would report it with reservation, 4.8 per cent said they would intervene, and 3.7 per cent did not know.[48] The hesitation could be due to a fear of reprisal, a lack of faith in the ability of the state to respond, or perhaps even a lack of sympathy and support for the state itself, among other plausible reasons. Given the number of civilians, judges, mayors, and other collaborators who were killed by Sendero, a fear of reprisal would be understandable. Considering the low citizen confidence in the state, it is not surprising that many Peruvians would be hesitant to risk their lives to cooperate, even if they did not support Sendero or other groups.

Sendero's intimidation of citizens impeded participation and functioning of the state. Officials and candidates were threatened and killed by Sendero. In addition, Sendero violently encouraged citizens to either abstain or to cast blank votes. Moreover, it is plausible to infer that the repressive state response of invocations of states of emergency and the placement of areas under military control, with the suspension of individual liberties, further undermined integration. Many citizens, students, and refugees reported the reaction of others, citizens and officials, who suspected them of being terrorists.

Spanish rudimentary purpose of the state: integration

How did the violence affect the rudimentary purpose of the state, integration in Spain? Certainly, the killing of 289 civilians and non-professional military personnel did not bolster feelings of a community of equals and peers. However, there is evidence of the state acting to improve integration by resolving long standing disagreements about regional autonomy. It is plausible that the state efforts may have ameliorated some of the negative consequences of terrorist violence on integration.

To many regional groups, resentment against the central state was the legacy of the Franco regime. Although the restrictions against regional language and culture disappeared under the new democratic state, some of the distrust remained. Many citizens felt persecuted and discriminated against because of their regional origin. However, these feelings of discrimination appear to be fading over time. The worst dispersion of the community was ameliorated by the new democracy. In fact, the state acted to improve integration by conceding to regional demands.

Feelings of regional patriotism were especially high in Catalonia and in the Basque country. In a 1979 study, half of the Basque natives identified as only Basque. An additional 15 per cent identified as more Basque than Spanish. Only 24 per cent felt as Spanish as Basque. In Catalonia, only 20 per cent of the Catalan natives identified as only Catalan. An additional 16 per cent identified as more Catalan than Spanish. Forty-two per cent felt as Spanish as Catalan. The citizens in these regions demanded autonomous status.[49]

Almost immediately, the new democracy acted to reconcile regional demands. In 1977, the regional Catalan *Generalitat*, the former self-government of Catalonia, was restored and steps were made to accommodate Basque autonomy.[50] The new constitution of 1978 included an autonomous community clause. Catalonia and the Basque country moved first to apply and the autonomy statute was approved on 18 December 1979.[51] Many more regions acted to gain autonomy. In spite of the enthusiastic response of some regions, many on the right were strongly opposed to regional autonomy, which they viewed as an attack against national unity. Even regions not historically recognized were granted autonomy. By the end of February 1982, seventeen regions had approved statutes of autonomy.[52]

In many of the regions, a majority of citizens felt discriminated against by other Spaniards. For example, the Basques complained that they paid more in taxes than they received in benefits from the state. Under Franco, this was often the case.[53] Feelings of discrimination can be documented in limited public opinion data. Data for two years only are available, in 1979 and 1982. In two of the three major historical regions, Galicia and the Basque land, feelings of discrimination were significantly lower in 1982, down from 61 per cent to 30 per cent in Galicia and from 51 per cent to 36 per cent in the Basque country. In Catalonia the numbers were slightly higher, up to 26 per cent from 24 per cent.[54] The state's actions appeared to have improved integration in at least the regions of Galicia and the Basque country.

Purposes of the state summary

Uruguay

The available data measuring the purposes of the state in Uruguay suggest that both security and integration were undermined in this period by both terrorist violence and the state's response to it. Congruent with hypothesis one, as the activity of the Tupamaros increased, decreases in security are evident. This was indicated by an increasing proportion of Uruguayans who described their country as disorderly and who described the Tupamaros as a dangerous group. In addition, there is evidence that many industrialists, frequent targets of the Tupamaros, were fearful. Similarly, a decrease in integration can also be seen in the secondary literature supporting a general decline in tolerance. The evidence is also consistent with hypothesis two. Some evidence is available to support the notion that state violence also undermines security. For example, many on the legal left were frightened. They were targeted by violent groups, some of which were associated with state officials. It is also plausible to infer that the indiscriminate arrests, torture in interrogation, and suspension of liberties reduced the security of those suspected by the authorities of being involved in subversive activities. Evidence of a decrease in integration caused by state policies can be seen in the incident in which the Communist Party charged that the new laws designed to punish public support of subversion would also implicate those on the legal left who believed in class struggle.

Peru

The available data measuring the purposes of the state in Peru suggest that both security and integration were undermined in this period by terrorist violence and the state's repressive and violent response. A decrease in security is indicated by the death toll and public opinion data substantiating that the violence of Sendero and other terrorist groups caused fear in almost 80 per cent of the population. Decreases in integration can be measured by the electoral disturbances and lack of tolerance. Officials and candidates were assassinated. Many positions were unfilled due to lack of candidates. The pressure by Sendero to enforce electoral boycotts was effective as abstentions and blank votes were predominant in many areas. A decrease in security is also attributable to state actions. One instrument of the state responsible for the violence, the National Police, inspired more fear than security in a majority of citizens. This signifies that the security of the citizens was being undermined by the state as well as by the terrorist groups. Decreases in integration due to state violence and repression are shown by the stated fear of lack of tolerance for those on the legal left and by the suspicion of being Senderistas reported by students and residents of areas plagued by Sendero activities.

Spain

In Spain, the data are consistent with hypothesis one. Although public opinion data are limited, concern for terrorist violence was evident. No conclusions can be drawn in terms of integration due to the terrorist violence. In terms of hypothesis two, there is evidence that state actions actually improved feelings of integration for two historically alienated communities, the Basque country and Galicia.

Citizen confidence

Uruguayan citizen confidence in the state

> We were getting tired of it... The police nearly always lost to the Tupamaros, and the jails couldn't hold them even when they were captured.[55]
>
> (José Romero, a waiter in Montevideo)

Public opinion data allow us to examine the reaction of Uruguayan citizens to terrorist violence, to the state's policies, and to state violence. Citizen confidence can be measured by public opinion data on the general mood of the country, electoral support for traditional parties, the emergence of non-traditional presidential candidates, and public opinion data on satisfaction with the state and its policies. The indicators show a thorough dissatisfaction with the state that continues to worsen even after the end of Tupamaro violence.

Some public opinion data are available assessing the general situation of the country. In general, Uruguayans did not positively assess the state of their country in the late 1960s. In the years 1967–1969 consistently over half the population listed the situation of the country as poor or very poor. Only 6–7 per cent of those questioned replied that the country was in a very good or good situation.[56] An excellent measure of the general situation in Uruguay is the desire to emigrate. In 1968, only 55 per cent of the population preferred to stay in Uruguay, while 33 per cent expressed a desire to emigrate. Only one year later, only 39 per cent preferred to stay in Uruguay, while 42 per cent stated they would emigrate if they could.[57] Moreover, many Uruguayans followed through with their desires to emigrate. Although comprehensive emigration statistics are unavailable, anecdotal evidence is available. For example, there were a large number of absentee ballots in the 1971 election. Of a total of Montevidean 700,000 ballots, 150,000 people voted absentee from abroad.[58]

Generally, the evaluation of the state continues to worsen even after the end of Tupamaro violence. The disillusionment with the National Assembly's performance is evident as early as 1968. One of the early state strategies for dealing with both labour unrest and terrorist actions was the state of siege or prompt security measures. However, this strategy was not popular among Uruguayans. In August 1968, a question probing the public's opinion about the MPS and other restrictions uncovered that only 33 per cent believed the MPS to be helpful, 58 per cent believed that the MPS was not helpful, and 9 per cent were unsure.[59] The respondents were asked whether or not the National Assembly should lift the MPS. A strong majority, 62 per cent, said lift them, only 29 per cent said allow them to remain, and 9 per cent were unsure.[60] Then, respondents were asked why the National Assembly would not lift them. More than one third, 39 per cent, chose the irresponsibility of the National Assembly, 30 per cent chose political reasons, and only 5 per cent chose the actual situation of the country. Only one out of twenty Uruguayans believed that the situation of the country merited the continuation of the MPS. A small minority, 3 per cent, feared that the National Assembly would be dismissed if the MPS were lifted. Some additional questions about the MPS were asked in late 1971. Although individuals were more likely to view the MPS as beneficial the older they were, no age group reported a majority positive view of the measures. Only 29 per cent of those aged 18–32, 40 per cent of those aged 33–47, and 44 per cent of those over 48 viewed the measures as beneficial. Among all age groups there was a majority view that the measures were not beneficial. Seventy-one per cent of those aged 18–32, 60 per cent of those aged 33–47, and 56 per cent of those over 48 viewed the measures as not beneficial. Three years later, there is still a strong rejection of the MPS. A strong majority of Uruguayan citizens viewed the MPS as harmful.

Some polls assessed the public reaction to other repressive policies and actions in 1968. A prohibition on public gatherings was rejected by almost half of respondents, 47 per cent, while 40 per cent supported the measure. In another question, people were asked if they supported the detention of people without judicial intervention. Of those questioned, 69 per cent disagreed and only 11 per cent approved. In the same year, after the clashes between police and university students that resulted in the death of one student, respondents were asked, 'Who is responsible for the death of Liber Arce [the student killed by state forces on 14 August 1968]?' Almost half, 46 per cent, of the people blamed the police and the state, 11 per cent blamed the students, 13 per cent blamed Liber Arce himself, 0.5 per cent blamed the Communists, and 0.5 per cent blamed the university authorities. Twenty-nine per cent did not know whom to blame.[61] The repressive response of the state to the troubles was rejected by a large majority of citizens.

Until 1971, the main agent of the state to respond to the disorder was the police. The unrest at this time was a mixture of both seditious activity and labour protest. In August 1968, respondents were asked to rate the attitude/position of the armed forces and the police during recent events. As early as August 1968, the armed forces, with 48 per cent believing that their attitude was correct, were twice as popular as the police, with only 26 per cent. They also received half the negative rating, with 24 per cent believing that their attitude was incorrect, of the police, with 46 per cent.[62] *Cuadernos de Marcha* in late 1971 followed up on an earlier question, asking whether or not the police posture or attitude was correct. In response to this question, a slight majority (53 per cent) of those over thirty-three supported the police. However, a strong majority (64 per cent) of younger citizens did not approve of the police posture. This reflects the greater suspicion of young Uruguayans for participating in illegal activity. Overall, the police were viewed more negatively than before.[63]

The record of Uruguayan presidential voting also demonstrates a growing frustration with the two main political parties. The share of the vote for the traditional party significantly declined in the 1970s. The leftist coalition group Frente Amplio had 30.1 per cent of the electoral support in Montevideo by 1971. The combination of the vote for the Blanco and Colorado parties shrunk from 83 per cent in 1966 to 69 per cent in 1971. The interior vote is typically more conservative than the vote in Montevideo. In the interior, non-traditional parties had only 10 per cent of the support.[64] By 1971, electoral results showed a three way split in Montevideo for the Colorados, the Blancos, and Frente Amplio. Only the interior vote saved the traditional parties from defeat.[65]

In addition to looking at the electoral success of non-traditional parties, disillusionment with traditional candidates can be seen by the sudden appearance of military men as political candidates. In 1966, Colorado Oscar Gestido, a sixty-five year old retired air force general, was elected to the presidency.[66] Later other generals served as ministers. The appointment of military men was also seen as a strategy of military appeasement. General Antonio Francese served as minister of defence from 1967–1970, under President Pacheco. In May 1970, Francese became minister of the interior and General César Borda became police chief. Rumours reported by *Latin America* alleged that 'only by the appointment of military men to these two key posts, it was said, were the army and the police persuaded to give up the idea of a bloody revenge on the best known left-wing figures in the country in reprisal for the killing of police inspector Héctor Morán Charquero by the Tupamaros on 13 April.'[67] Later, in January 1971, Pacheco replaced Francese as minister of the interior with General Rafael Milans. Colonel Julio Vigorito was appointed undersecretary of the ministry. General Borda was then minister of defence.[68] President Bordaberry continued the trend with Defence Minister General Enrique Magnani. The trend grew to include generals as presidential candidates in the 1971 elections: General Seregni for the Frente Amplio, General Aguerrondo for the Blanco party, and General J. Ribas for the Colorado party. The candidacy of General Aguerrondo for the Blancos is especially important since his political ambitions were usually reported within the context of speculation of possible coup attempts. However, at the time of the election, he had supposedly been persuaded to think in terms of a Peruvian style programme of reform.[69]

The increasing frequency of military officers serving as ministers and running for office seems to reflect the growing confidence in the military as opposed to the rest of the state. The credibility of the state continued to fall in 1971. In one study, only 13 per cent of Montevideans thought that the National Assembly was acting well and only 23 per cent said the president was acting well. The military received the highest rating, with a 41 per cent approval score.[70] Lack of citizen confidence hit critical levels during the first severe confrontation between the state and the military in February 1973. An Instituto de Opinión Pública poll recorded that 89 per cent of Uruguayan citizens believed that the state bureaucracy was corrupt, 60 per cent agreed with military proposals for reform, 60 per cent believed a coup was immanent, and 88 per cent believed that state corruption should be dealt with severely.[71] It appears that democracy, in practice anyway, and the leading politicians of the time, had lost the support of the people. The evidence suggests that by 1973, the rejection of the state had progressed to a rejection of democracy. These negative numbers continue even though the threat from the Tupamaros had ended. The Uruguayan people who had rejected the state's repressive policies were not only rejecting the state, but ultimately democracy.[72]

Peruvian citizen confidence in the state

Citizen confidence in the Peruvian state can be measured in five ways. First, an increasing dissatisfaction with the main political parties and a growing preference for new and independent parties indicate a lack of confidence in the leading politicians. In addition, public opinion data concerning desires to emigrate indicate a low level of citizen confidence in the state. More specific data are available to measure citizen confidence in the state. Presidential popularity polls indicate a level of satisfaction with particular leaders, with implications for their parties. Questions of confidence and performance of institutions can measure citizen confidence and approval of state performance. Finally, public opinion data assessing support for reform plans also reflect on the level of support for those institutions.

Electoral results indicate a growing dissatisfaction with the traditional parties. The traditional parties in Peru began to lose broad public support as early as 1985 with the emergence of Izquierda Unida (IU) candidate Barrantes. In that year APRA candidate Alan García received 47 per cent and United Left; Barrantes 22 per cent of the vote. However, Barrantes declined to participate in the runoff since he doubted he would win and he feared an outbreak of violence between APRA and IU militants.[73] By 1989, independent candidates had started to win. For example, in the 1989 municipal elections Ricardo Belmont Cassinelli, founder of the independent Workers' Movement (Movimiento Obras), won the mayoral election in Lima in November and again in 1993. According to Wilson Jaime Barreto, 'the triumph of Ricardo Belmont... indicated that the electorate was searching for new options, and as a consequence, rejecting the old parties and old politicians'.[74] There was a general increase in the popularity of the independents and a turning away from the traditional parties that began to dramatically increase after the 1986 municipal elections. Since 1980, support for independent parties had varied from 3–8 per cent. In the general elections of 1985 and the municipal elections of 1986, the conservative parties AP and PPC did not gain many votes. To maintain support in the 1990 elections, they formed a coalition party, FREDEMO (Frente Democrático). By 1990, the independents had secured the vote of a third of the population and the independent candidate, Alberto Fujimori, won the presidential election in the runoff. The share of the votes for the independents had increased from just 3 per cent in 1985 to ultimately 62.5 per cent in the second round presidential election.[75] A majority of voters had repudiated the traditional parties and politicians.

Another general indicator of low citizen confidence in the state's ability to solve national problems is the percentage of Peruvians who desired to emigrate. The available evidence about the willingness to emigrate reflects a deep pessimism about the direction and future of the country. In July 1988, 52 per cent of those polled said they would emigrate if they could. By May 1991, that number had peaked at 71 per cent wishing to emigrate. Not until the presidency of Fujimori did the numbers begin to decline. By November 1991, the numbers had begun to decline, reaching 56 per cent in May 1992 and 46 per cent in May 1996.[76] When asked why they wished to emigrate, in October 1989, 55 per cent chose the reason that there are more possibilities to develop/flourish abroad, 33 per cent chose the economic crisis, and 9 per cent blamed the violence. Another drop occurred one month after the *autogolpe*, from 62 per cent to 56 per cent, indicating the confidence gained by the election of Fujimori.

Public opinion tracking presidential popularity is also informative of the level of citizen confidence in the state. Of all the democratically elected presidents in Peru from 1980–1992, only Fujimori maintained reasonably high and constant approval ratings throughout most of his first two terms as president. Considering that Fujimori was an independent, this reflects a thorough dissatisfaction with the traditional parties and perhaps even reflects on democracy as practised in Peru. President Belaúnde began his term with a 67 per cent approval rating. However, for more than the last two years of his presidency, from April 1983 until the 1985 presidential elections, his approval rating was consistently lower than 25 per cent, with disapproval ratings ranging from 60–70 per cent.[77] Belaúnde's successor, García, started his term with extremely high ratings, at 96 per cent.[78] However, his popularity plummeted in October 1988. During 1989 and 1990, his approval ratings did not exceed 15 per cent.[79] The percentage of Lima residents who rejected the president in 1988 rose from 71 per cent in October to 74 per cent in December. Only 21 per cent approved of García's administration, down from 24 per cent in October. However, at this time, 71 per cent of the respondents did not believe a coup would solve the crisis.[80]

This pattern of optimism, followed by high dissatisfaction, was broken with the election of Alberto Fujimori. Fujimori did have a few low points in his popularity, especially in the summer of 1991 with approval ratings between

25 and 35 per cent, but he later recovered to his original high levels of approval. In December 1991, his approval rating was measured at 69 per cent by the polling firm DATUM and 60 per cent by APOYO.[81] In March 1991, at the beginning of a summer of low popularity, the displeasure with Fujimori had also spread to members of his government and party. Vice-President Carlos García indicated that he would not oppose the removal of Fujimori as head of state. However, even at the lowest point in Fujimori's popularity, he was viewed more positively than Alan García. In an APOYO poll conducted in Lima between 25 and 26 July 1991 during a point in Fujimori's lowest popularity, when asked who had a better administration, 41 per cent believed Fujimori had done a better job than García. Only 23 per cent believed that García did a better job than Fujimori. Some of the respondents, 28 per cent, believed that neither administration was good.[82] After December 1991, Fujimori's approval ratings continued to improve. The December poll came after his successful handling of a border conflict with Ecuador.[83]

Public opinion data in the late 1980s and the early 1990s reveal a deep dissatisfaction with the performance of most state institutions. For example, in 1988 only 10 per cent believed the government was doing a good job, about half thought the government performance was average, about 30 per cent responded that the government did a poor job, and about 10 per cent were undecided.[84] As Peru moved into the 1990s the evaluation of the state worsened. Only President Fujimori, the Catholic Church, and the military maintained positive evaluations.

The state was not judged to be efficient or effective in its attempts to quell the violence. Moreover, perhaps because of the paramilitary groups and the repressive response to the terrorist threat, the state was not perceived by the population as pursuing peace. In the 1988 National Questionnaire about Violence, when asked which institutions worked for national pacification, the state was not mentioned often. When asked to identify organizations that worked for peace, 58.1 per cent identified the Catholic Church, 18.2 per cent identified the Commissions of Human Rights, 3.0 per cent identified the police, and only 4.5 per cent identified the state.[85]

In 1991, only President Fujimori and the military received favourable ratings. While Fujimori's popularity continued to increase after the summer of 1991, other institutions lost more citizen confidence. *Debate*'s annual survey of the 'power in Peru' ranking, in May 1991, included a question about institutional rankings. Less than one year before the coup, the legislative branch was viewed as doing a poor or very poor job by 92 per cent of those questioned. The judiciary fared only slightly better, with 82 per cent responding that it was functioning poorly. The police force received a 74 per cent negative rating. Only four institutions had a majority of those questioned rate them as average, good, or very good in terms of their performance: the executive branch (82 per cent), the armed forces (60 per cent), the Catholic Church (74 per cent), and the press (66 per cent).[86] This dissatisfaction is corroborated by later polls. In July 1991, in an Imasen poll conducted in Lima, 88.5 per cent of the respondents believed that the political parties did not fulfil their functions that year.[87] In the same month, Congress's disapproval rating reached 80.8 per cent. In August, Congress's disapproval rating remained high at 71.3 per cent.[88] Not only were Congress and the political parties held in low esteem, but the populace seemed to view them as insignificant. In 1991, 40 per cent of the population could not identify a single leader of the opposition.[89] Also in 1991, the political parties received a low approval rating of 13 per cent.[90]

Other studies conducted by APOYO corroborate the dissatisfaction. In an October 1991 poll conducted in Lima, respondents were asked which institutions they trusted. Only the Church (85 per cent trust, 11 per cent distrust), the media (55 per cent trust, 32 per cent distrust), and the armed forces (47 per cent trust, 42 per cent distrust) generated more trust than distrust. Congress had an overwhelmingly negative rating of 72 per cent distrusting it and only 19 per cent trusting that branch. The judicial branch fared only slightly better, with 22 per cent trusting it and 68 per cent distrusting it.[91] A separate APOYO poll conducted on 26 October 1991 asked respondents 'should the national police be dismantled?' Fifty-one per cent agreed, 40 per cent disagreed, and 9 per cent did not respond. On the contrary, the executive branch was rated as average or good by 83 per cent of people. The armed forces were positively rated by 60 per cent of the population. Those were the only groups evaluated positively.[92] A series of studies conducted by APOYO corroborated the increasing rejection of institutions. All branches except the armed forces and the executive had low ratings of approval. The Catholic Church and the media were also held in relatively high esteem. One month before the coup, only the armed forces, the Catholic Church, the media and the president had high confidence ratings. Political parties and the judiciary were rated favourably by less than 15 per cent of the population. The confidence rating of Fujimori, the armed forces, and of the police increased after the *autogolpe*.

By late 1991, citizen dissatisfaction with the state seemed to be progressing into a rejection of democracy as it existed in Peru at the time. Fujimori took advantage of the lack of popularity of the other institutions to push through reforms and ultimately to seize power. Public opinion data seem to suggest a growing confidence in Fujimori, independent of his office, and in the military. For example, Fujimori's reform plans for Congress and the judiciary were well supported. In a December 1991 poll, Fujimori's proposal to renew one third of Congress at two year intervals was approved by 80 per cent of those questioned. His proposed reorganization of the judiciary was approved by 89 per cent and the reorganization of the comptroller's office received 69 per cent approval. Fujimori's motives for his reform were

Table 6.6 Peru: average or good rating of institutions, 1990–1992

Institution	Sept. 1990	Mar. 1991	Sept. 1991	Mar. 1992	Sept. 1992
Council of Ministers	52	25	24	27	37
Armed forces	58	53	47	54	57
Church	81	83	85	80	81
Media	60	48	55	57	58
Political parties	21	13	13	12	13
Judiciary	23	16	22	14	28
National Police	47	31	33	20	48
President	57	29	26	42	54

Sources: APOYO, *Informe de Opinion*, Lima, October 1991, August 1993.

viewed positively by a strong majority of the citizens. When the respondents were asked why Fujimori criticized Congress, 47 per cent believed Fujimori wanted to make them work harder, 27 per cent believed he wanted to make the Congress more efficient, 7 per cent believed in a smoke screen theory, 6 per cent believed Fujimori wanted to dissolve Congress, and 4 per cent believed he wanted to legislate through decree. Overall, Fujimori's confrontations with Congress and the judicial branch were approved by 72 per cent of those questioned.[93]

Spanish citizen confidence in the state

Citizen confidence in the Spanish state can be measured in different ways. First, data are available outlining what sort of response to terrorism Spaniards wanted the state to undertake. The actual actions of the state can be compared with these wishes. Second, questions evaluating the general mood and direction of the country are available. Finally, public opinion data of satisfaction with different governments according to policy area are available.

Public opinion data analysing citizen evaluation of state policy towards terrorism are available. Few Spaniards desired a repressive response to the terrorism. The state basically followed those demands. At the beginning of the transition to democracy in March and April 1977, Spaniards were asked how they thought the state should react to the claims of regions and the terrorist threats. A strong majority, 78 per cent, agreed with the following statement: 'In Spain, the most important thing is to maintain the order and the peace.' Interestingly, only 22 per cent supported a more firm police response to the disorder, agreeing with the statement that 'the police should be more firm to avoid public disorder.' Spaniards wanted peace, but did not want a heavy handed police response to achieve it. Moreover, a majority of Spaniards supported total regional autonomy: 55 per cent agreed with the statement 'The different regions should have total autonomy.'[94]

In an earlier study in December 1976, respondents were asked how the state should respond to terrorist kidnappings. From these early data, it appears that Spaniards were unwilling to sacrifice liberties for more order. On the contrary, almost one third of respondents preferred a widening of political liberties, agreeing with either the statement that the state should 'negotiate and widen political liberties' or 'stay firm and widen political liberties'. Eleven per cent were in favour of negotiation and ultimately freedom for terrorists in exchange for prisoners. Thirty-six per cent agreed that the state should 'stay firm to avoid future kidnappings'.[95] This same principle can be seen three years later, under even more prevalent terrorism. In 1979, 55 per cent of Spaniards preferred that the state maintain order within the law. The willingness to accept terrorist demands or to negotiate was low at 2 per cent and 16 per cent respectively. However, there was much more support for negotiation among the regional left, at 67 per cent, compared with 16 per cent nationally. Support for a harsher reaction was low. Overall only 20 per cent favoured making a 'war on terrorism'. Most of the support came from the AP (34 per cent) and the extreme right (48 per cent). Similarly, only 7 per cent favoured the return of military rule. Over one out of four (27 per cent) in the extreme right favoured this response.[96]

In September 1979, Spaniards were asked to predict the future performance of their democracy. Citizens were optimistic about the country. Forty-two per cent of those questioned believed that the country's problems would be solved, 26 per cent believed they would continually get worse, and 33 per cent believed they would stay the same.[97] A separate study conducted in September 1980 asked citizens to assess the performance of the new democracy up to that point. The results were mixed. Only 23 per cent of the respondents believed that the country had progressed better than expected. Thirty-six per cent stated that things had gone worse than expected.[98] A separate study conducted two months later probed anticipated state performance in particular areas. The numbers for November 1980 reveal a low level of satisfaction and pessimism for the future. Belief about the direction of prices was strongly negative, with only 9 per cent believing things would get better and 55 per cent believing they would worsen. Results were slightly better in regard to unemployment but still pessimistic, with only 19 per cent believing unemployment would improve, 24 per cent predicting it would remain the same, and 37 per cent believing the situation would get worse. The response about terrorism was split (20 per cent better, 27 per cent the same, and 29 per cent worse), but with a leaning towards a more pessimistic view.[99]

In 1980, people were asked to evaluate whether or not the following problems had improved or become worse since Spanish democratization. In 1980, many important indicators of state performance were highly negative. On the following issues, more respondents believed that things had changed for the worse than for the better: unemployment (3 per cent for the better and 89 per cent for the worse), delinquency (2 per cent for the better and 81 per cent for the worse), the economic situation (12 per cent for the better and 72 per cent for the worse), security and public order (11 per cent for the better and 63 per cent for the worse), labour conflicts (22 per cent for the better and 47 per cent for the worse), corruption (7 per cent for the better and 63 per cent for the worse), and the principle of authority (22 per cent for the better and 31 per cent for the worse). In spite of the severity of the terrorism and economic crisis in 1980, the state received high marks in areas that affected integration. Interestingly, citizen liberties (53 per cent for the better and 27 per cent for the worse), regional autonomy (48 per cent for the better and 20 per cent for the worse), and information (61 per cent for the better and 12 per cent for the worse) all received significantly higher marks of improvement. Regardless of the effectiveness of the state's policies towards the economic crisis and terrorism, it appears that state action or inaction did not exacerbate the strains on security or integration caused by other crises. In fact, the policies seemed to somewhat compensate for the negative effects of the terrorist violence on security and integration.[100]

Within the next two years, Spaniards became more optimistic. By October 1982, the level of satisfaction had improved. Many fewer people believed that problems would get worse. The response in regard to terrorism was much improved. Now only 11 per cent believed it would get worse and 40 per cent believed it would improve. In terms of unemployment, 30 per cent thought the situation would improve, 26 per cent believed it would stay the same, and 23 per cent thought it would get worse. Views of prices remained negative. Only 15 per cent thought they would improve, 28 per cent thought they would stay the same, and 30 per cent thought they would get worse.[101]

In another Gallup survey, citizens were asked to indicate their level of citizen satisfaction with different governments according to policy area on a scale of one to ten, with one representing the lowest level of satisfaction and ten representing the highest. In general, the level of satisfaction increased as time progressed. In 1978, the average score was 4.46. In 1980, the average score was 4.49. By 1984, the average had increased to 4.81. Franco received his highest ratings in law and order and in living standards. In fact, his 1980 rating of 5.15 was the highest received in that category. In 1984 the PSOE government outscored the memory of Franco 4.7 to 4.31 for the level of citizen confidence. The Socialists received the highest rating for social equity and living standards. In all categories, the PSOE received the highest ratings. The most popular figure in Spain was the King. Of the politicians, González and Suárez fared best.[102] With time, Spaniards evaluated the state in a more positive manner in every category.

Citizen confidence summary

Uruguay

In Uruguay, citizen confidence levels decreased as the amount of terrorist violence increased. From 1967 to 1969, many citizens evaluated the situation of the country as generally poor. In addition, there was evidence of many Uruguayans wishing to emigrate and anecdotal evidence of many who carried through on their desire. There was a growing repudiation of the traditional parties. However, after the elimination of Tupamaro violence in September 1972, citizen confidence continued to decrease, suggesting that the state response to the violence was also a factor. Specifically, the poll conducted in February 1973 documents the highest rejection of the state. This lack of citizen confidence remains even after the demise of terrorist violence. The evidence is congruent with both hypotheses.

Peru

Citizen confidence levels in most Peruvian institutions, except the executive, the Catholic Church, and the armed forces, continued to worsen until the *autogolpe* in 1992. As terrorist violence increased and then stabilized at a high level, citizen confidence decreased. As repressive policies were pursued and state violence introduced, citizen confidence levels decreased. Separation of the causation is difficult since both the terrorist and state violence persisted in the same time period. Nonetheless, the evidence is clear that approval ratings of the state and its institutions, with the noted exceptions, continued declining until the *autogolpe* of Fujimori. In addition to poor approval ratings, a strong majority of citizens expressed a distrust of Congress, the judiciary, and the National Police. Only Fujimori, the military, the Catholic Church, and the media received good approval ratings. In addition, Fujimori had broad support for his drastic reform proposals, signifying a rejection of the existing institutions. The lack of citizen confidence in the state appeared to progress to a rejection of democracy as practised in Peru before April 1992.

Spain

An evaluation of the Spanish experience meets the expectation that the differences in security, integration, and citizen confidence derive from the fact that the Spanish state did not violently and repressively react to the terrorist violence. The evidence of citizen confidence supports hypothesis one in the sense that as incidents of terrorist violence increase, there is a decrease in citizen confidence. In 1980, ETA killed ninety-two people. In that year, the public was pessimistic about the state's ability to ameliorate terrorism; only 20 per cent thought the state response had improved, 29 per cent responded that it had remained the same, and 27 per cent said the situation was worse. However, by 1982 violence had decreased by approximately two thirds. ETA killed thirty-seven people that year. In that year, respondents were more optimistic about the state's ability to respond to terrorism. Only 25 per cent believed the situation was worse, 11 per cent responded it was the same, and 40 per cent believed things were improving.[103] The difference in the level of satisfaction looking towards the future in regard to terrorism and public order from 1980 to 1982 is consistent with hypothesis one. The levels of citizen confidence and measures of terrorist violence seem to be related in a manner consistent with hypothesis one.

During the years of 1979 and 1980, terrorist violence peaked. This decrease in the terrorist violence is followed by an increase in citizen confidence in the state. In regard to the second hypothesis, we do not have an indiscriminate, violent, and repressive state response. Interestingly, during 1980, a low point in satisfaction with the new democracy referred to as the 'desencanto' or period or disenchantment, the state received positive marks in areas that are related to integration. Specifically, the state performance in terms of an improved political situation, the quality of political leadership, citizen liberties, regional autonomy, and freedom of information was viewed positively by most Spaniards. The state maintained support in spite of overwhelmingly negative evaluations in regard to unemployment, the economic situation in general, security and public order, corruption, labour conflicts, and the principle of authority. These data are consistent with hypotheses one and two, since the effects of terrorist violence can be seen while the negative consequences of a violent and repressive state response are absent.

Democratic stability

In each of the three cases, it is easiest to measure democratic stability by looking at its opposite, democratic instability. Democratic instability can be indicated by successful coups. It can also be measured by other indicators, depending on available information in each country.

Uruguayan democratic stability

In addition to the final breakdown of Uruguayan democracy in June 1973, democratic stability can be measured by looking for signs of instability. In any constitution, broad support for seditious groups is an indication of instability. Another indicator of instability is electoral irregularities. Public opinion data concerning choice of regime and perception of risk of instability to the existing constitution can also indicate instability. Public statements encouraging military intervention and calling for the resignation of the president indicate instability. A supportive public reaction to a coup also demonstrates democratic instability.

Although the Tupamaro violence was rejected by a majority of Uruguayans, a sizable minority of citizens admitted supporting the aims of the Tupamaros. *Marcha* reported consistent minority support, at least indirectly, for the Tupamaros. In June 1971, 41 per cent believed the Tupamaros were at least partially justified in their actions. This number shrank to 36 per cent in September, with 49 per cent of the respondents denying them reasonable justification.[104] However, the Tupamaros still had much support. This support was corroborated by a similar poll conducted one year later, in July 1972. A Gallup poll revealed that 20 per cent of the public were Tupamaro sympathizers.[105]

Another indicator of democratic instability became apparent in the 1971 presidential elections. Instead of the typically peaceful elections, the campaigns were marked by violence. However, this violence did not originate from the Tupamaros. A frequent target of attacks was General Liber Seregni, the sole presidential candidate for the Frente Amplio.[106] For example, on 7 November 1971 Seregni was stabbed in the chest by a youth member of a far right group. Another time, a boy was killed by a bullet intended for Seregni. These incidents were the first attacks made on an Uruguayan presidential candidate in thirty years.[107]

The 1971 election results were also hotly contested. In the end, Juan Bordaberry was announced as the winner, in spite of documented charges of electoral fraud.[108] In a public opinion poll the following question was asked: 'Recently there have been a lot of protests about the elections. In your judgment, were these elections as clean as any, or was there fraud?'[109] Only the victorious party, the Colorados, had a majority response (72 per cent) affirming the fairness of the elections. Almost half (48 per cent) of those affiliated with the Blanco party and three quarters (72 per cent) of those affiliated with the Frente Amplio believed fraud occurred. The credibility of the Bordaberry government was questioned and fewer than half of Uruguayans believed the elections to be honest.

Public opinion polls conducted in 1971 investigated citizen perceptions of a risk to the democratic system. In late 1971, citizens were asked whether or not the democratic system was at risk. In almost every age group, a majority believed that the democratic system was either at risk or had already been damaged. Of those aged 18–32, 68 per cent agreed. In the middle age group of 33–47, 60 per cent agreed. Of those 48 or older, 55 per cent agreed.[110] In spite of the belief that democracy was at risk in Uruguay, the general preference among Uruguayans for democracy remained strong. When asked what form of regime or constitution do you prefer, in January 1971, 73 per cent chose democracy. In October 1971, 79 per cent chose democracy. However, it is striking that approximately one out of eight citizens (16 per cent in January 1971 and 13 per cent in October) admitted a preference for a 'strong and orderly military state' in a country with seventy years of stable, democratic rule.[111]

In addition, seditious statements came from across the political spectrum. An early statement was made on 9 June 1969. Eugenio Baroffio, the managing director of *El Diario*, signed an editorial asking for a coup, 'because the parliament [the National Assembly], by constitution, cannot be dissolved, which would allow an appeal to the electorate, the executive power must free itself from constitutional norms'.[112] Calls to sedition were also made from the left. Even the Frente Amplio's 1971 presidential candidate, General Seregni, said after the contested elections

> We have encountered the dirtiest elections that are recorded in our memory ... They want us to get used to behaving ourselves like a herd, but the oriental republic [Uruguay] was not born for tameness! This means struggle, means organized popular resistance. The struggle and resistance will be stronger than yesterday![113]

Seditious calls were also made by the extreme right. In April 1972, *Azul y Blanco*, an ultra rightist publication that is considered to be the voice of *golpista*, or pro-coup, members of the military, ran an editorial entitled 'Govern or Resign'. It advocated eliminating legislative and judicial branches of the state.

In addition to public calls for a military intervention, both of Bordaberry's competing presidential candidates in the 1971 election called for his resignation. On 9 February 1973 General Liber Seregni, candidate for the Frente Amplio, stated:

> The government, Mr. Bordaberry, not only has not known how to correct the disorder, but has contributed to its aggravation. The government has been transformed into the main agent of the disorder from which society suffers. Mr. Bordaberry has not had the capacity or the will to correct the situation in which the country lives and has tried to hide his ineptitude by blaming the popular discontent.... For these reasons, we believe that Bordaberry should resign.[114]

A main leader of the other major political party, the Blancos' Wilson Aldunate Ferreira, stated on 30 March 1973 in *Marcha*,

> I believe that all of this is a direct consequence of the weakness of the executive... Uruguay needs a strong executive power through a broader political base and the growth of prestige. Is it possible with Mr. Bordaberry as the first magistrate?[115]

Instead of opposing factions joining to defend the president, Bordaberry was attacked by some as others courted military action.

Another indicator of democratic stability is the reaction of citizens to attacks against the state. By using the concept of the purposes of the state, it can be understood why so few citizens supported Uruguayan democracy and why there was support for the military action that began in February 1973. Citizens from across the political spectrum supported the idea of further military involvement. Factions within the military were still active, and different groups of Uruguayans supported the idea of military intervention, expecting different outcomes. Unfortunately, public opinion data during the slow coup are scarce. Other than one poll in February 1973, the data are unavailable. When the army and the air force rebelled in February, Bordaberry made an emotional plea to the people to support the state. The paper *Opinion Nacionalista* reported that 'when he [Bordaberry] made the emotional call, only twenty to twenty-five girls... stopped themselves in the front path. But the public was not there.'[116] In a February poll, 60 per cent agreed with military proposals.[117] Support for military intervention also included some leftists. An 11 February 1973 editorial called 'Proposed Objectives of the Armed Forces' in the Communist leaning newspaper *El Popular* stated, 'we are essentially in agreement with the proposed measures of the armed forces as an immediate solution for the situation in which the Republic finds itself. Certainly, the proposed measures are not incompatible with the ideology of the working classes.'[118] Their support for the intervention was stated again in June. In June, at the same time most politicians in the National Assembly were coming together to resist military demands, a general strike was organized by the Communist led labour union, the Confederación Nacional de Trabajadores,[119] five days before the coup. Those leading the strike called for increased wages 'in the spirit of army communiqués four and seven' in addition to calling for the resignation of Bordaberry.[120] After the coup, other than the pre-planned strike, the public reaction was calm.

Peruvian democratic stability

In Peru, in addition to the *autogolpe* in April 1992, there are other indicators of democratic instability. For example, publicly acknowledged support for seditious groups is an indication of instability. Public opinion data concerning choice of constitution or regime and perception of risk of instability to the existing constitution can also indicate instability. Finally, calls for military intervention also indicate democratic instability.

Two studies track empathy for terrorist acts. In the 1988 National Questionnaire about Violence, a rejection of terrorist means prevailed. Only 9.9 per cent understood the terrorist acts, 73 per cent rejected them, 12 per cent were indifferent to them, and 1 per cent reacted otherwise.[121] Two years later, the results were almost equivalent; when Peruvians were asked how they felt about terrorist acts, 72 per cent replied they were repulsed, 11 per cent were indifferent, and 9 per cent were empathetic. Among Peruvians in the lowest economic stratum there is slightly more support of and indifference to terrorist acts: 14 per cent were indifferent to terrorist attacks and 12 per cent were empathetic.[122] In spite of a frustration with democracy as practised in Peru, a majority of citizens rejected violent protest. Three years later, most citizens still did not condone subversion. In June 1991, the bloodiest month in terms of death toll casualties in ten years, APOYO conducted a poll to assess subversion. Overall, only 17 per cent believed that subversion was justified; 78 per cent did not. APOYO used a stratification of A–D. Stratum A includes about 5 per cent of the population of Lima, including mostly the upper class. In this category, 78 per cent did not believe subversion was justified. Stratum B includes 24 per cent of metropolitan Lima, including professionals, merchants, and the upper middle class. In this category, 96 per cent believed that it was not justified. Stratum C includes 39 per cent of metropolitan Lima, including wage-earners, workers in the private sector, and merchants in the informal sector of the economy. In this group, 78 per cent believed it was not justified. Stratum D includes 33 per cent of the metropolitan population, including public sector employees, the unemployed, and poor merchants in the underground economy. Justification for subversive actions increased among the lower socioeconomic strata of the respondents. Among those in the lowest socioeconomic strata (D), over one in five thought terrorism was justified. This constant minority support for terrorism is an indication of democratic instability. Even in the lowest category, however, 66 per cent of those questioned rejected subversion.[123]

Another indicator of democratic instability can be found in public opinion data of desired regime type. Many Peruvians were frustrated with democracy as practised in Peru. The first democratically elected president since the 1980 return to democracy, Fernando Belaúnde, was not considered very democratic by a majority of Peruvians. When asked to evaluate his administration in 1987, 58 per cent of those questioned stated that it was only 'a little' or 'not at all' democratic.[124] Although the affirmation of democracy in Peru increased from 1982 until June of 1986, support began to falter afterwards. As the gap between the popularity of Fujimori and the armed forces, on the one hand, and the popularity of the rest of the institutions on the other, increased, support for democracy declined. As the actions of Sendero, and other groups; spread throughout the country and as the state implemented a violent and repressive response, the affirmation of democracy declined. A sixteen point decline occurred from 1988 to 1989. In this time period, there was a significant increase in the incidents of subversive actions and deaths from MRTA, Sendero, and paramilitary groups; at the same time the percentage of provinces under a state of emergency increased from 30 to 50 per cent.

Table 6.7 presents data from public opinion from three sources. Datum, APOYO, and a Peruvian scholar, Eduardo Ballón, conducted polling during this time. In 1989, we see a dramatic drop in support for democracy, down to only 61 per cent. This is evident in both Ballón's data and APOYO's study. By 1991, a significant number of citizens, 30 per cent of those questioned, admitted a preference for military rule, reflecting a significant and persistent disillusionment with democracy. In addition, some civilian sectors of society expressed support for a coup. For example, prominent banker Francisco Pardo Mesones suggested that García be removed from power in 1988.[125] Support for military rule peaked in March 1991. As Fujimori became more popular, support for democracy increased and those believing that a coup was probable fell to 31 per cent from 41 per cent. With Fujimori's approval ratings as high as they were in 1992, few people believed a coup was immanent.

Public opinion about the autogolpe

Fujimori's *autogolpe* was very popular among Peruvians. It was supported by 80 per cent of the population.[126] In a Peruvian public opinion poll, 12 per cent of Lima residents thought Fujimori's measures to create a new constitution, dissolve Congress, and reorganize the judiciary were excellent, 14 per cent thought they were very good, and 41 per cent thought they were good. Only 9 per cent thought they were bad, 2 per cent thought they were very bad, and 3 per cent considered them terrible.[127] Interestingly, after the coup only 25.8 per cent of the respondents in the popular sector of Lima considered the coup an attack against democracy.[128] In fact, in an APOYO survey on 13 April, it was discovered that 50 per cent of those polled believed the post-coup Fujimori rule to be democratic, with only 30 per cent of all respondents thinking it was a dictatorship.[129] The rest of the population approved of Fujimori's actions on the grounds that he acted to improve the country. When asked if they approved of the armed forces controlling the country, 60 per cent approved of military control for a time, 18 per cent approved of permanent control, and 22 per cent disapproved of military control.[130] In a May 1992 APOYO study, the poll found overwhelming support, 73 per cent, for the use of military courts to try alleged terrorists. Fujimori's proposal

Table 6.7 Peru: choice of regime, 1982–1992

	Democratic (%)	Military/by coup (%)	Marxist/Socialist by Revolution (%)	Coup probable (%)	Coup improbable (%)
February 1982D	66	11	16		
January 1984D	72	9	13		
June 1986D	88	3	6		
April 1987B	86	7	10		
1988B	77				
March 1988D	75	7	13		
April 1988A	77	9	4		
April 1988D	81				
September 1988A				44	51
1989B	61				
March 1989A	61	14	8	23	65
March 1990A	78	13	5	27	47
June 1990A	76	15	4	38	48
September 1990A	70	17	6	33	57
March 1991A	59	30	6	41	47
September 1991A	65	22	6	31	57
March 1992A	73	16	2	30	63

Sources: Dates noted with an 'A' come from *Informe de Opinion*, APOYO, March 1992. Data with a 'D' after the year are from Datum polls. Question: 'Which of these types of government do you consider to be the most adequate for a country such as ours?' 400 < n < 800. Table 4, Cynthia McClintock, 'The Prospect for Democratic Consolidation in a "Least Likely" Case: Peru', *Comparative Politics* Vol. 21, No. 2, January 1989, pp. 127–149, p. 140. Data with a 'B' after are from Eduardo Ballón's work in Pablo González Casanova and Marcos Roitman Rosenmann (eds), *La democracia en América Latina: actualidad y perspectivas* (Mexico DF: La Jornada, 1995), p. 276.

for the death penalty for some terrorists was approved by 64 per cent. In sum, Peruvians supported Fujimori's *autogolpe* precisely because they thought that he would improve the state.

Spanish democratic stability

In Spain, democratic stability can be indicated in numerous ways. General public opinion data are available. Overall, perceptions of the state and levels of optimism are probed. These general questions allow an examination of levels of satisfaction with democracy in general. Finally, although the attempted coup in 1981 may be considered by some to be an obvious sign of instability, the strong public rejection of that attempt indicates an underlying stability.

Throughout the difficulties of the transition, Spain's democracy gained in support. According to Peter McDonough, Samuel Barnes, and Antonio López Pina's study of system support, the citizen's view of the state improved from 1978 to 1984.[131] The numbers of those who trusted the state increased from 27 per cent in 1978 to 41 per cent in 1984. More Spaniards believed that the state was for the many in 1984 (58 per cent, up from 35 per cent in 1978) as opposed to for the few (42 per cent, down from 65 per cent in 1978) as the democracy consolidated in those six years. A separate study corroborates the increasing satisfaction with democracy during the same periods. The respondents were asked to indicate their level of satisfaction on a scale of one to ten, with one representing the lowest level of satisfaction and ten representing the highest. The idea of democracy, alone, fared better than democracy under any particular government.[132] It should be noted that these numbers are rebounding from what has been called the 'desencanto' or disillusionment of the early 1980s. This disillusionment, according to José Ramón Montero, was caused by the 'high expectations raised during the first stages of the transition from authoritarian rule'.[133]

In spite of the ongoing problems, both economic and violent, the citizens maintained a strong support for democracy. Three studies are available to document the increase in support for democracy. First, a study begun before the death of Franco and continuing until 1982 shows a growing support for democracy as a constitutional form. In 1966, when Franco was still alive, only 35 per cent agreed that 'it is better that officials, elected by the people, decide'. Eleven per cent agreed that it was 'better that a distinguished man decide for us'. In 1974, one year before his death, a majority of 60 per cent preferred democracy. Immediately after Franco's death, support for an authoritarian rule was highest, at 24 per cent. However, as the transition progressed, democratic principles enjoyed a stable, strong majority. Care should be taken with the interpretation of the 1966 and 1974 data, since more respondents may have felt pressured not to answer or to choose the 'distinguished man' option. By May 1976, only 8 per cent agreed that one man should decide and 78 per cent chose elected officials. These numbers remained stable until 1982. A second study covers 1980 to 1985. In 1980, respondents were asked to agree or disagree with the statement that 'democracy is preferable to any other form...'. In 1980, only 49 per cent did. By 1984, 69 per cent did and in 1985, 70 per cent.[134] This improvement in the support for democracy is corroborated by data from 1983–1986. Respondents were asked if they were satisfied with democracy. By November 1986, 57 per cent of Spaniards believed democracy functioned very well or well enough, compared with 47 per cent in December 1983.[135] All three studies, although different measures of democratic stability generally, indicate a growing support for democracy.

As popularity of democracy increased, the fear of a coup subsided. When asked in November 1983, 'Do you believe that in Spain today there exists the possibility of a new attempted coup?' 42 per cent said yes. Only 30 per cent believed that a new coup was possible in 1986. Those most confident that there would be no further coup attempts were the Socialists (PSOE) at 59 per cent, and the Nationalists at 61 per cent.[136] Nonetheless, 30 per cent still believed that a coup was possible.

Public opinion after the coup attempt

Many politicians blamed terrorism for the attempted coup. Conservative Manuel Fraga stated, 'if things simply went on as before, there would be a new attempt to seize power because the causes which led to the attempted coup – terrorism and the absence of proper communications between politicians and the military and between the military and the king – would remain'. Surprisingly, even ETA-pm accepted that terrorist violence was partially to blame. ETA-pm instead embraced a negotiated solution instead of more violence.[137] The conspirators themselves blamed terrorism. At the end of the attempted coup, Tejero described the army and civil guard members who participated in the attempted coup.

> They do not accept separatist autonomies and they want a decentralized Spain, not a broken one. They do not accept the impunity of the assassin terrorists against those who apply the law. They do not accept a situation in which the prestige of Spain diminishes daily; they do not tolerate public insecurity that prevents us from living in peace.[138]

Terrorism and the granting of autonomy to regions, in the view of some in the military, precipitated the crisis. However, the Spanish citizens did not support the coup attempt, in spite of Spain's troubles.

Democratic stability was indicated by the actions of the Spanish citizens in reaction to the attempted coup in February 1981. Days after the attempted coup on 27 February 1981, large demonstrations broke out in major cities in favour of democracy. In Madrid, the demonstration was led by diverse political leaders, from Manual Fraga of the Popular Alliance to Socialist leader Felipe González and to Communist leader Santiago Carrillo.[139] Approximately 1.4 million people participated in the Madrid march in support of democracy.[140] This anti-coup sentiment was corroborated by polls. In a post-coup survey, 76 per cent were against the coup and only 4 per cent admitted being in favour of it. In addition, 47 per cent stated that they would personally defend democracy.[141] Another survey conducted two days after the failed coup showed that only 9 per cent of those questioned supported the coup attempt.[142] A repeat survey in October 1982, after news of another plot, demonstrated that less than 5 per cent of the population would support a coup attempt.[143]

Democratic stability summary

Uruguay

In Uruguay, democratic instability followed terrorist and state violence. The violence of the Tupamaros and the other seditious groups created an atmosphere of hostility, paranoia, and fear in the political community, undermining both security and integration. The repressive state response aggravated both the rudimentary purposes. The censorship, suspicion of the opposition, repression, and politicization weakened the integration of the political community and also created fear and distrust. The violent and contested elections, public assessment of the risk to democracy, a small but persistent preference for a strong and orderly state, and the disparate calls for sedition, all reflect democratic instability. The democratic instability until the end of the Tupamaro violence in 1972 is difficult to separate from the instability due to the state violence. However, the calls for the resignation of the president, the calls for military intervention, the public opinion poll of February 1973, and finally the public reaction to the dissolution of democracy in June 1973 cannot be attributed to the terrorist violence. Despite the end of terrorist violence, state violence and repression continued. Consequently, the severe democratic instability of 1973 occurred after the end of the terrorist violence.

After the beginning of the slow coup in February 60 per cent of respondents approved of the military proposals for political involvement and the same number expected a full coup. This continued decrease cannot be accounted for by the previous amounts of terrorist violence. Moreover, specific evidence of citizen rejection of state repressive policies is available. Uruguayans supported the final dissolution of the National Assembly in June in hopes of obtaining a more practicable constitutional form.

This conclusion is corroborated by evidence gathered by Charles Gillespie. Gillespie conducted interviews in 1984, attempting to map the deterioration of Uruguayan democracy. Gillespie asked politicians to rank factors causing the democratic breakdown. The question was: 'In 1973, Uruguay experienced a crisis that led to a new system of government. Contradictory explanations have been given for this process...What importance would you assign the following statements (ranking them from most important to least important)?'[144] As we would expect, overall, violence (47 per cent) and the military (49 per cent) were marked as most or second most important factor causing breakdown. Gillespie's research also corroborates the broad lack of support for the state, by examining perceived loyalty to democracy according to parties and factions. The question was: 'In the crisis of a democracy political parties may be judged by their behaviour as loyal to the rules of the democratic game, whether they are in office or in the opposition; semi-loyal when they are only sometimes loyal; or disloyal (anti-system parties). Thinking about parties and their factions from 1968 to 1973, if "1" represents an unimpeachably loyal democratic conduct, and "10" one totally antidemocratic, where would you place the following?' It is interesting to note no faction gave themselves a perfectly democratic score of 1. The Colorado party gave themselves the most antidemocratic rating, with a 3.5, followed by the Frente Amplio, 3.1, and the Blanco party, 2.2. This communicates that many politicians were courting subversives, either of the left or the right.[145] Gillespie's data also corroborate the dual responsibility of both the state and the terrorist violent groups. Gillespie asked: 'In your opinion, which groups were principally responsible for the disorder and violence which the country faced 1968–73?' The state (59 per cent), the extreme left (81 per cent), and the extreme right (51 per cent) received most of the blame. Only 34 per cent blamed the police and the military.[146] Gillespie's later public opinion research significantly corroborates both hypotheses.

Peru

Violence in Peru had a devastating effect on democratic stability. The violence of Sendero, MRTA, and the other violent groups created widespread fear. The state was unable to protect citizens or even judges from the violence. In addition, this violence harmed the integration and functioning of the community. In many areas of the violence, participation in politics or even voting was dangerous. In addition, citizens suspected each other of being members of either Sendero or MRTA or a member of one of the death squads. The state's response to the violence was repressive. In a country in which much of the population has limited contact with the state, much of that contact was violent. The repression of the state resulted in more resentment towards state institutions. The state's policy also reflected a greater suspicion and harassment of its citizens. Finally, the military, along with the general population, lost faith in the traditional parties and institutions. Many Peruvians did not view the democratically elected presidents as democratic. Moreover, state institutions demonstrated an extreme inability to meet the challenges facing the nation. The governments of Belaúnde and García undermined both security and integration of the political community, all without improving institutional effectiveness. The terrorist and state violence in Peru undermined democratic stability. The democratic instability is demonstrated by some public support for terrorist groups, a decline in the choice of democracy, and calls for military intervention. The instability culminated in Fujimori's *autogolpe* of April 1992. For the average Peruvian, the situation was sufficiently desperate that they supported the only institution and man who appeared capable of doing something: the armed forces and Fujimori. Only the military, the Catholic Church, and Fujimori maintained support. Under the pretext of the Congress and the judiciary's gross inability to function, the military and Peruvians supported Fujimori in his 1992 *autogolpe* with the hopes that it would be a more practicable solution for Peru.

Spain

Despite grave challenges to democracy, Spanish democracy retained the support of its citizens. However, public opinion data demonstrate that citizens were not rating state performance very well in terms of inflation, unemployment, order, or terrorism. Indeed, violence was prevalent and the economy suffered. Why did the citizens support democracy? The use of the purposes of the state allows an understanding of the basis upon which citizens support a state with poor performance in key issues. Instead of just focusing on state performance in economic issues or order, it looks to how the state responds to these challenges and how that response affects the political community. The new Spanish democracy improved integration of the community by attempting to reconcile demands for regional autonomy with national unity. How did the state actions affect the political community and the purposes of the state? In general, the state opted for a legal response and accommodation of regional demands. In prosecuting only the perpetrators of violence, as opposed to indiscriminate repression, the state furthered, instead of harmed, reciprocal justice. In other words, the state tried to return evil for evil and good for good. By not pursuing a policy of repression and suspension of individual liberties, the state did not further harm the political community. The state restored freedoms and minimized repression. The state improved integration and did not further harm the security of the political community by pursuing indiscriminate repressive responses to the terrorism. Instead, citizens were free to participate, to deliberate, and to act politically, without restrictions on their participation. This state response encouraged a political community based more upon civic friendship as opposed to one plagued by enmity. Although the attacks from ETA, GRAPO, and others continued to threaten security and integration, the state did not worsen the situation by introducing its own indiscriminate violence, with the exception of GAL. It appears that the citizens took this into account when evaluating democracy. In spite of negative performance evaluations in regard to economic and order related issues, Spaniards still supported democracy. Improvement in areas of citizen liberties, autonomy, and information seem to matter more. Measures of democratic stability overall showed an increase from the beginning of the transition until the end of the study in 1986. Although the attempted coup of February 1981, attributed to terrorist violence by the elites involved demonstrates some threat to democracy, the bold affirmation of democracy by Spanish citizens reflects an underlying democratic stability in Spain.

Notes

1 Informe Gallup 1970, *Futuro Inmediato y Previsible del Uruguay* (Montevideo: Gallup Uruguay, 1970), p. 12; also Gallup Uruguay O.P. 130/131. The size of the study was between 750 and 900 respondents.
2 Informe Gallup 1970, p. 13; also Gallup Uruguay 107, ex19.
3 The data are compiled from Republica Oriental del Uruguay Junta de Comandantes en Jefe, *La Subversión* (Montevideo: Las Fuerzas Armadas al Pueblo Oriental, 1977). Republica Oriental del Uruguay Junta de Comandantes en Jefe. Tomo 1.
4 *Generals and Tupamaros*, p. 15.
5 Howard Handelman, 'Labor–Industrial Conflict and the Collapse of Uruguayan Democracy,' *Journal of Interamerican Studies and World Affairs* Vol. 23, No. 4, November 1981, pp. 371–394, p. 377–379.

6 Comisión de la Verdad y Reconciliación, *Informe Final* (Lima: Comisión de la Verdad y Reconciliación, 2003).

7 Comisión Especial de Investigación y Estudio sobre la Violencia y Alternativas de Pacificación, 1992, pp. 185–199. The senate commission acknowledged some of the difficulties involved in its study, especially in terms of methodological issues. The commission lists the lack of adequate information in parts of the country, the anonymous character of much of the violence, the fear of many people to denounce abuses, the clandestine and mimetic nature of the seditious action, the cover-up of the actions of the government forces, and the lack of an adequate census as problematic; p. 17.

8 Fumerton, p. 477.

9 Enrique Obando, interview in Lima, July 2006.

10 'Violencia y pacificación: un informe que debe ser escuchado', *QueHacer* No. 54, August/September 1988, pp. 18–28, p. 19.

11 FBIS LAT 89-143, p. 43, 'Survey Published Reveals Fear of Civil War', Madrid EFE, 25 July 1989.

12 Comisión Especial de Investigación y Estudio sobre la Violencia y Alternativas de Pacificación en el Perú, 1989, p. 372.

13 'Poll Reveals Public Perception on Terrorism', *Peru Económico*, in Spanish, January 1991, p. 16, FBIS LAT 91 047, p. 44.

14 'Public Poll Reveals Low Police Prestige', Lima Panamericana de Televisión, 28 October 1991, FBIS LAT 91 211 pp. 40–41.

15 Starn, p. 562.

16 Organization of American States, *Report on the Situation of Human Rights in Peru* (Washington, DC: OAS, 1992), p. 2.

17 Manuel Castillo Ochoa, 'Fujimori and the Business Class,' *NACLA* Vol. 30, No. 1, July/August 1996, pp. 25–30, p. 26.

18 'Nadie sabe dónde está seguro, nadie: ni el policía que espera en caulquier momento un ataque ni el habitante que teme, si no la detención, el prepotente registro de su domicilio por una policía que busca terroristas y que cree que todos son senderistas'; author translation. Raúl González, 'Ayacucho: por los caminos de Sendero,' *QueHacer* No. 19, October 1982, pp. 39–77, p. 41.

19 Gallup 16:41. Respondents were asked: 'You have a card with a list of problems that affect the country in general. Please tell me the three that you consider the most important. If there is something not on the list, you may express it in two words.'

20 Gallup – published 4 May 1980, IG 600/081, IG 600/085.

21 *El Pais* 4 May 1986, p. 30. See also Aguero, 1995, p. 143.

22 *Generals and Tupamaros*, p. 12.

23 *Generals and Tupamaros*, p. 43.

24 Gillespie, 1991, p. 32.

25 Handelman also interviewed 100 of Uruguay's industrial, commercial, and agricultural leaders.

26 Handelman, pp. 377–379.

27 Perelli, p. 31.
28 Langguth, p. 297.
29 'Va a ser muy difícil, porque los estigmas del pasado, de las divisions étnicas y culturales son muy fuertes y muy profundos. Este es un país racista. El *apartheid* no está escrito en leyes, pero funciona en la vida cotidiana y eso no sé cuánto tiempo tomará cambiarlo'; author translation. Quoted in Forgues, p. 41.
30 Mauceri, 1991, p. 97.
31 Graham, p. 166.
32 Americas Watch, 1992, p. 65.
33 John Crabtree, *Peru Under Garcia* (Pittsburgh: University of Pittsburgh Press, 1992), p. 194.
34 Sandra Woy-Hazleton and William A. Hazleton, 'Sendero Luminoso and the Future of Peruvian Democracy,' *Third World Quarterly*, Vol. 12, No. 2, 1990, pp. 21–35, p. 29.
35 'Alcaldes muertos', *Caretas* No. 1062, 19 June 1989, pp. 32–35, p. 33.
36 US Government Printing Office, *Committee Report of Human Rights Practices 1991* (Washington, DC: US Senate, 1992) p. 718.
37 Fernando Tuesta Soldevilla, *Perú Político en Cifras* (Lima: Fundacion, 1994), pp. 142–201.
38 Palmer, 1986, p. 129.
39 Soldevilla, p. 163.
40 Woy-Hazleton and Hazleton, p. 31.
41 US Senate, *Committee Report of Human Rights Practices 1991*, (Washington, DC: US Senate), p. 718.
42 'La izquierda socialista tiene que optar, sincera y conscientemente por la democracia representativa, y rechazar el camino de la violencia, de la cual ella resultaría sin duda la primera víctima'; author translation. 'Guerrillas en Ayacucho', *Equis X* No. 204, 12–14 August 1980, pp. 12–14, p. 11.
43 'Más temprano que tarde, una repression militarizada no podría coexistir con los espacios democráticos. Esto, que es algo que no le importa a "Sendero," sí resulta vital para la izquierda'; author translation. 'Sendero: conciencia de la inzquierda?', *QueHacer* No. 16 April 1982, pp. 14–20, p. 20.
44 'Los estudiantes universitarios somos sospechosos de ser terroristas ... todos y especialmente los que estamos en universitarios estatales'; author translation. 'Los jóvenes dicen: 'somos sospechosos de ser terroristas', *QueHacer* No. 24, September 1983, pp. 28–31.
45 'Es posible gracias al apoyo que muchas veces le prestan los habitantes' y porque 'pueden confundirese con mucha facilidad con los lugareños'; author translation. Raúl González, 'Ayacucho: por los caminos de Sendero', *QueHacer* No. 19, October 1982, pp. 39–77, p. 41.
46 Enrique Mayer, 'Patterns of Violence in the Andes,' *Latin American Research Review* Vol. 29, No. 2, 1994, pp. 141–171, p. 153.

47 'Violencia y pacificación: un informe que debe ser escuchado', p. 22.
48 'Violencia y pacificación: un informe que debe ser escuchado', p. 25.
49 Medrano, p. 175.
50 Edward Malefakis, 'Spain and its Francoist Heritage', in John Herz (ed.), *From Dictatorship to Democracy* (Westport: Greenwood Press, 1982), p. 227.
51 Robert Clark, 'The Basques, Madrid, and Regional Autonomy: Conflicting Perspectives between Center and Periphery in Spain,' in William D. Phillips, Jr and Carla Rahn Phillips (eds), *Marginated Groups in Spanish and Portuguese History* (Minneapolis: Society for Spanish and Portuguese Historical Studies, 1989), p. 225. For more recent discussions of the evolution of the autonomous communities in Spain, see Rafael Banon and Manuel Tamayo, 'The Transformation of the Central Administration in Spanish Intergovernmental Relations,' *Publius*, Vol. 27, No. 4, Fall 1997, pp. 85–115; Luis Moreno, 'Federalization and Ethnoterritorial Concurrence in Spain', *Publius* Vol. 27, No. 4, Fall 1997, pp. 65–85; and Robert Agranoff and Juan Antonio Ramos Gallarin, 'Towards Federal Democracy in Spain: An Examination of Intergovernmental Relations,' *Publius* Vol. 27, No. 4, Fall 1997, pp. 1–39.
52 Newton with Donaghy, p. 119. After the attempted coup and in an attempt to placate opponents of regional autonomy, the government changed the rules for regional autonomy. LOAPA, one of the Agreements on Autonomy approved in July 1981, was an effort to contain the autonomy of the Basque and Catalan regions, reducing their autonomy to a level more comparable to that of the other regions. Clark, 1989, p. 236. See also Newton with Donaghy, p. 123; Shabad, p. 118.
53 Zirakzadeh, p. 107.
54 Shabad, p. 125.
55 George Miller, 'A Lesson Learned in Uruguay', *New Leader* Vol. 76, No. 10, 9 August 1993, pp. 7–10, p. 8.
56 Informe Gallup 1970, p. 12; also Gallup Uruguay O.P. 132/133.
57 Informe Gallup 1970, p. 10; also Gallup Uruguay O.P 115/99.
58 McDonald, 1972, p. 36.
59 Instituto de Ciencias Sociales, *Uruguay: Poder, Ideologia y Clases Sociales* (Montevideo: Facultad de Derecho, 1970).
60 Instituto de Ciencias Sociales, p. 68.
61 Instituto de Ciencias Sociales, p. 72.
62 Instituto de Ciencias Sociales, p. 71.
63 Jellinek and Ledesma, part 1, p. 10; see also *Cuadernos de Marcha* No. 47.
64 Mieres, p. 209.
65 Mieres, p. 210.
66 Davis, p. 36.
67 *Generals and Tupamaros*, p. 10.
68 *Generals and Tupamaros*, p. 20.

69 *Generals and Tupamaros*, p. 26. Within Uruguay, however, he had a strong reputation as a fascist, earned while in charge of the Montevideo police from 1963 to 1967. During that time Uruguayan students used to chant 'Queremos a Aguerrondo, Colgado de un farol, y a todos sus secuaces con las tripas al sol' ('We want Aguerrondo, hanging from a street light, and all his henchmen and their guts drying in the sun.')

70 Gillespie, 1991, p. 46.

71 *Generals and Tupamaros*, p. 64.

72 Ronald McDonald stated: 'Uruguay's democratic heritage was the strongest hallmark of its traditions and culture, but the apparent acquiescence, if not outright support, of public opinion for the military's action suggests that, in face of daily challenges to individual economic and personal security, political commitments can run a poor second.' McDonald, 1972, p. 42.

73 Graham, p. 84.

74 Wilson Jaime Barreto, *Marketing Político: Elecciones 1990* (Lima: Universidad del Pacifico Centro de Investigacion, 1991), p. 156.

75 Soldevilla, p. 36.

76 *Informe de Opinion*, APOYO, Lima. November 1991 and May 1996.

77 DATUM, also in 'La batalla de Lima', *Caretas* 1119, July 1990.

78 FBIS LAT 88 207 p. 41, '2 Polls: 3 out of 4 "Reject" President Garcia', Madrid EFE, 25 Octorber 1988.

79 DATUM, also in '2 Polls: 3 out of 4 "Reject" President García', *Asunción Hoy* 25 October 1988, p. 9. *Caretas* 1119, July 1990.

80 FBIS LAT 88-239 p. 40, 'Survey says Garcia's Popularity Declining', Madrid EFE, 12 December 1988.

81 Data taken from FBIS 90-FBIS 92 and *Pretextos* Vol. 3, 1992, p. 43.

82 FBIS LAT 91 172 p. 55, 'Poll Compares Garcia, Fujimori Administration, Perú Económico, Lima, August 1991, p. 15.

83 FBIS LAT 91 242. 'Poll Says Fujimori's Popularity Increasing', *El Comercio*, 8 December 1991, p. A4; FBIS LAT 91 244, p 27, 'Poll Shows Fujimori's Popularity Rising', Lima, Panamericana Television, 16 December 1991, For an extensive overview of the conflict, see Beth Simmons, *Territorial Disputes and Their Resolution: The Case of Ecuador and Peru* (Washington, DC: United States Institute for Peace, 1999).

84 'Violencia y pacificación: un informe que debe ser escuchado', p. 23.

85 Other Churches were identified by 2.5 per cent, 'other' by 14.8 per cent, the Red Cross by 2.2 per cent, and 'no identifications' by 8.2 per cent. 'Violencia y pacificicación: un informe que debe ser escuchado', p. 26.

86 FBIS LAT 91-180, p. 36, 'Results Published', *Debate*, Lima, July–September 1991, pp. 21–41.

87 Adrianzén, p. 30.

88 Adrianzén, p. 30.

89 Philip Mauceri, 'State Reform, Coalitions, and the Neoliberal Autogolpe in Peru,' *Latin American Research Review*, Vol. 30, No. 1, Winter 1995, pp. 256–266, p. 22.

90 FBIS LAT 91 211, pp. 40–41, 'Public Poll Reveals Law Police Prestige', Lima, Panamericana de Television, 28 October 1991.

91 FBIS LAT 91 222, p. 54, 'Claims Journalist's Murder', Madrid EFE, 17 November 1991.

92 FBIS LAT 91 211, pp. 40–41.

93 FBIS LAT 91 244, p. 27.

94 'Encuestas y sondeos del Instituto de la Opinión Pública', July–September 1977. *Revista Española de la Opinion Publica* (Madrid: Instituto de la Opinion Publica), Vol. 49, p. 248.

95 *Revista Española de la Opinion Publica* (Madrid: Instituto de la Opinion Publica), Vol. 48, p. 348.

96 Gunther et al., Tables 26–27, p. 259.

97 Maravall, p. 123.

98 Maravall, p. 123.

99 Victor Pérez Díaz, 'Políticas económicas y pautas socials en la España de la transición: la doble cara del neocorporatismo', in Juan Linz (ed.), *Un presente para el futuro* (Madrid: Instituto de Estudios Economicos, 1985), p. 37.

100 Peter McDonough, Samuel Barnes, and Antonio López Pina, 'The Growth of Democratic Legitimacy in Spain', *APSR*, Vol. 80, No. 3, September 1986, p. 743. citing *La imagen de las instituciones politicas en la opinion publica: una perspectiva compavativa* (Madrid: Hispania senice), p. 148.

101 Linz, 1985, p. 39.

102 McDonough et al., p. 743.

103 Ministry of the Interior; Linz, 1985, pp. 37–39.

104 *Marcha*, No. 1264, 22 December 1972.

105 Kohl and Litt, p. 302.

106 Weinstein, p. 43.

107 McDonald, 1972, p. 40.

108 Porzencanski, p. 59. Some scholars, such as Cesar Aguiar, claim that the key to understanding the 1971 elections really has a foundation in 1958. In these elections, the Blancos achieved power. Aguiar argues that the social alliance of the rural forces of masses, small and medium producers, defeated a conglomeration of urban groups. Aguiar, p. 36. The Blancos, with a different set of alliances, won again in 1962. Aguiar characterizes this decade of one in which the state was unable to maintain stable, long term policies. He states, 'the instability of the public policies is a manifestation of the representational incapacity of the state, which is a consequence of the accumulation of the clientelistic politics automatically supported, holding the political system prisoner'; author translation, Aguiar, p. 39. According to Aguiar, if the neobatllistas had been a faction of the Colorados, instead of the Blancos, the Frente Amplio would have developed as a further faction

within them. Instead, the Frente Amplio formed with little possibility of an alliance with rural sectors. The split of 1958 made it difficult for any viable alliance with the vital rural modernizing sectors. Aguiar, pp. 40–45.

109 Gillespie, 1991, p. 44 citing *Informe de Opinion Publica*, No 186–7, February 1972.

110 *Cuadernos de Marcha*, No. 47 in late 1971.

111 Jellinek and Ledesma, part 1, p. 10; also *Cuaderno de Marcha*, No. 47.

112 Labrousse, p. 53.

113 'Hemos enfrentado las elecciones más sucias que recuerda nuestra memoria:... Nos quieren acostumbrar a comportarnos como un rebaño, pero el pueblo oriental no nació para la mansedumbre! Esto implica lucha, implica resistencia popular organizada. Lucha y resistencia que serán más duras que ayer'; author translation. Nelson Caula and Alberto Silva, *Alto el Fuego: FFAA,Tupamaros* (Montevideo: Monte Sexto, 1986), p. 30.

114 'El gobierno, el señor Bordaberry, no solo no ha sabido sorregir el desorden, sino que ha contribuído a agravarlo. El gobierno se ha convertido en el mayor agente de desorden que sufre la patria, opone entre sí a los orientales, que impede una verdadera concordia entre los patriotas de verdad. El señor Presidente no ha tenido la capacidad ni la voluntad de corregir la situación que vive la patria, y ha tratado de ocultar su inepititud reprimiendo toda manifestación del descontento popular... Por todas estas rezones, entendemos que el señor Presidente debería renunciar; author translation. Republica Oriental del Uruguay Junta de Comandantes en Jefe. Tomo 2, p. 133.

115 'Yo creo que todo esto es consecuencia directa de la debilidad del Poder Ejecutivo... Uruguay necesita un Poder Ejecutivo fuerte a través de una amplicación de su base política y fundamentalmente del señor Bordaberry en la primera magistratura'; author translation. Republica Oriental del Uruguay Junta de Comandantes en Jefe. Tomo 2, p. 133.

116 'Cuando hizo [Bordaberry] un llamado emocionado, respondieron 20 ó 25 niñas vestidas de voladitos que fueron a pararse en la vereda en frente. Pero el pueblo no estuvo'; author translation. *Opinion Nacionalista*, 15 February 1973.

117 *Generals and Tupamaros*, p. 64.

118 'Estamos de acuerdo en lo esencial con las medidas expestas por las FFAA como salidas inmediatas para la situación que vive la República y por cierto no incompatibles con la ideología de la clase obrera'; author translation. Jellinek and Ledesma, part 2, p. 82.

119 The Communists took over the unions in the 1960s. Miller, p. 8.

120 *La opinión*, 29 June 1973.

121 'Violencia y pacificación: un informe que debe ser escuchado', p. 24.

122 FBIS LAT 91 047, p. 44, 'Poll Reveals Public Perception on Terrorism', *Económico* Lima, in Spanish, January 1991, p. 16.

123 FBIS LAT 91 202, p. 38, 'What the Polls Say'; 'Poll Indicates Support for Insurents Rising', *Quehacer* July–August 1991, pp. 40–45.

124 McClintock, 1989, p. 142.
125 Mauceri, 1996, pp. 8–10.
126 Guillermo Rochabrún, 'Deciphering the Enigmas', *NACLA Report on Peru* Vol. 30, No. 1, July/August 1996, pp. 16–25, p. 20.
127 FBIS LAT 92 068, p. 23, 'Fujimori Issues Decree; Poll Shows Support', Mexico City Notimex, 7 April 1992.
128 Sandro Macassi Levander, 'Cultura politica de la eficacia,' *Socialismo y participacion* No. 58, June 1992, pp. 65–75.
129 FBIS LAT 92 072, p. 54, 'Poll Shows Extensive Support for Fujimori', Lima, Panamericana Television Network, 13 April 1992.
130 Macassi Levander, pp. 65–75.
131 McDonough, et al. Because of the variation from 1980 to 1984, which coincides with the Socialist control of the government, they conclude, 'None of these results corroborate expectations about crisp demarcations between government and regime or between popularity and legitimacy', p. 740.
132 McDonough et al., p. 743.
133 José Ramón Montero, 'The Business Sector and Political Change in Spain: Apertura, Reforma, and Democratic Transition', in Richard Gunther (ed.), *Politics, Society and Democracy: The Case of Spain* (Boulder: Westview Press, 1993), p. 166.
134 Gunther, 1993, pp. 146–147.
135 Del Campo, Vol. 7, p. 502.
136 Gallup IG 600/122.
137 Lancaster and Prevost, p. 113.
138 'No admiten las autonomies separatistas y quieren una España descentralizada, pero no rota. No admiten la impunidad de los asesinos terroristas, contra los que es preciso aplicar todo el rigor de la ley. No pueden aceptar una situación en la que el prestigio de España disminuye día a día; no admiten la inseguridad ciudadana que nos impide vivir en paz'; author translation. Buaquets et al., p. 89.
139 Aguero, 1995, p. 175.
140 Lancaster and Prevost, p. 113.
141 Maravall, p. 98.
142 Howard R. Penniman and Eusebio M. Mujal-Leon (eds), *Spain at the Polls 1977, 1979, and 1982* (Chapel Hill: Duke University Press, 1985), p. 301.
143 Penniman and Mujal-Leon, p. 301.
144 Gillespie, 1991, p. 37.
145 Gillespie, 1991, p. 48.
146 Gillespie, 1991, p. 35.

7
Prospects for stability

Introduction

This study has focused on three pivotal events. In Uruguay, democratic institutions were dissolved in the slow coup by the Uruguayan military. In February 1973, the army and air force rebelled, forced President Bordaberry to create a new advisory committee, and demanded the appointment of a new minister of defence and a new marine commander. Bordaberry appealed to the public to defend the institutions. Less than one hundred people showed up to protest the military defiance. In June, the slow coup was completed when the military, with the approval of President Bordaberry, closed the National Assembly. In April 1992, Peruvian president Alberto Fujimori dissolved Congress and the judiciary with the support of the military. His actions were strongly supported by the public. Eighty per cent of those questioned approved of the *autogolpe*. In Spain, the troubled democracy survived an attempted coup in February 1981. Immediately after the attempted coup, large demonstrations broke out in major cities in favour of democracy. Support for democracy and rejection of possible coup attempts were clear in the polls. Over three out of four Spaniards rejected the coup and almost half said they would act to defend democracy. Less than 10 per cent supported the attempted coup. Why did Uruguayans and Peruvians withhold support for their democracies? Why did the Spaniards defend theirs?

What caused democratic breakdown in Uruguay and Peru? How did Spain, a country with many of the same serious problems faced by Uruguay and Peru, avoid a democratic breakdown? The reactions of the citizens are crucial for understanding the fate of democracy. To discern these reactions, it is necessary to study both terrorist violence and the state reaction to the violence. The Aristotelian concept of purposes of the state illuminates how state and terrorist violence affected the citizens' support for democracy. Terrorist violence attacks both rudimentary purposes of the state: security and integration. An indiscriminate repressive state response further undermines the security and integration of the political community. As the purposes of the state are undermined, levels of citizen confidence fall and democratic instability rises. Although the focus of this study is on the breakdown of Uruguayan democracy in 1972, the dissolution of Peruvian democracy in 1992, and the attempted coup in Spain in 1981, these countries are currently evolving, demonstrating the continued importance of security and integration. This chapter extends the argument to a discussion of prospects for stability in these countries through 2006.

Why the purposes of the state is an appropriate concept

Legitimacy is usually recognized as based in belief, habit, or rational calculation. Socialization and habit are very important for identifying options of regimes, but are not very helpful in explaining changes in citizen support. Moreover, in Peru and in Spain, both authoritarian rule and democracy had existed, complicating the main source of habit based legitimacy, time. In Uruguay, the country had seventy years of solidly democratic rule. One would expect a well established habit and belief in the legitimacy of a democratic form of constitution. To explain changes of citizen support, it would seem reasonable to look at rational calculation. Linz focuses on efficiency and efficacy in the basic functions of a state, identified as basic economic and social policies in addition to the 'maintenance of civil order, personal security, the adjudication and arbitration of conflicts, and a minimum of predictability in the making and implementation of decisions'.[1] However, Linz's attempt at identifying basic functions of a regime is unable to differentiate why

Spaniards continued to support their democracy and why Peruvians and Uruguayans abandoned their democratic institutions. All three countries faced challenges of civil order and personal security, domestic conflict, and economic crisis. Each democracy had minimally predictable systems of making and implementing decisions. Without the concept of the purposes of the state, why citizens support or abandon their democracies is unclear.

As reported in chapter six, Spaniards supported democracy in spite of rating many problems as worse since the transition to democracy. The public judged the state's performance as ineffective. The citizens overwhelmingly rated unemployment, delinquency, the economy, security and public order, and corruption as worse than before. The political situation and the quality of leaders were overall rated as better than before, but by slim margins. Thirty-nine per cent said the political situation was better and 38 per cent said it was worse. Thirty per cent felt there was better leadership and only 24 per cent thought it was worse. With such a tepid endorsement of the democratic Spain, why did a majority of Spaniards say they would personally act to defend democracy? Why did only 10 per cent approve of the attempted coup? Only by examining public opinion data with the concept of the purposes of the state can this reaction be understood. The only areas where Spaniards rated state performance as better were citizen liberties (53 per cent better, 27 per cent worse), regional autonomy (48 per cent better and 20 per cent worse), and information (61 per cent better and 12 per cent worse). Interestingly enough, this corresponds to the restraint shown by the state in its response to terrorism. The state, in its response to terrorism, did not further undermine the purposes of the state by using indiscriminate repressive and violent measures. These are the only areas where the state received high marks. Without that support, upon what basis would citizens support democracy? By analysing public opinion according to the rudimentary purposes of the state of security and integration, it can be shown why Spaniards supported democracy and why Peruvians and Uruguayans did not. Uruguay and Peru faced the same difficulties. However, the state responses attacked security and integration, which had already been undermined by terrorist violence. Security was undermined by the increase in state violence and repression. Integration was undermined by the suspension of individual liberties and the decrease in tolerance as levels of suspicion increased.

> **Hypothesis one**
>
> Terrorist violence threatens democratic stability by undermining both rudimentary purposes of the state, security, and integration. As the purposes of the state are unfulfilled, citizen confidence in the state declines. As citizen confidence decreases, democratic instability increases.

In all three cases, Uruguay, Peru, and Spain, terrorist violence was viewed as a serious threat to the state. As reported in chapter six, in Uruguay, a strong majority of the population viewed the Tupamaros as highly dangerous. A concern about the violence was also evident in public opinion polls, with the social disorder and instability a concern for many. In Peru, approximately seven out of ten people were afraid of the violence, viewed it as serious, and were repulsed by it. Over half thought the country was in a state of civil war. In Spain, terrorism consistently was ranked as one of the top three problems facing the state. Moreover, citizens recognized terrorism as a threat to democracy. Interestingly, all three states received poor evaluations for their efforts in dealing with the terrorist threat. In Uruguay, only approximately one out of eight citizens characterized the National Assembly as doing a good job. The Peruvian Congress had overwhelmingly low approval ratings. Every democratically elected leader except for Fujimori ended his term with extremely low approval ratings. In addition, traditional parties in both Uruguay and Peru lost support in the last election before the coup. Even in Spain, the successfully consolidated democracy received high marks of dissatisfaction in regard to the economy, unemployment, corruption, public order, and security.

Clearly, the terrorism was viewed by the Uruguayan, Peruvian, and Spanish citizens as a serious problem. As the threat continued unabated, the states were held accountable in public opinion for the failure to promote the two rudimentary purposes of the state: security and integration. Citizens were afraid and the violence was viewed as a threat in these countries.

Hypothesis two

State repression and violence undermine the rudimentary purposes of the state, integration and security. Decreases in citizen confidence should follow a decrease in the fulfilment of the rudimentary purposes. Finally, as citizen confidence in the state decreases, increases in democratic instability should be identifiable.

In two of the three cases, Uruguay and Peru, the state responded to the terrorist violence with indiscriminate repressive and violent means. In Uruguay, the state broadly suspended rights, practised censorship, instituted torture in investigations, and used covert, state sponsored violent groups to combat terrorist violence. In Peru, the state suspended rights in the areas under a state of emergency, forced many to participate in armed peasant groups, and used torture and extrajudicial executions in its counterinsurgency policy. Spain, on the contrary, pursued a policy of national reconciliation. The state restored political liberties, granted amnesty to political prisoners, and allowed regional autonomy. Although there were scattered instances of allegations of torture, it was not a state policy. Some anti-terrorist legislation was introduced, but it was used sparingly. The citizens' reaction to the state was negative in Uruguay and Peru. The state policies of indiscriminate repression and violence further undermined the purposes of the state. Levels of citizen confidence and democratic stability declined. In Spain, however, the state's policy of national reconciliation helped to bolster the purposes of the state that were under attack from terrorist violence. Consequently, there is no evidence of a further degeneration in security due to state actions. Furthermore, the state actions seemed to improve integration.[2]

The indiscriminate state repression and violence further undermined the purposes of the state in Uruguay and Peru. As the citizens faced threats from terrorist groups, instead of being confident in an appropriate proportionate response by the state to those responsible, all citizens suffered from the repressive measures instituted by the state. The citizens began to look at the state as a threat to their security and integration, in addition to the terrorist groups. Only the military, in Uruguay, and the military, Catholic Church, and Fujimori, in Peru, maintained positive citizen support. With the state presenting more of a threat, instead of a solution, many citizens supported the coups in Uruguay and in Peru. In Spain, the state did not add to the pre-existing violence. Instead, its policies of a rational reconciliation buttressed the security and integration that were attacked by the terrorist violence, instead of further weakening them. Consequently, the citizens remained supportive of democracy, believing it to be the most practicable constitutional form.

An answer to a possible objection

One objection that can be raised is the following question. Why did the people support the military in Uruguay and in Peru when the military was involved in the repressive policies? The answer to this rests on the development of factions within each military. Given these factions, citizens could support the military with different hopes for and expectations of a military led state.

Uruguay

Four factions of military officers developed within the armed forces. The popular frontist group was composed of officers who supported the Frente Amplio, including its candidate, Liber Seregni and others. The second group was composed of the traditional legalist members. These officers were basically members of the traditional parties and some were candidates for office, such as General Juan Ribas, who ran for president under the Colorado banner, and General Mario Aguerrondo, who ran under the Blanco party. This group also included Generals Gravina and Francese. A third group, the nationalist reformist group, viewed itself as similar to the Peruvian revolutionary military regime of 1968. They advocated intensive economic development and social change. A prominent member of this group was General Gregorio Alvarez, who led the fight against the Tupamaros and who served as secretary general of COSENA. Finally, there was the developmental or 'guerilla' group. This group of the extreme right favoured a takeover of the state. They also believed in the promotion of unrestricted foreign investment in Uruguay. Members included commander-in-chief of the army General Hugo Chiappe Posse and General Esteban Cristi, who advocated the military's responsibility to eliminate subversion and political corruption.

The influence of the traditional legalist officers waned quickly. In July 1972, 559 officers condemned the attempt by the National Assembly to publicly name soldiers responsible for the death of a civilian. Despite being warned by constitutionalist commander-in-chief General Florencio Gravina that the proposed resolution was 'inopportune and inappropriate', the officers continued. General Gravina also disapproved of the military's investigation of economic crimes. He resigned in October 1972 in protest.[3] These incidents mark the increase in power of the hard-line, developmental faction in the military.[4] By the time of the crisis in February 1973, most of the popular frontist and traditional legalist factions were out of the military. The few that remained lost influence shortly after the crisis.[5] The Nationalist reformist group and the hard-line developmental groups were mainly responsible for the slow coup. The Nationalist reformist group remained visible and influential throughout the June dissolution of the National Assembly. This group was responsible for authorship of military communiqués four and seven. These communiqués called for the elimination of unemployment and subversion, the implementation of land reform and further benefits for citizens such as health care, the pursuit of modernization and development, and guarantees of sovereignty and security. One of the main Nationalist reformist generals, General Gregorio Alvarez, was a leader of the February rebellion and the June dissolution of the National Assembly. He also served as secretary general of COSENA. The hard-line developmental group, including General Esteban Cristi, also participated in the slow coup. General Esteban Cristi and General Gregorio Alvarez commanded the dissolution of the National Assembly in June. With two contrasting factions conducting the slow coup, it seems plausible that citizens could have very different expectations of a military state.

Peru

In Peru, it must be remembered that the military succeeded in implementing significant, although not entirely successful reforms, under the military rule of General Velasco Alvarado (1968–1975). In spite of the failures of the revolutionary military state of 1968–1980, in 1988, Peruvians rated General Velasco as the best president since 1950.[6] The military had different traditions to follow.

Although the military had been placed in charge of the counterinsurgency policy, it was not given a policy to follow by the governments of Belaúnde and García. Paralleling the inconsistency in the governments of Belaúnde and García, there was a similar lack of unity among the generals charged with the elimination of the threat during those two presidencies. In terms of controlling the counterinsurgency policy, the military was in complete control. However, this military had been divided over how to solve the problem. For example, General Clemente Noel Moral, the first commander in Ayacucho, viewed the conflict as an internal war. 'One misses the fact that Sendero Luminoso, whatever its political variation, is the armed wing of a large movement which attempts to disrupt the established order to favour international communism, and nothing less.'[7] General Adrián Huamán attempted to create a new counterinsurgency strategy that nurtured the alliance between the people and the armed forces. He spoke fluent Quechua, was born in Apurimac, and was the son of peasants. Huamán stated:

> Here the solution is not military, because if it had been military, I would have resolved it in minutes. If it were a question of destroying Ayacucho, the area would not exist for half an hour,

nor would Huancavelica. We would be done with the problem. But that is not the answer. What is happening is that we are talking about human beings from the forgotten pueblos who have been crying out for 160 years, and no one has paid any attention to them. Now we are reaping the result.[8]

General Adrián Huamán, the only general to be discharged by President Belaúnde, was military commander of Ayacucho from 1983 until September 1984. This disagreement among the generals was reflected in the seesaw-like policies of the military. In Ayacucho in 1988, General José Valdiva was in charge. He followed an internal war approach, complete with curfews and the prohibition of the presence of the Red Cross and other human rights organizations. The result was an increase in human rights violations. General Sinesio Jarama disagreed with those policies, stating in 1989 that the first thing that is needed to combat subversion is an examination of the political, economic, social, and psychological context. 'This context is what has still not been defined. It is the famous counterinsurgency strategy that so many speak of and which still does not exist.'[9] Later, in 1989, a different general, General Howard Rodríguez, lifted many repressive measures and involved the military in civic action programmes. In 1990, General Petronio Fernández Dávila continued the programmes of Rodríguez, but added a psychological campaign, which was later dropped.[10] The same inconsistency due to the turnover of generals occurred in the Huallaga Valley, a coca growing region with high levels of Sendero activity. General Alberto Arciniega reported on the battle for Huallaga in a *QueHacer* interview. The general communicated his sympathetic attitude towards the peasants:

> We must keep in mind that the peasants who grow the coca were accosted by the police and by whatever force of order existed, because they were considered a delinquent.... We are talking about 80 per cent of the population! What we need to do, then, is to modify this situation to prevent the harassment of the peasants growing the coca, the base Sendero needs to support its activities, by the government[11]

The general denied that the peasant who grows the coca should be treated like a drug trafficker. General Arciniega succeeded in ending the alliance between insurgents and Sendero. When his term ended, his successor changed strategies, targeting the peasants who grew the coca. As a result, Sendero's activity increased in the region.[12] As in Uruguay, it seems plausible that citizens initially had very different expectations of Fujimori's military supported state.

Prospects for stability to 2006

Although the focus of this study is on the breakdown of Uruguayan democracy in 1972, the dissolution of Peruvian democracy in 1992, and the attempted coup in Spain in 1981, this section extends the argument to a discussion of prospects for stability in these countries into more recent years.[13] The violence in Uruguay is over and the country has made significant progress in national reconciliation, although rumours of possible coups and conspiracies inspired by human rights prosecutions have emerged. In Peru, the violence of Sendero Luminoso continues, albeit at a greatly reduced level. Additionally, Peru has made significant progress in reducing impunity and punishing human rights violations. In Spain, the violence of ETA continues, although Spain recently experienced a time of peace. Moreover, two international factors have changed. In Peru, the Organization of American States has become a more active force for democracy in the region. Other non-governmental agencies and countries have pressured Peru to maintain the integrity of its democratic process and the Fujimori regime is being dismantled. In Spain, membership in the European Union has also strengthened Spain's ability to prosecute ETA and has also symbolized democratic progress and modernization to both Spanish elites and citizens.

Uruguay (1973–2006)

After the dissolution of the National Assembly in 1973 and contrary to the expectations of many, a period of intense repression began. Seven years later, in 1980, the Uruguayan military held a referendum to institutionalize its rule. The plebiscite failed, the military receiving only 43 per cent of the vote. The military announced its plans for a controlled liberalization of the regime, called the *cronograma*. Primaries were held and the traditional parties were allowed to participate. In August 1984, representatives from the Colorado party, the Frente Amplio party, and the Unión Cívica, a Catholic party affiliated with the military, met to discuss the transition. The Blanco party did not participate. In accordance with these talks, the military regime passed Institutional Act 19, which returned the country to its pre-1973 democratic institutions. Eventually, elections were held in 1984 and the country was returned to democracy in 1985. In 1984, Colorado party leader Julio Maria Sanguinetti was elected president, serving from 1985–1990 and again from 1995–2000.[14]

Although the main political parties won the presidency in the first three elections, the leftist Frente Amplio party has gained support, becoming a legitimate challenger. In 1989, the Socialist Tabaré Vázquez was elected mayor of Montevideo. In 1994, he lost the presidential election by only 35,000 votes.[15] Sanguinetti, the victor, had served in the National Assembly and as a minister of education in the previous democratic regime. He led the democratic delegation in the Club Naval talks with the military in 1984.

One issue that was not settled in the Club Naval talks was that of human rights violations during the military regime.[16] Under the military regime, there were 4000 long term prisoners in Uruguay, whose average length of detention was 6.8 years. The total number of prisoners during the period reached 600,000.[17] During the military regime of 1973–1985, virtually all political prisoners were tortured.[18] Although the number of people killed by the regime was relatively low at 168,[19] Uruguay had the highest proportion of political prisoners in the world. Amnesty International estimated that 1 out of 600 Uruguayans were jailed under the military regime.[20]

President Sanguinetti calmed civil–military relations by not calling for either trials or investigations. In March 1985, the National Assembly approved an amnesty law that freed political prisoners, except those who had intentionally committed homicide. However, this bill did not include an amnesty for members of the military or state security forces. Thus, a different amnesty bill was passed in August 1986, although the government maintained the right to investigate abuses. This 1986 'Expiry' law exempted all military and police personnel from liability for human rights violations during the dictatorship.[21] Many citizens challenged this amnesty, gathering over 600,000 signatures to force a plebiscite on the law. However, their efforts to annul the law failed. The law was approved in the 1989 plebiscite, 56 per cent to 43 per cent.[22] Initially, the government, the main political parties, and the military were content to honour the 1989 plebiscite. Despite this, significant numbers of Uruguayans still want the issue to be discussed. For example, in May 1996 50,000 people participated in a silent march held in remembrance of the disappeared.[23] During Sanguinetti's first term, civil–military relations normalized under civilian supremacy. In the presidency of Lacalle (1990–1995), new service commanders of the navy and air force were appointed against the wishes of the military command.[24]

Pressures for accountability for past human rights violations continued to build. Part of the 1986 impunity law, the 'Law Nullifying the State's Claim to Punish Certain Crimes', included Article 4, which allowed the executive to investigate the cases of lost and presumably abducted children. In 1999, Colorado Jorge Batlle was elected president. President Batlle (2000–2005) responded to public pressure and began a limited investigation. A prominent case, of the granddaughter of Argentine poet Juan Gelmén, born in Uruguayan captivity but raised without the knowledge of her family, was solved after President Batlle met with the family and located the daughter twenty-four years after her birth.[25] Other cases remained unsolved. In 2000, instead of opening prosecutions of military or civilians accused of human rights violations during the military regime, Batlle created a commission to investigate the cases of the disappeared. Twenty-six individuals were identified as victims of torture during the previous regime. As a result, in 2003 President Batlle ordered the government to pay families of the victims of both guerrilla violence and government repression.[26]

Upon the election of Tabaré Vázquez of the Encuentro Progresista–Frente Amplio (Progressive Encounter–Broad Front) in 2004, human rights became a higher priority. Moreover, former Tupamaros were now in prominent positions in the government which assumed power in March

2005. Former Tupamaros and current Frente Amplio members Nora Castro and Jose Mujica became the leader of the Chamber of Deputies and leader of the Senate respectively. Mujica had been imprisoned during the military regime because of his guerrilla activities.[27] In addition to the symbolic importance of having former guerrillas participating as part of a legal political party which enjoys broad popular support, the new government was interested in investigating and prosecuting the human rights violations of the military regime.

The amnesty law remains technically unchallenged. In December 2005, victims of military repression were found, after newly elected president Vázquez (2005–2010) ordered the excavations of suspected graves. Meanwhile, he has begun a debate on whether or not to open investigation of military human rights abuses.[28] However, under President Vázquez, prosecutions have been allowed to proceed by interpreting the 1986 law as only covering crimes that occurred in Uruguay, not in other countries, and by excluding civilians from coverage of the amnesty. In August 2006, eight former police and military members were listed for investigation by Uruguayan judge Mirtha Guianze for the kidnapping and disappearance of five Uruguayan leftists in 1976 in Argentina.[29] These five victims were the target of Operation Condor.[30] In November 2006, former president Bordaberry and his former foreign minister, Juan Carlos Blanco, were arrested for the kidnapping and murder of Senator Zelmar Michelini, House Leader Hector Gutierrez, Tupamaro William Whitelaw, and Tupamaro Rosario Barredo.[31] In December 2006, Bordaberry was charged with ten additional murder charges.[32] In February 2007, retired Colonel Manuel Juan Cordero was extradited from Brazil to face human rights abuse charges.[33]

These developments point to the resilience of Uruguayan democracy. However, efforts to prosecute human rights violations have been resisted. Many military officers viewed this as a campaign against them.[34] Moreover, at least one coup rumour has been reported. Before the 2004 elections, Colonel Gilberto Vázquez (who has since been charged with human rights violations) insinuated that a coup was possible if Tupamaros continued to lodge accusations against the military.[35] In October 2006, the Uruguayan army commander-in-chief, General Carlos Díaz, was relieved of his duties after inviting leading opposition leaders, former Colorado president Julio Sanguinetti and former Colorado defence minister Yamandu Fau, to a barbeque at the fourteenth battalion, without permission.[36] Generals Aguerre and Miguel Dalmao also attended. Some viewed this as the beginning of a possible conspiracy. Later, there were reports that former Blanco president Lacalle had also separately met with Díaz and the navy commander Fernández Maggio.[37]

Economically, Uruguay faces the challenges of a small, open economy sandwiched between Brazil and Argentina, as demonstrated in table 7.1. The new democracy faced sluggish growth from 1988 to 1990 and again in 1995. Despite this fluctuation, the early troubles were better than the twenty year stagnation experienced prior to 1973. Inflation picked up after the restoration of democracy, but the increases tapered off beginning in the 1990s, down from rates of 112 per cent in 1990 to 20 per cent in 1997, and 5 per cent in 2005. In terms of unemployment, the country entered a period of double digit unemployment in the late 1990s and early 2000s. Since 1991, Uruguay has been a member of Mercosur, along with Brazil, Paraguay, and Argentina. In 2006, Venezuela joined. Although this customs union integrated the small economy into the larger Argentine and Brazilian economies, it also increased the vulnerability of Uruguay to the economic problems of fellow Mercosur members. In particular, Uruguay suffered because of the contagion problems in the international market which started in 1998 and greatly affected both Brazil and Argentina. Argentina suffered a deep recession in 2001 and did not receive an IMF bailout. Both Brazil and Uruguay received IMF aid packages. In terms of economic growth Uruguay, despite the difficult regional economic situation in the late 1990s and early 2000s, and its own recession and banking crisis during the period,[38] has returned to economic growth. In fact, the Uruguayan economic situation has improved such that the country repaid its IMF loan ahead of schedule in 2006.[39] Moreover, in the last quarter of 2006 unemployment had fallen to under 10 per cent.

Citizen support for democracy is solid in Uruguay. According to *Latinobarómetro* polls shown in table 7.2, Uruguay has some of the strongest support for democracy

Table 7.1 Uruguayan economic indicators, 1980–2005

	Unemployment	Consumer Price Index (annual %)	GDP growth rate
1980	NA	63	6
1981	NA	34	2
1982	NA	19	−9
1983	NA	49	−6
1984	NA	55	−1
1985	NA	72	1
1986	10.1	76	9
1987	9.1	64	8
1988	8.6	62	0
1989	8.0	80	1
1990	8.5	112	1
1991	8.9	102	4
1992	9.0	68	8
1993	8.3	54	3
1994	9.2	45	7
1995	10.3	42	−1
1996	11.9	28	6
1997	11.4	20	5
1998	10.1	11	5
1999	11.3	6	−3
2000	13.6	5	−1
2001	15.3	4	−3
2002	16.9	14	−11
2003	16.9	19	2
2004	13.1	9	12
2005	12.2	5	7

Sources: World Bank Development Indicators, Inter-American Development Bank, Instituto Nacional de Estadística (www.ine.gub.uy).

within Latin America. For example, in 2006 77 per cent of Uruguayan respondents agreed that democracy was the most preferable type of government, down slightly from a high point of support (86 per cent) in 1997. Moreover, Uruguayan citizens are consistently more satisfied with democracy, compared with the rest of Latin America. The low points of satisfaction with Uruguayan democracy are in 2003 and 2004, after two economically difficult years and before the new Frente Amplio government assumed power. Despite some flagging of satisfaction with democracy, in 2005 76 per cent of respondents agreed with the statement, 'I would

Table 7.2 Views of democracy, 1995–2006

	Satisfaction with democracy (Very and fairly)[a] (%)			Support for democracy (Democracy is preferable to any other kind of government)[b] (%)		
	Uruguay	Peru	Latin America	Uruguay	Peru	Latin America
1995	57	44	38	80	52	58
1996	51	28	27	80	63	61
1997	65	21	41	86	60	63
1998	68	18	37	80	63	62
1999/2000	69	22	36	84	64	57
2001	56	16	25	79	62	48
2002	53	18	33	78	57	56
2003	44	11	29	78	52	53
2004	45	7	29	78	45	53
2005	63	13	31	77	40	53
2006	66	23	38	77	55	58

Sources: Latinobarómetro 1995–2006.

Note: [a] Satisfaction with democracy reflects respondents answering either 'fairly' or 'very' to the following question: 'In general, would you say you are very satisfied, fairly satisfied, not very satisfied or not satisfied at all with the way democracy works in Uruguay?' [b] Support for democracy reflects respondents choosing 'Democracy is preferable to any other kind of government' when asked the following question: 'With which of the following statements do you agree most? Democracy is preferable to any other kind of government/Under some circumstances, an authoritarian government can be preferable to a democratic one/For people like me, it doesn't matter whether we have a democratic or a non-democratic regime.

never support a military government under any circumstances'.⁴⁰

Uruguay summary

The outlook for Uruguayan democracy is positive. The country has not faced additional guerrilla violence since the restoration of democracy.⁴¹ The country has significantly improved integration, former guerrillas have been reintegrated, and past human rights violations are being prosecuted. Despite a polarization of the public in regard to the amnesty for the military and security forces, the country is mostly tranquil and, to date, rumblings within the armed forces have been contained. Citizen support for democracy remains among the highest in Latin America, although down slightly from its peak in 1997.

Peru (1992–2006)

In 2002, Héctor Béjar, former guerrilla leader of the Ejercito de Liberación Nacional de Peru, described contemporary Peru in the following terms: 'we are experiencing both a useless democracy and a useless violence. And the corruption has been useful for those enriched by it.'⁴² Certainly, the country has suffered from waves of terrorist violence and government violence, in addition to persistent corruption scandals and institutional instability. Nonetheless, Peru is making progress in increasing transparency, holding both government and guerrillas responsible for past human rights violations, and promoting a more open society that is moving towards increased security and integration. The country recovered from the economic disaster of the 1980s, although the recovery has yet to reduce the stubbornly high rates of poverty in the country. The violence of Sendero Luminoso continues, although at a lower rate. Moreover, the international environment, specifically the OAS, has changed, allowing for a more robust defence of democracy in the region.

A main goal of Fujimori's *autogolpe* was to create a new set of governing institutions. The new Democratic Constituent Congress was elected on 13 November 1992.

Municipal elections were held in February 1993, and a new constitution was created and ratified in a referendum in October 1993 by 52.3 per cent of the population.[43] Fujimori was reelected in 1995 with 65 per cent of the vote. His party, Cambio 90/Nueva Mayoria, held 69 seats of the unicameral 120 member Congress.

The new democracy, however, lacks an effective balance of power among different branches and many aspects of the constitution are problematic. The new judiciary is weak in relation to the executive. A preponderance of judges and prosecutors are provisional and appointed. Without a tenured, permanent position, the judges are more vulnerable to political pressure. For example, in 1997 of the 1,473 judges, only 403 had permanent appointments and half of the Supreme Court judges had temporary or provisional status.[44] In December 1997, Congress granted provisional judges the same authority as tenured judges in the Jurado Nacional de Elecciones (National Electoral Board), thus allowing them the right to vote and to participate in the Board.[45] However, in response to critics, in 1996 two new institutions were created: the Defender of the People (Defensoria del pueblo) and the Constitutional Tribunal. The power of the Constitutional Tribunal is limited since there must be six out of seven votes for a law to be deemed unconstitutional.[46] Another troubling aspect of the new constitution is Article 173, which created separate military courts. In addition, due to presidential decrees, these courts were presided over by anonymous judges. Individuals accused of terrorism were tried in faceless civilian courts and those accused of treason were tried in faceless military courts. These decrees also allowed extended times of police detention and a restriction of the right to a defence.[47] Moreover, the majority of these judges were military officers with little or no legal training, the trials were secret, and access to defence attorneys limited. Human Rights Watch estimated that at least 10 per cent of those convicted by the faceless courts were innocent. After intense criticism by human rights groups, the faceless courts were abolished in October 1997.

The new legislature is very weak compared with the executive branch. The Congress is now unicameral with 120 members elected at large. Under Fujimori, the Congress did not invoke its powers of oversight and refused to investigate cases of alleged wrongdoing. One commission was formed in May 1996, after more than forty requests.[48] In addition, critics have complained that the legislature was little more than a rubber stamp body. For example, despite broad public rejection, Congress passed the law of 'authentic interpretation', allowing Fujimori to run for a third term in 2000. Congress declared that the limitation of two presidential terms did not apply to Fujimori since the 1993 constitution was not in force at the time of his first election in 1990.[49]

The lack of balance of powers became clear in the case of the drive to force a referendum on the issue of Fujimori's attempt to run for a third term. The importance of the dependence of individual judges was highlighted in 1997 when Congress removed three of the judges from the constitutional tribunal who had voted against the 'authentic interpretation' law of 1996. Because of this, the tribunal could not function because of a lack of quorum. By 1999, the tribunal was still inactive.[50] In response to the passage of the 'authentic interpretation' law, a grass roots effort formed to force a referendum on the issue. At least 1.4 million signatures were gathered to force the referendum. However, the National Board of Elections ruled that a referendum would occur only if forty-eight members of Congress voted for it. On 27 August 1998 only forty-five members voted for it. In short, the constitutional right to a referendum was undermined by Congress without opportunity for judicial review.[51] This exemplified a growing concern that Fujimori had undermined the rule of law in Peru.

As support for and confidence in Fujimori declined, more Peruvians described him as dictatorial. In an APOYO study, Peruvians were asked their opinion of his government. Although 52 per cent of those polled believed that Fujimori's government was democratic one month after his *autogolpe*, by June 1997 only one third of those asked described him as democratic. A strong majority, 59 per cent, described him as dictatorial.[52]

Fujimori's party Vamos Vecino lost in the municipal elections of October 1998. Incumbent mayor Alberto Andrade beat Fujimori's Juan Carlos Hurtado Miller in Lima's mayoral election. Other pro-Fujimori candidates won in only seventy-nine provinces while opposition candidates won in one hundred. Moreover, protests against Fujimori running for a third term continued to grow.

During the April 2000 first round of presidential elections, APOYO asked Fujimori's supporters why they supported him. In the poll, 60 per cent responded because he ended terrorism, 48 per cent responded for other things he had done, 28 per cent for assisting the poor, and only 26 per cent for providing economic stability.[53] On the eve of the 2000 election, Fujimori was the candidate with the most support, but was projected to lose a close race in the second round, against opposition candidate Toledo.[54] However, citing continued electoral irregularities and Fujimori's refusal to postpone the second round elections to correct the problems, Toledo withdrew from the race in May 2000. Despite consistent criticism from the opposition about corruption and abuse of power, Fujimori enjoyed positive evaluations of over 50 per cent through out the autumn of 2000. Fujimori won a third term in the 28 May 2000 runoff election that was boycotted by the opposition and international observers.

Within a few months however, his regime rapidly unfolded. On 14 September, TV stations aired film of Vladimiro Montesinos bribing a member of the opposition with US $15,000 to join Fujimori's ruling bloc. In an attempt to contain the scandal, two days later Fujimori announced the deactivation of the SIN, shortened his third presidential term, and called for new elections in 2001 in which he would not be a candidate. Fujimori resigned on 20 November 2000 in response to the growing scandal. His resignation was rejected by Congress, which instead declared him 'morally unfit' and ousted him on those grounds on 22 November 2000. Valentín Paniagua was installed as interim president. Fujimori fled to Japan. Eventually, an international arrest warrant was issued in September 2001, with the charges of treason, human rights abuses, and corruption. (He was arrested in Chile in November 2005.) Within the next year many leaders suspected of collaborating with Fujimori and Montesinos resigned, including the heads of the army, navy, and air force, and other top officials were replaced, including the president of the Supreme Court and nine other senior judges. After fleeing to Venezuela, Montesinos was incarcerated in June 2001 due to charges of government corruption, voter fraud, constitutional manipulation, and abuse of power. Eventually Montesinos had multiple trials. In 2002, he was tried for corruption and sentenced to nine years. In 2003, he was charged with abuse of power and embezzlement, resulting in five and eight year terms. In 2006, he was tried for the 1997 extrajudicial deaths of fourteen MRTA members and was sentenced to twenty years.

President Alejandro Toledo Manrique was elected in June and assumed office on 28 July 2001, becoming the first president of Indigenous heritage. Toledo, known as 'el cholo', grew up in a family of sixteen children and worked as a shoeshine boy. Despite his poor upbringing, he earned a PhD in economics at Stanford and worked for many of the premier international economic institutions, such as the World Bank, Inter American Development Bank, International Labour Organization, and the OECD. He was elected with promises of free trade, optimizing social spending, increasing government worker salaries, creating jobs by increasing exports, and the six monthly monitoring of the social goals of reducing poverty, inequality, and malnutrition.

Peruvian economic performance

In general, Peru continues to face economic challenges, as shown in table 7.3. However, inflation has been contained, down from the massive increases in the late 1980s. Similarly, as inflation fell from a high of 7650 per cent in 1990, so did the number of strikes. By 1996, strikes were ten times less frequent than in 1988. Fujimori also was successful in restarting economic growth, especially during the first three years after the *autogolpe*. However, growth rates slowed significantly in 1998 and 1999. Despite Fujimori's success in containing inflation and restarting growth, poverty remained very high. In 1998, half of Peruvians lived in poverty. Moreover, 14.7 per cent of Peruvians live in extreme poverty, unable to access the basic necessities of sufficient food and water.[55] Compounding the problem of persistent poverty was the perception that poverty figures were being politically manipulated. Javier Herrera, author of *Informe de Pobreza 2003*, found higher estimates of poverty in Peru than publicly admitted, resulting in a scandal about poverty statistics. According to Herrara, there are 190,000 additional

Table 7.3 Peruvian economic indicators, 1993–2005

	Unemployment	Consumer Price Index (annual %)	GDP growth rate
1993	10	40	5
1994	9	15	13
1995	7	10	9
1996	7	12	2
1997	8	9	7
1998	8	7	−1
1999	8	3	1
2000	7	4	3
2001	8	2	0
2002	10	0	5
2003	10	2	4
2004		4	5
2005		2	7

Source: World Bank Development Indicators.

instead of 420,000 fewer people in poverty, as stated in a recent presidential address. Moreover, depending on different classifications, as many as eight out of ten Peruvians are impoverished.[56] The difference in statistics was due to INEI's comparison of annual statistics with trimester estimates. Another source, the World Bank, estimated the 1997 national poverty rate as 49 per cent, with 65 per cent rural and 40 per cent urban poverty. It also estimated the malnutrition prevalence for children under five, in terms of height at 25 per cent and in terms of weight at 7 per cent in 2000.

Sendero Luminoso after the autogolpe

The capture of Guzmán significantly affected the operations of Sendero Luminoso. After the capture of Abimael Guzmán in September 1992, Oscar Ramirez Durand, better known as 'Feliciano', and Miguel Aranda Montanez took over leadership roles. The incarcerated Guzmán proposed peace talks in 1993. The government allowed Guzmán to read his proposal on television. Sendero Luminoso divided over the issue of whether or not to heed the call of their imprisoned leader.[57] In 1994, almost 6,000 members accepted an amnesty offer from the government to reintegrate in society. The original Sendero Luminoso, led by Aranda Montanez, reiter-

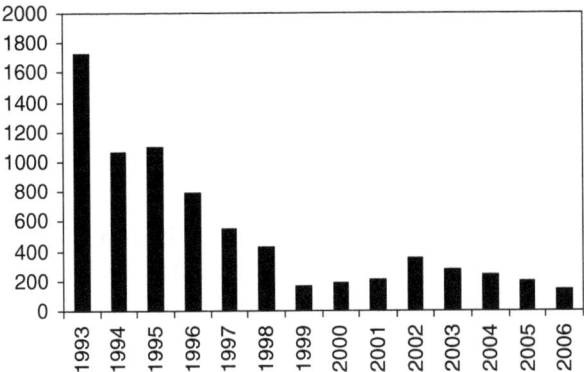

Figure 7.1 Peru: terrorist violent incidents, 1993–2006
Source: Ministry of the Interior.

ated its desire to begin peace talks in December 1997. The group also promised to crush the dissident Red Path branch of Sendero Luminoso. However, some members continued to fight. The Red Path faction of Sendero Luminoso, led by Oscar Ramirez Durand, 'Feliciano', continued to operate and kill. It rejected Guzmán's calls from prison for an end to violent action and a peace accord.[58]

Figure 7.1 presents the downword trend in terrorist violence. In 1997, Sendero Luminoso killed 12 peasant leaders[59] and an additional 158 in the first six months of 1998.[60] Throughout the late 1990s, Sendero Luminoso was still active in the Upper Huallaga Valley and in the departments of Piura, La Libertad, and Ayacucho, and was attempting to regain control of parts of Lima. However, the state continued to make progress arresting leaders. In December 1998, a top military leader of Sendero Luminoso, Juan Carlos Rios, was captured in the slums of Lima.[61] In July 1999, Red Path leader 'Feliciano' was captured and in November was sentenced to life in prison. By 2000, terrorist incidents had fallen to fewer than 200 incidents a year from over 1700 in 1993. Incidents increased in 2002 and 2003, creating some concern that the movement was regrouping. Specifically, there were prominent attacks including a car bomb outside the US embassy in March 2002 which coincided with a visit from US president George W. Bush (killing 10 and wounding 20), another car bomb in Lima's El Polo shopping district, and the kidnapping of 71 Argentine workers in Ayacucho (who were released a day later). Some of the recent activity can be attributed to the Proseguir group, led by Victor Quispe Palomino, also known as Comrade 'José' or 'Martín'.[62] Another group, 'Los Sanguinarios', is said to be under the control of 'Alipio'. This group ambushed and killed a group of eight police officers and officials who were on an antinarcotics mission in December 2006. In response, García sent a 500 man force to confront the guerrillas. He announced plans to legalize the death penalty for terrorism, contrary to the terms of multiple international agreements.[63] In January 2007, García protested the decision of the Inter-American Court of Human Rights, which ordered the government to pay compensation to the families of imprisoned Sendero members killed in the 1992 prison raid and commemorate the victims.[64] Some analysts are concerned about the resilience of some pockets of Sendero Luminoso activity in Ayacucho and Huancayo and the efforts to gain support among the coca growers, but most remain optimistic about the government's ability to respond and the public's rejection of the group.

The other main group, MRTA, had been active mainly in Junín. However, its last major campaign took place on 17 December 1996. On this day, MRTA took hostages in the Japanese embassy. Special forces finally stormed the complex on 22 April 1997. Seventy-two of the hostages were freed and one died in the process. Of the special forces, two were killed. All fourteen MRTA members were killed in the actions. Reports allege that many were summarily executed, laying the grounds for later human rights trials. Late 2006 reports suggest that some surviving members are attempting to regroup in Bolivia.

Peruvian state reaction after the autogolpe

Under Fujimori, the state continued to pursue a tough strategy to combat terrorism. States of emergency were declared, anti-terrorism laws were passed, and general amnesties were granted to the military and police. In addition, some attempts have been made to confront accusations of human rights violations of the accused.

After the establishment of the new constitution, much of the country remained under a state of emergency. In 1994, almost half of the population, 48 per cent, was living under a state of emergency.[65] By 1997, 16 per cent of the country and over 20 per cent of the population remained under a state of emergency.[66] Interestingly, many of the areas still under decree did not have a major guerrilla presence.[67] By 1999, only 6 per cent of the country was under a state of emergency.[68] More states of emergency were extended in the departments of Junín, Huancavelica, Ayacucho, Apurimac, and Cusco by President Toledo in 2003.[69] Additional states of emergency were declared for Puno in 2004 because of protestors. In 2005, parts of Ayacucho, Cusco, and Junín were under a state of emergency because of Sendero Luminoso activities. Figure 7.2 provides a trend of the state counterterrorism actions. The number of counterterrorism actions and the number of National Police killed mirror the decreasing trend of non-state violence seen in figure 7.1.

Due to the passage of the anti-terrorism (DL 25475) and treason (DL 25659) laws, 5,003 people had been jailed for terrorism as of 1994 (about 25 per cent of the prison population). About 66 per cent were members of Sendero Luminoso and 10 per cent were members of MRTA. The affiliation of the rest was undetermined. Peruvian human rights groups are concerned that the cases in which the affiliations of the prisoners were unclear indicate unjust imprisonment.[70] Since 1995, Peru has both granted amnesty to its military and has responded to criticisms from international human

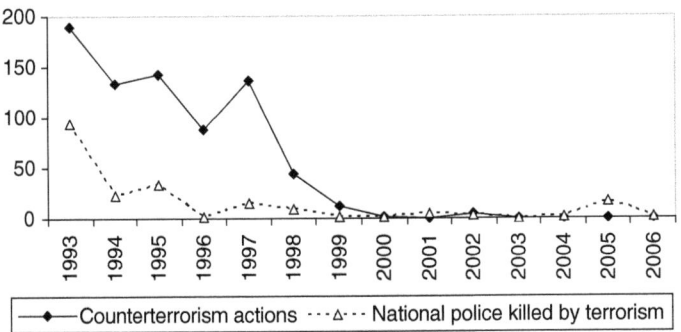

Figure 7.2 Peru: state counterterrorism actions and National Police deaths, 1993–2006
Source: Ministry of the Interior.

rights groups. In June 1995, laws 26479 and 26492 were passed, granting amnesty to members of the armed forces from responsibility for the human rights abuses that occurred from 1980–1995.[71] In the same year, decree law 26248 was passed, restoring the right of habeas corpus to people charged under anti-terrorism laws.[72] In addition, the office of the Defensoria del Pueblo was created and the Court of Constitutional Guarantees was reactivated.[73] In 1996, the Ad Hoc Pardons Commission was formed to investigate charges of unjust incarceration. By the close of 1998, a total of 462 prisoners had been released. In that year, the commission's mandate was expanded to look at those who had been convicted of terrorism and treason but who had repented. The life of the commission was expanded until 31 December 1999.[74] In February 1999, the state seemed to be moving away from the condoning of torture, which was made a specific offence in the Peruvian legal code. In 1998, there were no cases of disappearances. This favourably compares with the total of 2,371 people reported as disappeared during the internal conflict as recognized by the Human Rights Ombudsman.[75]

Despite the institutional and legal improvements, problems were still common under Fujimori. Torture was still commonly practised.[76] In addition, charges of illegal monitoring of prominent Peruvians and journalists were frequent. For example, former UN secretary general Javier Perez de Cuellar was allegedly the target of wiretaps. The Peruvian media investigate and report these charges, even though they occasionally receive anonymous threats for doing so.[77] Human rights groups, such as the Pro-Human Rights Association APRODEH, have also reported harassment. In 1999, Fujimori withdrew Peru from the Inter-American Court of Human Rights. Officially, it was in response to the Court's decision that Peru would have to retry four Chileans convicted in military courts. Others suspected that it was to prevent review of the cases of the three former Constitutional Tribunal judges who were involuntarily replaced, the constitutionality of Fujimori's intent to run for a third presidential term, and the case of Baruch Ivcher in 1997. Ivcher, after airing a report of human rights violations, had his Peruvian citizenship and his TV station confiscated from him.[78]

Under President Valentín Paniagua, the Comisión de la Verdad was established. The commission was composed of seven members who were charged with investigating the processes, incidents, and responsibilities of both the terrorist violence and the human rights violations from May 1980 to November 2000 (supreme decree no. 065-2001-PCM, article 1). In August 2001, President Toledo ratified its existence, changed its name to the Comisión de la Verdad y Reconciliación, and added five new members. Its mandate ended on 13 July 2003.[79] Paniagua also created the Comisión de Indulto (Pardon Commission) in November 2000. More than 300 Peruvians were pardoned and released before the commission's mandate expired at the end of Paniagua's term.[80] In 2003, in response to the commission's final report, President Toledo announced plans to invest in areas that suffered most of the violence.[81]

Efforts to prosecute human rights violations of both the state and the guerrillas continue. In January 2003, the Constitutional Tribunal ordered new trials for all those convicted by the military courts under Fujimori, including Guzmán. Guzmán was retried and sentenced to life in prison in October 2006. President Toledo also returned Peru as a member state of the Inter-American Court of Human Rights. One of the more egregious cases of human rights violations occurred in 1992, when a professor and 9 students were abducted from La Cantuta University and killed by the Colina counterinsurgency group, which had links to Fujimori and Montesinos. Fujimori was charged in 2001 with responsibility for these crimes and the deaths of 15 people in Lima in 1991.[82] Despite the earlier amnesty, 56 members of the group believed to be responsible were tried and are being detained while they await sentencing.[83] The government agreed to pay US $3.3 million to 15 victims of Colina in 2001.[84] Efforts to try Fujimori continue – 12 cases of human rights abuses and corruption charges have been filed against him. In November 2005, he travelled to Chile, en route to Peru with the intention of running for president (despite being banned until 2011). Chilean officials have restricted him to house arrest while he awaits extradition.

Police reform was also highlighted in Toledo's inauguration speech. His reform plan was based on Paniagua's Foundations of Police Reform document. President Toledo involved prominent civilian reformers such as Fernando Rospigliosi (new interior minister), Gino Costa (later minister, former head of the UN police reform unit in El Salvador), and Carlos Basombrio (former director of Instituto de Defensa Legal).[85] Although former interior minister Costa did not view the effort as a conventional success, he believed that it at least increased expectations for later success in police reform.

Peruvian security

In terms of public opinion measured by the polling group APOYO, there is a declining trend of concern about terrorism as shown in table 7.4. Months after the *autogolpe* and the capture of Guzmán, only one out of four Peruvians listed terrorism as one of the country's main problems. As incidents decrease through time, less concern has been reported. In October 1992, the most pressing problem was terrorism. By 1996, the focus had changed to the ongoing high unemployment and recession (57 per cent) and poverty and hunger (54 per cent). Only 4 per cent of those polled believed that terrorism was one of the top three problems facing the

Table 7.4 Peru: four principal problems, 1993–2006

	Unemployment	Terrorism	Human rights violations	Inflation	Poverty/hunger
1993	44	33	12	11	45
1994	48	15	16	10	54
1995	67	12	11	6	53
1996	57	4	15	9	54
1997	57	17	17	11	51
1998	66	4	37	10	36
1999	74	4	15	17	38
2000	79	4	16	3	65
2001	68	5	12	9	65
2002	71	7	11	6	68
2003	61	5	11	11	71
2004	53	4	11	11	63
2005	65	6	18	10	45
2006	54	13	22	5	46

Sources: APOYO, *Informe de Opinion*, January 2006.

country. The confidence of Peruvians that terrorism would decrease also vastly increased after Guzmán's capture.[86] However, fear of increases of terrorism in the future returned in 1997, after some increase in the number of terrorist actions. In that year, according to APOYO, the population was almost evenly split among believing that terrorism would increase (35 per cent), decrease (29 per cent), or stay the same (31 per cent). Although the number of disappearances and extrajudicial executions also decreased, concern for human rights violations interestingly remain somewhat steady.[87] As Sendero Luminoso regrouped, concern increased. By 2006, concern about terrorism was up slightly to 13 per cent, but still far below concern about unemployment (54 per cent) or poverty and hunger (46 per cent).

Peruvian citizen confidence

Fujimori enjoyed high levels of citizen confidence in the early period of state restructuring. However, the ratings of Fujimori and his institutions began to drop precipitously in 1996. Two months after the coup, at the beginning of June, Fujimori's support was still strong. In a Lima based poll, 65 per cent of those questioned still approved of the coup. Among middle class adults and young adults, support reached 70 per cent. Fujimori's personal approval rating was 76 per cent, and among the middle class and young adults that number increased to 83 per cent. The opposition received a 69 per cent disapproval rating.[88] In July, Fujimori's rating fell to 60 per cent. Carmen Rosa Balbi attributed his drop in approval to the increase of terrorist violence.[89] After the capture of Guzmán, Sendero Luminoso's master computer files, and some key subordinates[90] on 12 September 1992, Fujimori's approval rating rose to 74 per cent and the approval of the anti-subversive policy rose to 66 per cent.[91] In the same May APOYO poll, opposition leader Máximo San Roman only received a positive rating of 10 per cent, with a 79 per cent disapproval rating.[92] The June APOYO poll occurred the day after Fujimori announced a date for new elections. New Congressional elections were held in 1992. Elections for a new constituent assembly were held in 1993. However, Fujimori's popularity began to drop after his reelection in 1995. In 1997, his average approval rating slipped to 34 per cent. By that year, Fujimori and his top advisor, SIN advisor Vladimiro Montesinos ranked at the top of the most disliked officials in Peru.[93] APOYO reported that Montesinos was chosen as the most disliked official by 26 per cent and Fujimori by 20 per cent. Roughly the same trend can be seen in the levels of confidence in institutions. As Fujimori's approval ratings drop in 1997, so does confidence in the institutions that are affiliated with him, according to APOYO polls. The approval of the military dropped from 57 per cent in 1992 to 38 per cent in 1997. Approval of the National Police also slid from 48 per cent to 32 per cent. The approval of the presidency dropped from 54 per cent to only 35 per cent. By 1997, the only institutions with positive ratings were the Catholic Church, the provincial and district government, and the media. Confidence in Congress, the council of ministers, and the judiciary had dropped to under 30 per cent. Political parties were only held in confidence by 14 per cent.[94]

This concern is also reflected in the growing distrust in the National Police. In August 1993, 44 per cent trusted the National Police and 42 per cent distrusted them. By the summer of 1997, only one out of every three Peruvians trusted the National Police, almost two out of three reported distrust. This corroborates the steady concern about human rights in Peru during the time.[95] However, after police reform attempts, some modest improvement can be seen in the image of the police. The percentage of respondents expressing confidence (using a different question and polling agency from before) in the National Police increased from 14.5 per cent in August 2001 to 21.7 per cent in November 2003. The armed forces, rating also improved, from 17 per cent in August 2001 to 27.4 per cent in November 2003.[96] As shown in table 7.5, throughout 2006, most of the institutions suffered from continuing declines in confidence. Almost all institutions were at their lowest confidence ratings since 1993, with the exception of the armed forces, the media, and the Catholic Church. Only the Church and the media had ratings greater than 50 per cent.

Despite the frustration with the regime of Fujimori, support for democracy in general continued to grow. APOYO asked Peruvians what kind of regime they preferred: a democracy, a dictatorship, or a revolutionary regime. By June 1997, 90 per cent of those questioned preferred a

Table 7.5 Peru: confidence in institutions, 1993–2005

	Council of Ministers	Armed forces	Church	Media	Political parties	Judiciary	National Police	President
1993	43	66	81	54	11	34	53	60
1994	44	59	82	66	14	33	44	63
1995	48	68	81	63	19	36	49	72
1996	43	55	81	69	18	39	44	56
1997	6	38	81	59	14	21	32	35
1998	30	46	80	53	18	25	35	34
1999	33	59	79	54	18	31	45	44
2000	37	48	75	47	18	27	42	41
2001	47	47	74	58	28	33	41	49
2002	23	38	65	52	20	20	41	18
2003	25	37	62	53	10	15	33	17
2005	15	48	69	52	8	14	33	13

Sources: APOYO, *Informe de Opinion*, September 2003; APOYO, *Informe de Opinion*, September 2005 (all dates are September).

democracy. This was an increase from 72 per cent in 1992. This affirmation of support for a democratic regime did not benefit Fujimori, who by then was predominantly viewed as dictatorial. The possibility of further instability was very real to many Peruvians. When APOYO asked Peruvians about the probability of a military coup, approximately one third of the population believed it to be a strong possibility. By June 1997, the belief in the probability of a coup reached its highest point since 1994, with 36 per cent believing that it was probable. However, still over half disagreed.[97] Undoubtedly, any attempt to remove Fujimori's regime would have needed the support of at least part of the armed forces. As discussed in chapter three, it must be remembered that the Peruvian military historically contained very progressive elements. However, when Fujimori first assumed the presidency, he took control of the institution, politicizing it, but making it his political ally.

Before the 2000 elections, Fujimori mobilized state resources to support his reelection. Fujimori's FONCODES (Fondo Nacional de Compensación y Desarrollo Social) programme was founded in 1991. Before the 1995 election, spending had increased dramatically.[98] Some scholars charge that FONCODES resources were allocated according to the expected political benefit for Fujimori, as opposed to objective need.[99] Moreover, it has been charged that the government food distribution agency, the Programa Nacional de Asistencia Alimentaria, tied the supply of aid to support for Fujimori in the 2000 elections.[100] In addition, the Carter Center reported that the 2000 presidential election is widely believed to be flawed. There are numerous reports of a lack of media fairness, harassment of opposition candidates, and the use of public resources to support the incumbent Fujimori.[101] Moreover, it has been reported by the Peruvian newspaper *El Comercio* that one million signatures used to register Fujimori for a third term were forged.

Public opinion documents the concern about corruption. An autumn 2002 ENAHO study surveyed Peruvians about the scope and cost of corruption. Overall, 5.2 per cent of respondents reported incidents of corruption, costing them on average 48 *soles*, representing 1.1 per cent of their food budget. Of respondents, 30 per cent characterized the police and 14.9 per cent viewed the judiciary as corrupt.[102] Despite the fall of Fujimori, corruption remains a persistent problem. Transparency International documents an increase in perceived corruption throughout Toledo's term, deteriorating from a score of 4.1 in 2001 to 3.3 in 2006. This pessimistic assessment is mirrored by *Latinobarómetro* polls. In response to this question, 'during the last two years, have you seen progress in reducing corruption in state institutions?', only 23 per cent answered 'yes' in Peru in 2003. In response to the same question in 2005, only 24 per cent answered 'yes'. At the beginning of the Toledo administration, some promising reforms were made. After the Montesinos scandals of the Fujimori regime, the SIN was replaced by the Consejo Nactional de Inteligencia (CNI). However, soon after, Toledo began accumulating corruption scandals of his own. The CNI, in turn, had to be disbanded in March 2004 because of corruption scandals such as dirty tricks on journalists. During its three years, the CNI had seven intelligence directors, many resigning due to allegations of misconduct or corruption. For example, Cesar Almedya resigned in May 2003 and is currently imprisoned, accused of bribing judges. In September 2003, Alfonso Panizo resigned because of allegations of spying on journalists. On 18 March 2004, Daniel Mora resigned, accused of conspiring against Interior Minister Rospigliosi. His replacement, Ricardo Arboccó, resigned four days later because of alleged corruption and ties to Montesinos. Outside of intelligence, Interior Minister Rospigliosi was censured for his ineffective response to protests that led to the lynching of the mayor in Ilave. It was the first Congressional censure since Toledo took office. In April 2004, angry Aymara Indians lynched the mayor, who had been accused of embezzlement. In June 2004, the minister of agriculture, José Leon Rivera, resigned because of allegations of running a brothel with underage prostitutes. Personal issues have dogged Toledo as well. During the presidential campaign, he faced charges of drug use. Also surfacing during the campaign were allegations that he had an unacknowledged illegitimate child. After refusing to take DNA tests to confirm or deny paternity, he eventually acknowledged his daughter in October 2002. Although the charges against Toledo were originally archived in September 2002, accounts of a TV scandal with implications for freedom of the press resurfaced in May 2003. First Lady

Elaine Karp was accused of embezzling funds from a World Bank loan. Moreover, Toledo had to publicly apologize for her remarks twice in November 2003. Additionally, his sister is accused of running a signature forging racket. In June 2004, Toledo's wife, sister, and brother were unable to leave the country until the corruption charges against them were completely investigated. In July 2004, the imprisoned Cesar Almedya alleged that Toledo received a five million dollar bribe. In response to all of these charges, Toledo and his cabinet offered to open all their bank accounts to public scrutiny.

In addition to the substantial economic constraints, the political challenges facing Toledo have been formidable: devolution, a minority political party presence, and ongoing corruption scandals. Political problems have resulted in frequent cabinet reshufflings (major reorganizations in July 2002, December 2003, July 2003, February 2004, February 2005, and September 2005 and a minor reorganization in January 2003). His approval ratings were so low that his ability to finish his term was questioned by many. For example, in February 2004 *El Comerio* ran a front page editorial asking him to step down. In May 2004, Foro Democratico ran a 'No lo Toledo campaign', calling for him to resign so that new elections could be held before April 2006. At this time, *Latinobarómetro* reported that only 47 per cent responded in 2004 that 'under no circumstance would [we] support a military government'. In response to the calls for him to resign, Toledo received statements of support from regional groups such as the OAS, Rio Group, and Mercosur. Ironically, some of his strongest domestic support – in terms of staying in office – came from the opposition.[103] In June 2004, the opposition helped pass a law that increased the necessary votes to remove the president from 61 to 80. However, by mid-2006 his approvals had begun to climb, reaching 45 per cent by June 2006, higher than at any time since autumn 2001. Newly elected president Alan García started his term with an approval rating of 69 per cent.[104]

Peruvian democracy is challenged. Table 7.2 also provides information on the view of democracy in Peru. Although satisfaction with democracy is consistently lower than Latin America in general, the trend finally began to improve in 2006. Much of the recent disenchantment with democracy can be attributed to the constant corruption scandals since the fall of Fujimori. Despite all the economic, political, and violent difficulties faced in Peru, the support for democracy has remained at over 50 per cent, except in 2004 and 2005. In 2006, the trend was more optimistic, with support for democracy increasing to over 50 per cent. Although recent trends are positive, the next few years are crucial to solidify support and maintain the progress that has been made.

Peru summary

Improvements have been made in reducing threats to security from both state and non-state forces. Sendero's activities have been minimized by a mixture of successful apprehensions, amnesties, and lack of popular support. Integration is improving due to the thorough examination of the past mistakes in countering Sendero and because of the increased attention to the peasants in the highlands. Economic performance has been stable and positive. Satisfaction with democracy remains tepid, due to ongoing corruption scandals and persistent poverty.

Spain (1986–2006)

Since 1986, Spain's democracy has continued to succeed. Economic performance has been stable and the stubbornly high unemployment has decreased. Initial progress had been made with a long ETA cease-fire in 1998 and a brief cease-fire in 2006, although both failed. The Spanish government has made efforts at peace talks, banned a radical Basque party, and opened the prospect of renegotiating the statutes of autonomy. However, internal politics are becoming polarized about how to respond to ETA.

Spanish economic performance

Economically, the country has been doing well, as shown in table 7.6. In the last twenty years, there has only been one year of negative economic growth. Most importantly, unemployment has decreased from the pressing highs of the mid-1990s. Additionally, inflation has been confined to the single digits. After receiving billions in EU economic assistance,

Table 7.6 Spanish economic indicators, 1987–2005

	Unemployment	Consumer Price Index (annual %)	GDP growth rate
1987	21	5	6
1988	20	5	5
1989	17	7	5
1990	16	6	4
1991	16	6	3
1992	18	5	1
1993	23	5	−1
1994	24	5	2
1995	23	5	3
1996	22	4	2
1997	21	2	4
1998	19	2	4
1999	16	2	4
2000	14	3	4
2001	10	4	4
2002	11	3	3
2003	11	3	3
2004	11	3	3
2005		3	3

Source: World Bank Development Indicators, Instituto Nacional de Estadística.

Spain achieved the convergence criteria of Maastricht in time for the 1999 launch of the Euro. Symbolically, the Spanish economy had matured, changing from a leading recipient of EU structural and cohesion funds, to only having eligibility for further cohesion funds on a transitional basis from 2007–2013.[105]

ETA violence

Despite the successful continuation of democracy and the granting of autonomy to all communities of Spain, violence continues, as shown in table 7.7. ETA continues to operate with kidnappings and killings. Each year from 1987 to 1997, ETA kidnapped one person a year, with the exception of 1996, in which two individuals were kidnapped.[106] The two people kidnapped that year were later released, after being held for an extensive amount of time. For example, Jose Antonio Ortega, a Spanish prison officer, was held for 522 days. A better indication of the trend of ETA's activity can

Table 7.7 Spain: non-state terrorist incidents with attributions of responsibility and by type of attack, 1987–2004

	Terrorist incidents with attributions of responsibility					Terrorist incidents by type				Deaths from ETA Violence
	ETA	Violent right	Violent left	Other separatist	Unknown	Bombings	Armed attacks	Arson	Kidnapping	
1987	7	0	0	24	0	30	1	0	0	52
1988	20	0	6	6	0	20	8	1	1	21
1989	37	0	7	2	0	23	19	0	1	19
1990	19	0	3	5	0	25	2	0	0	25
1991	24	0	0	0	0	13	1	0	0	46
1992	10	1	0	0	0	5	2	0	0	26
1993	9	0	4	0	0	10	2	0	1	14
1994	4	0	0	0	0	1	3	0	0	12
1995	10	0	0	0	0	5	3	0	1	15
1996	25	0	0	0	0	20	2	0	2	5
1997	19	0	0	2	0	8	7	0	1	13
1998	8	0	0	2	0	8	2	0	0	6
1999	0	3	0	0	0	1	0	3	0	0
2000	26	0	0	0	1	10	10	0	0	23
2001	21	0	0	0	1	15	5	0	0	15
2002	12	0	0	0	0	10	1	0	0	5
2003	14	0	0	0	0	11	2	0	0	3
2004	24	0	0	0	0	23	1	0	0	0

Source: TWEED; deaths from ETA violence are from Ministry of the Interior, www.mir.es/DGRIS/Terrorismo_de_ETA/esp/p12b-esp.htm.

be seen in the number of people killed and the number of ETA incidents. The years of 1987 and 1991 were the bloodiest. After 1991, a general decrease in deaths due to ETA occurred. However, ETA remained dangerous. For example, in 1995 ETA almost killed opposition leader and future prime minister José Maria Aznar of the Partido Popular in a car bomb. After the breakdown of the 1998 cease-fire and return to violence in 2000, twenty-three people were killed that year alone. However, violence began tapering off, with two years of relative peace until 2006, reflecting the fitful peace process and changing public opinion about the use of violence after both the 11 September and 11 March attacks. After the attacks in the United States, ETA suggested that violence would end in response to a vote on independence in the Basque country, but Aznar rejected the proposition.[107]

Despite the general decrease in ETA activities, there has been an increase in other ETA activity; specifically the actions of the ETA youth wing, Jarrai, and street violence (kale borroka). Jarrai attacks utilize Molotov cocktails, arson, and so on, and target homes, businesses, political offices, and cars. For example, in 1997 these actions caused millions of dollars of damage.[108] Additionally, the street violence continued during the fourteen month ETA cease-fire of September 1999.[109]

As of 1998, ETA's strength was estimated to be limited to forty gunmen, eighty more individuals ready to be trained, and five hundred active supporters.[110] There have been two significant changes in ETA. First, new recruits to ETA have differed from original members. Since the mid-1980s, a majority of new recruits have been from urban areas and many new members lack 'primordial traits as part of their individual profile'.[111] Second, the targets of ETA violence have expanded, especially since the mid-1990s. In the past, mostly military or police were targeted. Table 7.8 describes the victims of terrorist violence. Recently, many more civilians have been targeted, including Basque politicians, professors, business people, journalists, non-nationalist Basque citizens, and others critical of ETA violence.[112] This is especially true in regard to the street violence.[113] Reflecting the changing targets of ETA, it is evident that the relative composition of the typical victim has shifted, from a

Table 7.8 Spain: characteristics of victims of non-state violence

Demographic characteristic	TWEED (1987–2006)				Ministro del Interior (1968–2006)	
	ETA	Violent right	Violent left	Other separatists	ETA violence	
Military or police	107	0	7	2	*Location*	
Senior civil servants	9	0	0	0	País Vasco	547
Politicians	20	0	0	0	Madrid	123
Business executives	1	0	0	0	Cataluña	55
Union leaders	0	0	0	0	Navarra	40
Clergy	0	0	0	0	Others	54
Civilians	82	1	3	4	*Demographic class*	
Total	219	1	10	6	Military or police	478
					Civilian	341
					Total	819

Sources: TWEED, Ministry of the Interior.

predominantly military or police target to a slight majority of civilian and politician targets.

Spanish state response

As noted in chapter five, part of the early problems of excessive arrests and indiscriminate response can be linked to the fact that the institutions charged with counterterrorism were Francoist institutions undergoing reform. However, since the late 1980s there has been significant improvement. GAL activity ended in 1987 and its leaders prosecuted. In the summer of 1998, José Luis Barrionuevo, former minister of security (interior) from 1982–1988, Secretary of State for Security Rafael Vera Vizcaya civil governor Julian Sancristobal, and nine others were found guilty of kidnapping and murdering suspected terrorists. They each received sentences of ten years, although in December 1998 Barrionuevo and Vera were released pending appeal. The victims' families have received compensation. Although there were questions about the complicity of former prime minister Felipe González, he avoided being charged in the November 1996 proceedings in the Supreme Court.

Since 1988, police counterterrorist actions have become much more targeted. 'No single episode of illegal violence in the state response to ETA has been reported since that time [1988]' and the number of people arrested for terrorism and eventually prosecuted went up to 60 per cent.[114] The improved and professionalized effort had paid off. For example, in 2003 more than 150 members and supporters, including ETA commando leaders, were arrested in Spain and France.[115] From 2002 to 2003, more than 250 suspected ETA members and supporters were arrested. This roundup may have captured most of the existing leadership, which may provide opportunities for the emergence of a new, younger, and possibly more radical, leadership. This occurred previously after the 1992 arrest of top leaders. After their arrest, there was a change in ETA strategy, as reflected by the increasing use of street violence.[116]

Leaders of the main parties were committed to cooperation in regard to terrorism until recently. In January 1998, El Pacto de Ajuria Enea was signed. This agreement between the main political parties (Basque Nationalists and Spanish parties) in País Vasco was to work together towards the pacification and normalization of País Vasco. Signatories included leaders of the Alianza Popular, Centro Democrático y Social, Euskadiko Ezkerra, Partido Nacionalista Vasco, and the Partido Socialista de Euskadi–PSOE). All agreed that the recovery of liberties and democratic freedoms and the approval of the Estatuto de Gernika created a radically different situation from that before the transition and removed the justification for terrorism in Basque society. 'We Basque parties through the legitimacy conferred upon us through democratic defence and the peaceful self-government for our community reject and condemn ETA.'[117] Later that year, another agreement was struck. The Acuerdo de Lazarra/ Pacto de Estella Pact of 12 September 1998, between PNV, HB, EE, and other Basque Nationalist parties, created a process of open dialogue and negotiation to end the conflict, without limitation on which agents can participate (for example ETA). This declaration also proclaimed the right of the Basque people to determine their own future. This effort initially succeeded. ETA declared its first unconditional cease-fire on 16 September 1998, shortly before the elections. Prime Minister Aznar rejected the call for a referendum and instead called for ETA to disarm and renounce violence before any talks between parties could begin.[118] In November 1998, Prime Minister Aznar approved talks with groups linked to ETA.

ETA organized its demands around five points: the end to police prosecution in Spain and in France, the transfer of ETA prisoners to the Basque countries, a solution for ETA members in exile, the easing of conditions for prisoners who had completed most of their sentences, and the improvement of conditions of the imprisoned leaders of HB.[119] The cease-fire ended in November 1999. ETA blamed the government for the lack of progress on peace talks. The truce was broken by ETA in January 2000.[120] In response, an estimated one million Spaniards protested in the streets in response to the recent attacks. As these attempts with the moderate Nationalists to broker a peace failed after the cease-fire of September 1998 ended, the PP and the PSOE agreed to work together in 2000.[121] Moreover, a prerequisite for any agreement would be acceptance of the 1978 constitution and the Estatuto de Guernica. After the failure of the 1998 cease-fire, the main Spanish parties became more intolerant of radical Basque parties, culminating in the banning of Batasuna. Herri Batasuna was part of the ETA network. In the past, its spokesman had been convicted of kidnapping and a parliamentarian was convicted of terrorism. In 1996, Judge Garzon linked ETA to HB via a shared propaganda campaign.[122] In December 1997, twenty-three leaders of HB were imprisoned for collaborating with ETA. A desire to ban HB can be seen in the Ley Orgánica de Partidos Políticos (LOPP), passed in June 2002. LOPP targeted certain parties by excluding members who had been convicted of certain crimes, allowing the banning of parties that justify or excuse attacks on individuals because of nationality, ideology, beliefs, and so on, and preventing new parties that refer to previously banned parties. Typically, the party would refer to terrorist attacks as incidents or lay blame on the central government for provoking them.[123] HB, founded in 1978, has had many names, partially in response to attempts to ban it. In 1998, it was called Euskal Herritarok, in 2001 Batasuna. Similarly, its youth organization changed names in response to legal pressure from Jarrai to Segi, after Jarri became an illegal organization.[124] In August 2002, Batasuna was suspended for three years due to alleged links to ETA. By March 2003, the party had been banned indefinitely by the Tribunal Supremo, which based its decision on the LOPP. Much of the outrage that led to the banning was precipitated by HB's refusal to condemn the August 2002 bombings in Alicante. In November 2001, the leadership of Gestoras pro Amnistía, an organization that supported the families of ETA prisoners, was arrested and group activities were declared illegal, due to the presumption that the group was part of ETA. The following month the organization was added to the EU's, list of terrorist groups and entities. In February 2003, the only exclusively Basque language paper, *Euskaldunon Egunkaria*, was closed and ten of its employees arrested.[125]

Security

Spanish rejection of ETA is well illustrated by the case of a twenty-nine year old small town councilman, Miguel Angel Blanco. ETA kidnapped him in 1997, demanding the transfer of 500 prisoners from all over Spain to the Basque country in exchange for his release. The Spanish state refused the demand. The Pope and Amnesty International called for his safe release. Its demands rejected, ETA executed the young politician and abandoned his body to be found. In response, approximately six million Spaniards marched to protest his assassination by ETA. At the same time, ETA's political party HB led a march of 30,000 in support of ETA and independence from Spain. However, even in País Vasco, support for ETA has declined. In 1987, 7 per cent of those surveyed thought ETA was totally or somewhat justified, an additional 12 per cent supported the ends but not the means, 19 per cent said they had supported ETA earlier but not currently, and 34 per cent completely rejected the group. By the end of 2006, only 4 per cent of those surveyed thought ETA was totally or somewhat justified, an additional 13 per cent supported the ends but not the means, 19 per cent said they had supported ETA earlier but not currently, and 50 per cent completely rejected the group.[126]

In October 1997, the Spanish government accused the leaders of HB of being little more than a front for ETA. They were charged with condoning terrorism. The charges were precipitated by HB's distribution of an ETA video during the 1996 general election campaign. The leaders were arrested and sent to trial. The twenty-three leaders of the party were tried and convicted. Each was sentenced to seven years in prison. Although the numbers killed were relatively low, the targets were very salient. In a region normally insulated from ETA violence in southern Spain, in the city of Seville, ETA killed a local politician Alberto Jimenez Becerril and his wife on 30 January 1998. Jimenez Becerril was the first town councillor killed outside the Basque country. The same month, another councilman was killed by a bomb in Zarauz on the northern coast of the country. Later that year in June, another town councillor was killed by ETA in Renteria, in northern Spain.[127] In August 2002, two people (including a six year old girl) were killed by a car bomb in Alicante. Other high level victims of the forty-eight killed since 2000 included the shooting of the PSOE spokesman of the Basque parliament, the killing of seven town councillors, the deaths of two members of the Ertzaintza, and the murder of a general.

Table 7.9 presents both Basque and Spanish public opinion data. Concern about ETA terrorism remained high.

Table 7.9 Spanish public opinion, 1993–2006

	Basque public opinion						Spanish public opinion			
	Satisfaction with democracy		Principal problem				Satisfaction with democracy		Principal problems according (top three)	
	Very and satisfied enough	Little or not at all satisfied	Unemployment	Violence and terrorism	Social inequality		Very and satisfied enough	Little or not at all satisfied	Terrorism/ ETA	Unemployment
1993	28	71					41	55		
1993a							40	55		
1994							29	67		
1994b							39	58		
1995a	32	65	60	17	8		41	56	19	58
1995b	45	48	53	23	4					
1996			44	34	4					
1997	33	63					55	41		
1998			53	23	5		50	44		
1999a	50	43	60	14	7		72	25	61	77
1999b	54	43					68	28		
2000a	52	45	40	28	9		81	19		
2000b	42	56	29	36	10		73	25		

2001a	51	45	29	36	10			63
2001b	51	44	26	39	8	63	32	63
2002a	37	59	34	30	9			55
2002b	38	58	32	29	13			66
2003a	31	65	35	25	9			42
2003b	37	61	31	24	12			63
2004a	43	55	30	25	8	65		66
2004b	45	52	26	20	10		32	60
2005a	43	55	27	22	15			41
2005b	38	55	32	14	20			58
2006a	43	46	24	7	23			25
2006b	40	57	21	18	17			50

Source: Euskobarómetro, www.ehu.es/cpvweb/paginas/series_eusko/series_08.html, *Euskobarómetro*. www.ehu.es/cpvweb/paginas/series_eusko/series_05.html. Centro de Investigaciones Sociológicas 'What are, in your opinion, the three principal problems that exist in Spain?' (Maximum three responses.) Note, all the national survey figures are from April. Eurobarometer http://ec.europa.eu/public_opinion/.

Note: The *Euskobarómetro* poll only allows one choice, whereas the national poll allows up to three selections.

According to Gallup España polls, interestingly, concern was much higher in 1997, even though fewer people were killed than in 1995.[128] However, two of those killed were from Seville, a city usually immune from ETA activity. The concern about terrorism had more than doubled since 1986, increasing from 28 per cent to 61 per cent. The comparison between the Basque country and the whole of Spain is complicated by the fact that the national data allow three choices of principal problems, whereas the Basque poll only allows one choice. Nationally, concern for terrorism is high in 2004, after the Al Qaeda attacks in Madrid, but it drops as incidents of terrorism fall and during the ETA cease-fire. A more revealing comparison is the concern about terrorism compared with unemployment. In the Basque country, concern about terrorism is higher in 2000 and 2001, after ETA's return to violence in 2000.

Integration

Recently, there have been both positive and negative trends in Spain in terms of integration. On the positive side, nationally, in 2001, the Spanish parliament recognized the maquis, Republican guerrillas who fought against Franco, symbolizing national reconciliation. In the Basque country, there has been a significant growth of the peace movements. Gesto por la Paz began to mobilize after ETA killings in 1986. In 1988, multiple groups created the Coordinadora Gesto por la Paz de Eskal Herria, which by 2001 had over 130 participating groups. Other groups, such as Denon Artean, Bakea Orain, and Eklarri were formed in the early 1990s in support of peace.[129] However, a troubling development is the split of Basque Nationalist parties from Basque peace groups.[130] Moreover, in the Basque country many citizens who do not support ETA or violence continue to report threats, harassment, and violence. For example, according to an open letter from university professors in the Basque country, 'Many Basque citizens suffer an intolerable limitation on our liberty and security by peacefully opposing ETA and the groups that benefit from terrorism.'[131] Additionally, some fear that the banning of parties is counterproductive. 'The banning of Batasuna has been instrumentalized to reinforce a nationalist discourse aimed at delegitimizing Spanish democracy ... it also fulfils ETA's wishes of polarization.'[132]

Since the attacks and elections of March 2004, there has been a growing polarization about how to deal with terrorism and this disagreement about how to respond to terrorism has become politicized. Days before the 2004 elections, on 11 March, four commuter trains were bombed in Madrid, killing 191 and injuring an additional 1755. The next evening, approximately a quarter of Spaniards demonstrated against the attacks. However, by the next day additional demonstrations focused on demands that the PP government provide more information about the attacks.[133] There was growing concern that the PP was politicizing concern about terrorism and was attempting to take advantage of the attack before the elections. Prime Minister Aznar had an aggressive media campaign that blamed ETA for the attacks. Moreover, the diplomatic corps also blamed ETA for the attacks. In fact, Aznar convinced the UN Security Council to condemn ETA for the attacks.[134] Eventually, the Al Qaeda related group, the Moroccan Islamic Combatant Group, was blamed and Aznar had to apologize to the UN for insisting on ETA's culpability.[135] In the end, the PSOE candidate Zapatero won the election in an upset, despite the significant economic improvement under Aznar's PP and the PP's tough anti-terrorism stance against ETA. Post-election polls confirmed a wide belief (80.8 per cent) that information had been manipulated or withheld by Aznar's government, with 28.8 per cent believing that the PP attempted to use the attacks for electoral gain.[136]

The period since the elections has been marked by a sharply different relationship between the PP and PSOE, which had pledged to work together for national pacification in 2000. This divergence can be seen in terms of major party support for new autonomy statutes. When Zapatero assumed office in 2004, he stated his desire to have all seventeen regions renegotiate the autonomy statutes. By the end of 2006, Andalusia and Catalonia had revised their autonomy statutes. The Catalan was accepted by the Cortés in Madrid and accepted via referendum in June 2006 in Catalonia. The PP opposed the Andalusian statute and the Catalan. Furthermore, the PP considered the statute unconstitutional and appealed to the Supreme Court in autumn 2006. An attempt to revise the Basque statute of autonomy passed the Basque parliament in December 2004, but was rejected by the national Congress in early 2005. Despite the failure in Madrid, the leader of the EA described the rejected Plan Ibarretxe as the minimal foundation to solve the Basque conflict.[137]

The increasing tension is also evident in relation to continued attempts at peace talks. In May 2005, Prime Minister Zapatero offered peace talks with ETA if the group disarmed. However, a protest of between 240,000 and 850,000 people ensued against the proposition of talks with ETA, organized by the opposition PP.[138] In March 2006, ETA declared a cease-fire, and the next month Prime Minister Zapatero agreed to peace talks. Shortly after Zapatero announced the cease-fire, the PP withdrew support for the peace process because of government contact with members of the banned Batasuna. However, the process was ended after the December 2006 bombing at the airport in Madrid. Tension between the PSOE and the PP continued to increase after December 2006.[139] In February, the PP announced it would not meet with the PSOE for any additional meetings related to the Pacto Antiterrorista.[140] By March 2007, relations had worsened after the reduction of prison sentence of ETA prisoner Iñaki de Juana Chaos, who had been on a hunger strike. In response, the PP organized massive protests of 337,000 to 342,000 people, against the PSOE government's decision. Despite assurances by PP leader Rajoy that the protests were civil and democratic, PSOE leaders charged that the PP would 'pass into history as the first opposition party that called its militants to demonstrate in the streets against an antiterrorism policy of a democratic government'. In short, the PSOE accused the PP of politicizing counterterrorism policy.[141] Not only is this breakdown in cooperation troubling because of the increasing polarization over how to respond to terrorism, but it calls into question the viability of any future agreement the PSOE government may make with ETA or any moderate Nationalist group.

Citizen support and democratic stability

Table 7.9 provides measures of satisfaction with democracy, both in the Basque country and in Spain generally. In terms of satisfaction with democracy, the trend roughly mirrors major events related to ETA. There are dips in satisfaction in 1997 (the year twenty-three HB leaders were jailed) and a decrease in 2002 (suspension of HB). Evaluations are relatively positive in 1999 and early 2000, despite the return of ETA violence. Evaluations improved in 2006, during the ETA cease-fire. It is troublesome that since 2002, with the exception of one poll, more respondents were little or not at all satisfied with democracy, although the numbers are not as low as they were in 1993. National evaluations of Spanish democracy are consistently higher than in the Basque country. They improve in the late 1990s, as unemployment rates finally begin to fall. The peak in support tapers off in the second half of 2000, as ETA returns to violence. Nonetheless, moderate to strong support for democracy is consistently a majority view across the nation of Spain.

Although, in general, civil–military relations have been stable since 1986, some troubling signs remain. In accordance with the state's policy of preventing military intervention while mollifying the military, the state acted to appease military members after the coup attempt. A reform package, including early retirement with full pay and additional promotions, was put into practice to reduce the number of officers.[142] This expensive plan was successful without aggravating relations with the military. In addition, due to military pressure an emergency powers law was passed, although it was later modified to stress civilian control. At the same time, a law 'for the defence of the constitution' was passed, making it an offence to apologize for terrorists or plot against the constitution.[143] However, as late as January 2006, and before the June 2006 Catalan referendum on the new autonomy statute for the region, the head of the army was replaced and put under house arrest after suggesting military action as a way to curb autonomy in Catalonia.

Spain summary

Most scholars consider Spanish democracy to be fully consolidated. The violence of ETA is decreasing and the support for violent struggle has also decreased. Efforts to improve integration have improved as the activities of GAL have been prosecuted and uncovered, popular opposition to violence has increased, and new autonomy agreements are being discussed. However, since 2004 Spanish unity in dealing with violence has been strained as a new threat has emerged and disagreement in how to proceed has fallen along partisan lines. Satisfaction with democracy remains strong nationally, although less than half of those in the Basque country are satisfied. Disagreements over possible responses to ETA and new autonomy agreements continue to flare up. Moreover, Spanish democracy faces a new foe, as will be discussed in chapter eight.

Notes

1 Linz, 1978, p. 20.
2 My results are confirmed by a different analysis of G. Bingham Powell, see Powell, 1982. Powell concludes: 'I have suggested that party involvement in violence is particularly dangerous to the survival of the democratic regime ... In this decade [1967–1976], at least, deadly violence was virtually a precondition for the suspension of democratic politics ... The special role of party involvement in violence is also evident. In countries where the major parties presented a united front against the use of violence and kept themselves and their supporters from engaging in it, the democratic processes continued unchecked. Where violence involved the parties themselves, even in a limited way, it was much more difficult – for a variety of reasons, including the weakening of the regime's legitimacy and the inability of the democratic forces to join forces in defense of the regime – to sustain a democracy' (Powell, 1982, p. 169). In Powell's regression analysis the numbers of deaths (+.29) and the involvement of parties (+.62) were significant at the .05 level. In his study, when including only cases with more than one death per year, the two variables account for 80 per cent of the variance in the continuity of the democratic regime (Powell, 1982, p. 263, n. 27).
3 Kaufman, p. 58.
4 *Generals and Tupamaros*, pp. 48–49.
5 Kaufman, pp. 58–59.
6 *Caretas* 4 April 1988.
7 Moral cited in Mauceri, 1991, p. 91.
8 Bourque and Warren, p. 26; also *La República* 27 August 1984.
9 'Eso es la famosa estrategia contrasubversiva de la que tanto todos hablan y que no existe'; author translation. Guillermo Denegri, 'Entrevista al General Sinesio Jarama', *Debate* No. 55, March–May 1989, pp. 8–15, p. 9.
10 Mauceri, 1991, p. 98.
11 'Tenemos que tener en cuenta que el productor de coca, el campesino cocalero, era acosado por la policía y por cuanta fuerza de orden existía,

porque era considerado un delincuente... Estamos hablando del 80 per cent de la población! Lo que hacemos, entonces, es modificar esta situación para evitar que el campesino cocalero – la base de la que nutria Sendero para realizar sus actividades – sea hostigado'; author translation. *QueHacer* No. 62 December 1989–January 1990, p. 39.

12 Mauceri, 1991, p. 99.

13 Instead of reapplying an argument about democratic stability, some scholars would advocate the use of the term 'democratic consolidation' A typical definition of consolidation is 'a political regime in which democracy as a complex system of institutions, rules, and patterned incentives and disincentives has become, in a phrase, "the only game in town".' Juan Linz and Alfred Stepan, 'Toward Consolidated Democracies', in Larry Diamond, Marc Plattner, Yun-han Chu, and Hung-mao Tien (eds), *Consolidating the Third Wave Democracies: Themes and Perspectives* (Baltimore: Johns Hopkins University Press, 1997), p. 15. However, none of the main theorists of consolidation believe that consolidated democracies are invincible. As Linz and Stepan note, 'we do not preclude the possibility that at some future time it could break down'. Linz and Stepan, 1997, p. 16. Because of this, some scholars have questioned the utility of such a concept. As Guillermo O'Donnell stated, 'I see little analytical gain in attaching the term "consolidated" to something that will probably though not certainly endure'. Guillermo O'Donnell, 'Illusions about Consolidation', in Larry Diamond et al. (eds), *Consolidating the Third Wave Democracies: Themes and Perspectives* (Baltimore: Johns Hopkins University Press, 1997), p. 44. Moreover, the continuation of arguments of stability is consistent with an Aristotelian approach. Aristotle noted that 'to know the causes which destroy constitutions is also to know the causes which ensure their preservation' (*Pol.* p. 225).

14 Blanco leader Lacalle served as president from 1990–1995.

15 Peter Winn, 'Frente Amplio in Montevideo', *NACLA* Vol. 29, No. 1, July/August 1995, pp. 20–26, p. 20.

16 For an in-depth discussion of the contentious issue of human rights during the transition in Uruguay, see Alexandra Barahona de Brito, *Human Rights and Democratization in Latin America* (Oxford: Oxford University Press, 1997).

17 David Pion-Berlin, 'To Prosecute or to Pardon? Human Rights Decisions in the Latin American Southern Cone', *Human Rights Quarterly* Vol. 16, No. 1, February 1994, pp. 105–130, p. 111.

18 Servicio Paz y Justicia, *Uruguay: Nunca Más* (Philadelphia: Temple Press, 1992).

19 Servicio Paz y Justicia, 1992, pp. 417–430.

20 Servicio Paz y Justicia, 1986, p. 66.

21 Amnesty International, *AI Report 1998: Uruguay* (New York: Amnesty International), www.amnesty.org/ailib/aireport/ar98/amr52.htm.

22 Luis Roniger and Mario Sznajder, 'The Legacy of Human Rights Violations and the Collective Identity of Redemocratized Uruguay', *Human Rights Quarterly* Vol. 19, No. 1, February 1997, pp. 55–77.

23 US Department of State, *Uruguay Country Report on Human Rights Practices for 1996*, released by the Bureau of Democracy, Human

Rights, and Labor, 30 January 1997. www.state.gov/www/global/human_rights/1996_hrp_report/uruguay.html.

24 Felipe Aguero, 'Toward Civilian Supremacy in South America', in Larry Diamond et al. (eds), *Consolidating the Third World Democracies* (Baltimore: Johns Hopkins University Press, 1997), p. 184.

25 María Delgado, 'Truth and Justice in Uruguay', *NACLA Report on the Americas* Vol. 34, No. 1, July/August 2000, pp. 37–40, pp. 37–38.

26 Larry Rohter, 'Uruguay: Compensation for Dictatorship', *New York Times* 22 April 2003, p. A6.

27 BBC News, 'Ex-Rebel to Chair Uruguay Senate', http://news.bbc.co.uk/go/pr/fr/-/2/hi/americas/4269219/stm.

28 BBC News, 'New Find in Uruguay "Missing' Dig"', 3 December 2005, http://news.bbc.co.uk/2/hi/americas/4494286.stm.

29 YOW, 'Prosecutor in Uruguay Seeks to Try Military for Rights Abuses', 30 August 2006, Agence France Presse.

30 Lisl Brunner, 'Uruguay Indicts 8 for Operation Condor Disappearances', *Jurist* 12 September 2006.

31 BBC News, 'Uruguay's Ex-President Arrested', 17 November 2006, http://news.bbc.co.uk/2/hi/americas/6157418.stm.

32 'Uruguay: Bordaberry Charged Again', *Latinnews Daily* 21 December 2006.

33 Raul Garces, 'Uruguayan Ex-Colonel Detained in Brazil, Under Investigation in Military Abuses', Associated Press Newswires, 27 February 2007.

34 Raul Garces, 'Uruguayan Air Force Chief Likens Detention in Rights Probe to Campaign against Military Personnel', Associated Press Newswires, 13 September 2006.

35 'Justicia indagara amenaza de military', *El País de Uruguay* 29 August 2006.

36 Edouard Baibly, 'A Leftwing Government and an Environmental Struggle, Uruguay: Visible at Last', *Le Monde diplomatique* February 2007, http://mondediplo.com/2007/02/11uruguay.

37 'Uruguay: Keeping the Military in Check', Council on Hemispheric Affairs report on the Latin American Military, 20 November 2006, www.coha.org/2006/11/20/uruguay-keeping-the-military-in-check/.

38 Thomas Catan, 'IMF Poised to Grant Extra Funds to Halt Uruguay's Economic Slide', *The Financial Times* 2 August 2002, p. 2.

39 'Uruguay to Repay Debt', *The Grand Rapids Press* 31 March 2006, p. A6.

40 *Latinobarómetro Report 2005* (Santiago: Corporación Latinobarómetro, 2005), p. 51 (compared with 51 per cent in Peru).

41 However, it should be noted that some within the Tupamaro movement continued to contemplate the possibility of armed struggle into the 1990s. 'Hasta los años 90, Tupamaros discutieron lucha armada', *El País de Uruguay* 22 September 2006.

42 'Transitamos por una democracia inútil y una violencia también inútil. Y una corrupción que ha sido útil solo para quienes se

enriqucieron con ella'; author translation. Héctor Béjar, '25 años de Perú', *Socialismo y Participación* No. 94, 2002, pp. 17–26, p. 17.

43 Cameron, 1998, pp. 154–161.
44 US Department of State, *Human Rights Practices*, 1997, www.state.gov/www/global/human_rights/drl_reports.html.
45 Human Rights Watch, *World Report 1999*, www.hrw.org/worldreport99/.
46 Coordinadora Nacional de Derechos Humanos, *Informe Sobre la Situacion de los Derechos Humanos en el Peru en 1996* (Lima, CNDDHH, 1997).
47 For a complete analysis of the faceless courts see Human Rights Watch, *Peru: Presumption of Guilt* (Washington, DC: Human Rights Watch, 1996).
48 Cameron, 1998, p. 130.
49 Cameron, 1998, p. 130.
50 Miguel Jugo, 'Panoram sobre derechos humanos', *Actualidad Peruana* Vol. 8, No. 1, February 1999, http://ekeko.rcp.net.pe/aprodeh/public/acpe99/ap0199.htm.
51 US Department of State, *Human Rights Practices* (Washington, DC: United States. Department of State, 1998).
52 APOYO, Informe de Opinión, Lima, June 1997.
53 APOYO, Informe de Opinión, Lima, April 2000.
54 Poll conducted in Lima by Instituto de Investigaciones Económicas y Sociales, Universidad Nacional de Ingeniería, 18 March 2000.
55 Coordinadora Nacional de Derechos Humanos, *Informe Anual 1998* (Lima: Coordinadora Nacional de Derechos Humanos, 1999), http://www.cnddhh.org.pe/98_indice.htm.
56 'Se estaría jugando con la dignidad de los más pobres', *El Colmo* 30 July 2004, http://anteriores.epensa.com.pe/enlinea/ediciones/2004/jul/30/politica/pol01.asp.
57 Jo-Marie Burt and Jose Lopez Ricci, 'Shining Path After Guzman', *NACLA* Vol. 28, No. 3, 1996, pp. 6–9, p. 6.
58 Human Rights Watch, 1996, p. 31.
59 Human Rights Watch, 1999.
60 APRODEH,<gopher://gopher.rcp.net.pe:70/00/otros-gopher/nacionales/aprodeh/violencia/01>.
61 'World Briefing', compiled by Christopher S. Wren; *New York Times* 5 January 1999.
62 See W. Alejandro Sanchez, 'The Rebirth of Insurgency in Peru', *Small Wars and Insurgencies* Vol. 14, No. 3, autumn 2003, pp. 185–198 for a recent discussion about Sendero Luminoso and its potential to rebound.
63 'García Forges Ahead with His Own War on Terror', *Latin American Andean Group Report* 11 January 2007.
64 Marion Barbel, 'Insurgency/Human Rights Questions Dominate Peruvian Politics', *Global Insight Daily Analysis* 22 January 2007.

65 US Department of State, *Human Rights Practices* (Washington, DC: United States. Department of State, 1994).
66 US Department of State, 1997.
67 Human Rights Watch, *World Report 1999*. See also US Department of State, 1998.
68 US Department of State, *Human Rights Practices* (Washington, DC: Government Printing Office, 1999).
69 'War on Sendero to be Fought on New Front', *Latin American Andean Group Report* 7 October 2003.
70 Human Rights Watch, 1996, pp. 2–5. See also Coordinadora Nacional de Derechos Humanos, *Informe Sobre la Situación de los Derechos Humanos de el Perú en 1995* (Lima: Coordinadora de Derechos Humanos, 1996) and APRODEH et al., *Los Inocentes Tienen Nombre* (Lima: Grafimace S.A., 1995).
71 Coordinadora Nacional de Derechos Humanos, 1997, http://www.cnddhh.org.pe/96informe.htm.
72 Human Rights Watch, *Torture and Political Persecution in Peru* (New York: Human Rights Watch, 1998).
73 Human Rights Watch, 1996, p. 3.
74 US Department of State, 1997.
75 US Department of State, 1998.
76 Amnesty International, Peru: Legislation is Not Enough. Torture Must Be Abolished in Practice (New York: Amnesty International, September 1999). Amnesty International, Peru: Torture Continues Unabated (New York: Amnesty International, December 2000).
77 US Department of State, 1997.
78 Amnesty International, *Annual Report 1999: Peru* (New York: Amnesty International, 1999).
79 Carlos Ivan Degregori, 'Reflexiones sobre la Comisión de la Verdad y Reconciliación', *Socialismo y Participación* No. 94, 2002, pp. 93–98, p. 97, fn 1.
80 Amnesty International, *Annual Report 2001: Peru* (New York: Amnesty International, 2001).
81 'Thumbs Down for Toledo's Compensation Plan for Victims of Political Violence' *Latin American Andean Group Report* 2 December 2003.
82 See Comisión de la Verdad y Reconciliacón, *Informe Final*, Tomo, Capítulo 2: Los casos investigados por la CVR, Section 2.45. Las ejecciones extrajudiciales en barrios altos (1991).
83 US Department of State. Bureau of Democracy, Human Rights, and Labor, *Country Reports on Human Rights Practices – 2006* 6 March 2007, www.state.gov/g/drl/rls/hrrpt/2006/78902.htm.
84 'Violence – Sendero Sends Out a Brutal Reminder – But Are the Maoists Merely Hoping to Negotiate a Deal?', *Latin American Andean Group Report* 28 August 2001.
85 Gino Costa and Rachel Neild, 'Police Reform in Peru', *Australian and New Zealand Journal of Criminology* Vol. 38, No. 2, 2005, pp. 216–

229. See also the works of Instituto de Defensa Legal for an extensive collection of works covering the police and intelligence reform attempts in Peru: www.idl.org.pe/.
86 APOYO, Informe de Opinión, Lima, September 1997.
87 APOYO, Informe de Opinión, Lima, August 1997.
88 FBIS LAT 92 117, p. 38, Poll Shows Majority Supports Fujimori, Coup', Lima, Panamericana Television Network, 15 June 1992.
89 *Pretextos,* Documentos de trabajo (Lima: DESCO, División de Investigaciones), Vol. 3, p. 43.
90 Palmer, 1996, p. 72.
91 *Pretextos,* Vol. 3, p. 46.
92 FBIS LAT 92 097, p. 43, 'National Poll Reflects Approval of Fujimori', Lima, Panamericana Television Network, 18 May 1992.
93 FBIS LAT 97 363,'Peru: Poll gives Fujimori, Montesinos Lowest Popularity Ratings'.
94 APOYO, *Informe de Opinión,* Lima, September 1997.
95 APOYO, *Informe de Opinión,* Lima, August 1997.
96 Carlos Basombrio, *Seguridad ciudadana y actuación del estado: análisis de tendencias de opinion pública* (Lima: Instituto de Defensa Legal, 2004), p. 94.
97 APOYO, *Informe de Opinión,* Lima, July 1997.
98 Kenneth M. Roberts and Moises Arce, 'Neoliberalism and Lower Class Voting Behavior in Peru', *Comparative Political Studies* Vol. 31 No. 2, April–May 1998, pp. 217–247.
99 Carol Graham and Cheikh Kane, 'Opportunistic Government or Sustaining Reform? Electoral Trends and Public-Expenditure Patterns in Peru, 1990–1995', *Latin American Research Review* Vol. 33, No. 1 (1998), pp. 67–104. See also Norbert Shady, 'Seeking Votes: The Political Economy of Expenditures by the Peruvian Social Fund (FONCODES), 1991–95', Policy Research Working Paper, no. WPS 2166, World Bank.
100 'Mecánica naranja', *Caretas* 24 June 1999.
101 Carter Center, 'Statement of the NDI/Carter Center February 2000 Pre-election Delegation to Peru', Lima, 11 February 2000, www.cartercenter.org/REPORTS/perustatement.html.
102 Javier Herrera, 'Gobernabilidad, corrupción, participación ciudadana y pobreza en el Perú, 2002', working paper of the Ministerio de Economía y Finanzas, www.mef.gob.pe/propuesta/ESPEC/Gobernabilidad_en_el_Peru_2002.pdf pp. 13–14.
103 *Latin American Andean Group Report* 8 June 2004.
104 APOYO, *Informe de Opinión,* Lima, June 2006.
105 European Commission, <ec.europa.eu/regional_policy/sources/docoffic/official/regulation/newregl0713_en.htm>.
106 Spanish Ministry of the Interior, http:www.mir.es/oris/infoeta/esp/p9c-esp.htm.

107 William Shepard, 'The ETA: Spain Fights Europe's Last Active Terrorist Group', *Mediterranean Quarterly* Vol. 13, No. 1, 2002, pp. 54–68, p. 55.

108 US Department of State, *Spain Country Report on Human Rights Practices for 1997* (Washington, DC: United States. Department of State, 1998), http:www.state.gov/www/global/humanrights/1997_hrp_report/spain.html.

109 Hanspeter Van Den Broek, 'Borroka – the Legitimation of Street Violence in the Political Discourse of Radical Basque Nationalists', *Terrorism and Political Violence* Vol. 16, No. 4, Winter 2004, pp. 714–736, p. 730.

110 Adela Gooch, 'ETA Youths Test Ceasefire, Arson Greets Prime Minister's First Trip to the Region Since the Truce', *The Guardian* 28 September 1998.

111 Fernando Reinares, 'Who are the Terrorists? Analyzing the Changes in Sociological Profile among Members of ETA', *Studies in Conflict and Terrorism* Vol. 27, No. 6, 2004b, pp. 465–488, p. 480, 482.

112 Alonso and Reinares, pp. 266, 276.

113 Van Den Broek, p. 727.

114 Alonso and Reinares, p. 275.

115 Ingrid Van Biezen, 'Terrorism and Democratic Legitimacy: Conflicting Interpretations of the Spanish Elections', *Mediterranean Politics* Vol. 10, No. 1, March 2005, pp. 99–108, p. 100.

116 Fred Burton, 'The Resurgence of Spain's Basque Militants', 17 December 2004, Stratfor.

117 'Esta condena y rechazo de ETA la hacemos los partidos vascos desde la legitimidad que nos confiere la defensa democrática y pacífica del autogobierno para nuestro pueblo'; author translation, http://www.elmundo.es/eta/documentos/pacto_ajuria_enea.html.

118 Patty Li Peiyin, 'Will It Hold?', *Harvard International Review* Vol. 21, Issue 1, Winter 1998/1999, pp. 10–11.

119 Emma Daly, 'Spain's Basques See N. Ireland as Peace Model: Europe's Other War', *Christian Science Monitor* 13 November 1998.

120 See Ludger Mees, *Nationalism, Violence and Democracy: The Basque Clash of Identities* (London: Palgrave Macmillan, 2004), for an in-depth discussion of the emergence of the Basque conflict and the attempts to create a peace process in the 1990s.

121 'Acuerdo por las libertades y contra el terrorismo', www.elmundo.es/eta/documentos/pacto_libertades.html, 12 December 2000.

122 Katherine Sawyer, 'Comment: Rejection of the Weimarian Politics or Betrayal of Democracy? Spain's Proscription of Batasuna under the European Convention of Human Rights', *American University Law Review* Vol. 52, No. 6, August 2003, pp. 1540–1552.

123 Leslie Turano, 'Spain: Banning Political Parties as a Response to Basque Terrorism', *International Journal of Constitutional Law* Vol. 1, No. 4, October 2003, pp. 732–738.

124 Turano, p. 730, fn 2.

125 Human Rights Watch, 'In the Name of Counter-terrorism: Human Rights Abuses Worldwide: A Human Rights Watch Briefing Paper for the 59th Session of the United Nations Commission on Human Rights', 25 March 2003.

126 *Euskobarómetro,* www.ehu.es/cpvweb/pags_directas/euskobarometro FR.html.

127 Adela Gooch, 'Terror Campaign: ETA Gunman Kills Couple in Seville', *The Guardian* 31 January 1998 and 18 September 1998.

128 Gallup Spain, November 1997, OPP 302.

129 Benjamín Tejerina, 'Protest Cycle, Political Violence and Social Movements in the Basque Country', *Nations and Nationalism* Vol. 7 No. 1, 2001, pp. 39–57. See also Benjamín Tejerina, J. M. Fernández-Sobrado, and X. y Aierdi, *Sociedad civil, protesta y movimientos sociales en el País Vasco* (Vitoria: Eusko Jaurlarilza-Gobierno Vasco, 1995).

130 'Arzalluz dice que ¡Basta Ya! crea un "clima a favor de la guerra sucia"' *Deia* 24 February 2003, www.deia.com/es/hemeroteca/object.php?o=68916.

131 'Muchos ciudadanos vascos sufrimos una limitación intolerable de nuestra libertad y seguridad por oponernos pacíficamente a ETA y a los grupos que se benefician del terrorismo'; author translation; 'Profesores de la Universidad vasca denuncian que la mafia que apoya a ETA actúa impunemente', *El Mundo* 27 February 2002. http://www.elmundo.es/eta/documentos/manifiesto_upv.html.

132 Alonso and Reinares, p. 271.

133 'Miles de personas exigen en las calles españolas que se les diga la verdad antes de votar', *El País* 14 March 2004.

134 See the following articles on the March 2004 elections. Raj S. Chari, 'The 2004 Spanish Election: Terrorism as a Catalyst for Change?', *West European Politics* Vol. 27, No. 5, November 2004, pp. 954–963; Van Biezen; Charles Powell, 'Did Terrorism Sway Spain's Election?', *Current History* November 2004, pp. 376–382, p. 376; Paddy Woodworth, 'Spain Changes Course: Aznar's Legacy, Zapatero's Prospects', *World Policy Journal* Vol. 21, No. 2 Summer 2004, pp. 7–26.

135 Isabel Piquer, 'España se disculpa ante la ONU por insistir en ETA', *El País* 16 March 2004.

136 Van Biezen, p. 104.

137 A. Guenaga, 'EA asegura que el "plan Ibarretxe" es el listón mínimo para superar el "conflicto vasco"', *El País* 11 June 2006.

138 'Zapatero asegura que "escucha con respeto" a los que ayer le pidieron que no negocie con ETA El PP emplaza al presidente a elegir entre Batasuna o los manifestantes de Madrid' *El País* 5 June 2005.

139 'Zapatero afirma estar dispuesto a hacer "todo lo posible" para sumar al Partido Popular al consenso antiterrorista. El presidente pide a PP y PNV que no planteen condiciones previas para un nuevo pacto contra ETA', *El País* 17 January 2006.

140 Anabel Díez and Carlos Cué, 'El PP se niega a acudir a más reuniones preparatorias del Pacto Antiterrorista', *El País* 23 February 2007.

141 'Pasar a la historia como el primer partido de la oposición que convoca a sus militantes a manifestarse en la calle contra la política antiterrorista de un Gobierno democrático'; author translation. The protests were 'Blanco reprocha a Rajoy haber olvidado en su discurso a las víctimas de Irak y del 11-M', *El País* 11 March 2007.

142 Payne, 1986, p. 188.

143 Lancaster and Prevost, p. 114.

8

Al Qaeda in *al-Andalus*: lessons learned from domestic terrorism

The main questions addressed in this book are how both terrorism and the state response to terrorism affect democratic stability. The cases, thus far, have examined domestic terrorist groups. However, Spain has both domestic and international terrorists. How can the lessons learned in the domestic context help further understanding of the effects of international terrorism and the state's response to an international terrorist threat? The Peruvian, Spanish, and Uruguayan cases have clarified how both terrorist violence and state repression undermine security and integration, and ultimately citizen support of democracy. Does an approach based on understanding citizen support extend to an international threat? Can understanding these conflicts based upon security, integration, citizen support, and democratic stability inform discussions in democracies facing threats of international terrorism? This chapter will examine Spain's conflict with al Qaeda related groups using the lessons learned from the domestic context.

Security

Al Qaeda-related individuals were active in Spain before the Madrid attacks.[1] After the September 11 2001 attacks in the United States, one suspected sleeper cell of the Grupo Salafista para la Predicación y el Combate (GSPC) was discovered to be operating in five Spanish provinces. Later in 2001, Spanish members of Syrian origin were detained because of their membership in the Hamburg cell of al Qaeda.[2] The simultaneous attacks on four Madrid commuter trains near

Atocha station on 11 March 2004 killed 191 and injured an additional 1755.

Once attributions of responsibility had settled on the al Qaeda related neosalafist[3] jihadi groups, many blamed PP prime minister Aznar's participation in the war in Iraq and the increased ties to the United States for attracting the ire of al Qaeda.[4] Previously, in an October 2003 interview aired on al-Jazeera, Bin Laden threatened to punish Britain, Spain, Australia, Poland, Japan, and Italy for backing Bush in Iraq. Although Prime Minister Zapatero has removed Spanish troops from Iraq, this is unlikely to end the danger to Spain from al Qaeda related threats. Egyptian Islamic Jihad founder and al Qaeda second in command Ayman Al Zawahiri referred to *al-Andalus* 'as a promised land that one day would revert to Islamic rule'.[5] *Al-Andalus* refers to the past Islamic rule of parts of the Iberian Peninsula, including most of Spain and Portugal. Islamic rule of Spain ended in 1492 when the Catholic monarchs Ferdinand and Isabella conquered Granada, expelled the last Moorish king, Bilbao, and unified Spain. The repeated references to *al-Andalus* since 2003 by Osama Bin Laden and Al Zawahiri signify that Spain is likely to remain a target. In another warning found in a 2004 video left by terrorists before their death, threats and attacks would continue in *Andalus* until martyrdom in the land of Tarik ben Ziyad. This refers to the Moorish invasion of the Iberian Peninsula, led by Tarik ben Ziyad in 711, which resulted in an eight-century Moorish presence in Spain.[6]

Furthermore, Spain is strategically located near North Africa. The Spanish enclave cities of Ceuta and Melilla, which are surrounded by Morocco, are key transit points for people entering Spain and Europe from North Africa. Both cities are linked to Europe by ferries. Ceuta is only ninety minutes away from mainland Spain. These cities serve as preferred entrances for both typical illegal immigrants to Spain and for militant jihadis coming from North Africa, especially Morocco and Algeria.[7] This geographic overlap, added to the historical ties to Spain, reinforces the importance of Spain to al Qaeda related groups. These groups attempt to both hide among and recruit from the North African immigrant communities in Spain and throughout Europe. For example, in 1994 al Qaeda penetrated the

Soldiers of Ala (soldados de Alá) principally by recruiting Moroccan and Algerian neosalafists.[8] Moreover, many North Africans have relatives in Europe, which facilitates their immigration to Europe. 'That makes the region a great springboard not only for operatives looking to carry out strikes in Europe, but also for proselytizers seeking to unify and radicalize the large North African communities in the continent. Those communities can act as either support networks or as camouflage for jihadist operatives.'[9] Lessons from a domestic context suggest that success or failure of these groups to recruit may depend to a large extent on the posture and policies of the host governments.

Within the Maghreb, there is a long history of militant Islam and struggles against colonialism. Al Qaeda is active in North Africa and has succeeded in carrying out attacks, such as the May 2003 Casablanca bombing that killed forty-five people. Moreover, al Qaeda has created alliances with many of the existing radical groups in the Maghreb. For example, Algeria's GSPC recently aligned with al Qaeda. Furthermore, GSPC formed additional alliances with other radical Islamist groups, including Morocco's Islamic Combatant Group, Libya's Islamic Fighting Group, and the Tunisian Combatant Group, among others in the region. This new al Qaeda related umbrella group is called The Union of the Arab Maghreb. Presumably, this new group will try to recruit among North Africans in Europe.[10] This new strategy reflects the organizational changes of al Qaeda. Al Qaeda has evolved from a group to a movement or an 'operational model that encourages independent "grassroots" jihadists to conduct attacks, or to a model in which al Qaeda provides operational commanders who organize grassroots cells'.[11] In effect, the range is broader, while the operational depth and training of individuals within the movement may be diluted. Similarly, through the 1990s extremist groups in Spain were organized by nationality, such as Moroccan, Algerian, or Syrian. However, there is recent evidence of these groups cooperating and merging, mirroring changes among North African groups.[12] The goal for Europeans is to prevent the population of European based immigrants and Muslims from becoming a ripe recruiting ground for extremists. As Fidel Sendagorta, head of policy planning in the Spanish Ministry of Foreign Affairs notes, the combination of jihadism and immigration from North Africa makes Europe a top target for recruitment. To prevent recruitment, individuals in these communities need to choose integration into the European communities and the same European societies need to avoid creating a community chasm by equating Islam with terrorism.[13]

Terrorism has long been among the top concerns in Spanish public opinion, as documented in chapter seven. However, concern with immigration has grown considerably since the 2004 Madrid attacks, perhaps in response to the increasing numbers of North African immigrants and possibly also reflecting a conflation of concern of international terrorism with them. The following public opinion data reflect the top three problems facing the nation. In January 2004, only 16 per cent were concerned with immigration, compared with 38.1 per cent with terrorism, and 65 per cent with unemployment. However, by November 2005, 38.1 per cent were concerned with immigration and only 24.1 per cent with terrorism.[14] Spanish jihadism was not initially linked to the growth of the Muslim or Arab immigrants in Spain; however, by the mid-1990s recruitment and propaganda campaigns were directed at those communities. Moreover, increasing numbers of people are radicalized once they are in Spain.[15]

Within Spanish public opinion, there are telling differences between Muslims and non-Muslims. Concern with Islamic extremism was greater among the general population (66 per cent very or somewhat concerned) than among Muslims (46 per cent) in 2006.[16] Only 21 per cent of Muslims in Spain thought there was a struggle between moderate Muslims and Islamic fundamentalists in Spain,[17] and of those who believed there was a struggle, 68 per cent identified with the moderate Muslims and only 18 per cent with the Islamic fundamentalists (composing less than 4 per cent of the Muslim population in Spain).[18] Similarly, in 2006 there was a difference in perception of Spaniards in general and Muslims in Spain about the support for Islamic extremists like al Qaeda. Of all Spaniards, 41 per cent thought most or many Muslims supported them, compared with 12 per cent of the Muslims in Spain.[19] Another question asked about confidence in Bin Laden. Only 16 per cent of Muslims in Spain admitted to having a lot or some confidence in Bin

Laden in 2006, compared with 2 per cent of Spaniards in general.[20] Presumably, excluding the Muslim population, there is practically no support for Bin Laden in Spain. Depending on the comparison, this number is approximately the same proportion of the people in the Basque country who completely or partially support ETA (4 per cent) plus the additional 13 per cent who agree with ETA's ends but not their means.

Integration and immigration

In general, a broadly indiscriminate response undermines security and integration and causes a loss of regime support. However, in the case of an international threat, the question raised revolves around the definition of the community. Can immigrants be excluded or should they be included? Typically this plays into heated domestic debates about proper immigration policies. In the Spanish fight against al Qaeda related groups, the discussion focuses on immigrants from North Africa and the treatment of Muslims within Spain. In the case of domestic groups that fear the government, but have not yet turned to violence, increased scrutiny can be counterproductive by causing a security dilemma. Active investigation and infiltration may reinforce a belief that the government is out to get them. In order to avoid over-reaction, commitment to an inclusive political community must be maintained. Clutterbuck notes that a 'civilization which can accommodate dissent has a better prospect of prolonged survival'.[21] However, how does this relate to a community of foreigners, irregular or illegal immigrants? Are they to be considered part of the community or would the community benefit from exclusion or expulsion? How well integrated are the Muslim and immigrant populations in Spain?

Before the 1990s, on balance more Spaniards emigrated than foreigners immigrated to Spain.[22] However, that has changed. Since 1991, the number of foreign residents has increased five-fold – from 353,367 to 1,572,017, with the largest numbers of immigrants coming from Latin American countries such as Ecuador, Argentina, and Colombia,

North African countries such as Morocco, and Eastern European countries such as Romania.[23] Of those, Moroccans are the second largest group, with a 2005 estimate of 376,000 legal residents and an additional 200,000 undocumented.[24] Spanish census figures tabulate a total of 70,259 births to foreign mothers in Spain in 2005. Of those tallied, 26.73 per cent were from Africa. Overall, Moroccan mothers birthed over one fifth of the children (14,592).[25] The actual population is likely to be higher, since many are not counted in the census due to their irregular or illegal status. It should be noted that Spanish nationality is not granted on the basis of being born in the country, but also involves Spanish blood to gain nationality.[26]

The challenge for the Spanish government is to prevent the recruitment of Muslims or North Africans from the stock of people already in Spain or from those who may arrive in the future. In general, terrorism scholars such as Wilkinson recognize that 'democratic authorities need to defeat the terrorist leadership at the political level by showing that the government is capable of responding imaginatively to the legitimate demands and aspirations of the very social groups the terrorists seek to mobilize'.[27] Immigrants have complained about a lack of economic opportunity and discrimination. Responsiveness to understandable grievances may increase the government's popular support and decrease overt and tacit support for terrorists.

Al Qaeda has found a limited base in the Muslim immigrants from Syria, Morocco, and Algeria and from within the new mosques formed to serve those new immigrants.[28] More than half of those arrested for complicity in the 11 March 2004 attacks were Moroccans with Spanish residency. In a study of the 188 people imprisoned for ties to international Jihadi terrorist groups in Spain from 2001 to 2005, 36.7 per cent were born in Morocco, 35.6 per cent in Algeria, 11.7 per cent in Syria, 6.4 per cent in Afghanistan, and 4.3 per cent in Spain. Overall, the imprisoned were likely to be North Africans with low educational attainment: 75.5 per cent of those imprisoned were from North Africa, 66.7 per cent had either no schooling or just primary education. Interestingly, 57.7 per cent were legal residents, 33.7 per cent were illegal, and 6.3 per cent were naturalized Spanish citizens.[29] This suggests that the problem is not just within the illegal community, but within the Muslim and immigrant community in general. Moreover, almost 5 per cent are Spanish born, indicating a potential problem of recruitment from within more established segments of the community.

In Spain, the government has made efforts to normalize and improve the situation of immigrants. A first step has been to regularize the status of illegal immigrants to reduce or eliminate the pool of irregular immigrants. The general idea is to increase assimilation and improve their lot with the hopes of making the population less vulnerable to recruitment by radical groups. The government has amended the 2000 law which had previously governed the situation of illegal and irregular immigrants.[30] Efforts culminated in a new regularization programme in 2005, approved by all parties except the PP, in which the immigrant needs to provide proof of employment since before 7 August 2004 and prove that they do not have a criminal history, in addition to supporting documentation from an employer. Over 690,000 immigrants applied for this process to gain legal status.[31] Of those with a criminal record, the government has increased attempts to expel them. Foreigners with suspected ties to international terrorist groups are quickly deported. Moreover, the Spanish government has increased international cooperation, especially with the French, to identify and deport people with such ties.[32] Additionally, the Spanish government has attempted to work with source countries, such as Morocco, to limit illegal immigration, and is considering revising visa policies.[33]

The government has also attempted to avoid increases in xenophobia, especially in regard to Moroccans. Human Rights Watch, in a 2005 report, did not find evidence of indiscriminate actions against Moroccans in Spain. Moreover, the report quotes a leader of ATIME (Asociación de Trabajadores e Inmigrantes Marroquíes en España), El M'Rabet, who complimented the government's response as 'exemplary, that of a society that knows how to distinguish between a few terrorists and a community'.[34]

The government has also proposed both increased scrutiny of Spanish mosques and increased financial support of mosques in order to moderate the religious chiefs and emphasize collaboration. Although religious freedom is protected in Spain, it is also limited by the need for public order.[35] Previously, relations had been governed by the November 1992 Acuerdo de Cooperación between the Comisión Islámica (the leaders organization of Muslim representation) and the Spanish government (under the Socialists). Muslims view it both as a way to control the mosques and to collaborate and maintain a dialogue.[36] However, since then many new mosques have been formed, without government control or influence. Instead, in addition to being supported by the faithful, many of these new mosques are run and financed by Saudis directly or indirectly through Saudi related organizations.[37] Although some in the community view this attempt to increase funding, collaboration, and scrutiny as threatening, others note that it is not unusual. The leader of the Islamic Commission of Spain, Mansur Escudero, bristled at the suggestion of monitoring sermons as 'surreal'.[38] Contrarily, Mohamed El Afifi, spokesman of the Centro Cultural Islámico de Madrid, explained that the lack of control is due to the rapid growth of the Muslim population. He also noted that in Arab countries, mosques must be registered and imams qualified, neither of which had been required or controlled by Spain. There are an estimated half a million to one million Muslims in Spain.[39] Regardless, there are new efforts to create a registry of mosques and monitor or control local imams. Minister of the Interior José Antonio Alonso stated, 'A law to control the imams of the small mosques is necessary' after the 11 March attacks. Most imams report feeling watched or interrogated by security forces.[40]

Recent 2006 survey data provide some insight into the view of immigration, integration, and treatment of Muslims in Spain. Whereas of the general population 83 per cent associate Muslims with fanaticism and only 21 per cent with tolerance, among Muslims in Spain, 70 per cent of Muslims view non-Muslims to be tolerant and only 21 per cent view them as fanatical.[41] Despite these negative associations of Muslims among Spaniards, a strong majority of the overall Spanish population (62 per cent) believes that immigration from the Middle East and North Africa is a good thing. Among Muslims in Spain, the sentiment is even stronger (82 per cent).[42] Other questions probe whether or not Muslims have successfully integrated into the community. In terms of identity, there is a large divergence. Whereas 60 per cent of Spanish Christians view themselves as Spaniards first, only 3 per cent of Spanish Muslims view themselves as Spanish first.[43] This reinforces the notion of an increasing importance of Islam. Overall, 46 per cent of both the general population and Muslims believe there is a growing sense of Islamic identity among Muslims in Spain, but only 14 per cent of Spanish Muslims feel it is a bad thing, compared with 82 per cent of the general population.[44] However, there is evidence of a willingness to integrate among the Muslims in Spain. Whereas only 21 per cent of the general population view Muslim immigrants as willing to adopt Spanish customs, 53 per cent of Muslims in Spain expect new Muslim immigrants to do so.[45] On a positive note, more Spaniards in the general population perceive hostility towards Muslims (60 per cent replying most or many) compared with just 31 per cent of actual Spanish Muslims. In fact, among Spanish Muslims, 64 per cent replied only some or very few Europeans were hostile to Muslims.[46] Although there is evidence of trepidation among Muslims in Spain (69 per cent of those surveyed were either very or somewhat concerned) about the future of Muslims in Spain,[47] only 25 per cent of the Muslims in Spain have had a bad experience due to their religion, race, or ethnicity in the past two years.[48] Perhaps most telling is the question of how worried (very or somewhat) Muslims in Spain are about extremism among Muslims (46 per cent) compared with unemployment (83 per cent).[49] Everyday economic concerns are more pressing than other issues related to violence or extremism.

Some argue that these attempts to create a useful dialogue with the Islamic groups will fail. For example, Celso states that Muslim organizations are 'fairly impervious to co-option'; moreover, 'dialogues are likely at best to lead only to symbolic cooperation and at worst may end up legitimating many of the mosques and community organizations that are embedded in this network of terror'.[50] However, the choice for the government is either to pursue integration through modifying immigration patterns and policies, or to attempt broad expulsion. Expulsion would likely inflame passions and is of doubtful practicality. Although some commentators may prefer it as an option, it is simply not realistic, since Spain has always been a major transit point for Algerians and others between North Africa and Europe and is likely to continue to be so, regardless of Spanish policy. Moreover, the public opinion data suggest that the Muslim population in Spain is more open and pragmatic than the general Spanish population expects. Thus, efforts of outreach and collaboration may have a better chance to succeed – if not undermined by actions that increase suspicion and alienation. Additionally, policies that indiscriminately target immigrants and Muslims in Spain may hamper efforts at creating popular support abroad.[51]

Citizen support at home and abroad

Democracies may have unique strengths in maintaining support, and this strength is relative to how unified the population remains. For example, in the British case, according to Sir Robert Mark, 'the social conditions on the British mainland heavily favor the security forces in countering terrorism, because they are democratically accountable and enjoy almost universal support in discharging that particular task, a support which would be, of course, less certain if the task was more controversial. That is the essential condition for countering terrorism, without which the most efficiently organized, trained and led security forces could not succeed.'[52] To maintain (nearly) universal support, it is important that groups within the population remain supportive of the task of reporting suspicious activities. It must be remembered that it is difficult for terrorists to operate without safe houses and sources of local support. If the Spanish government succeeds in minimizing alienation of the immigrant and Muslim populations, this will greatly facilitate intelligence gathering and counterterrorism efforts related to the international jihadi threat. Despite a May 2005 statement that the principles of the Pacto Antiterrorista applied to the fight against all types of terrorists,[53] there has been a growing politicization of the counterterrorism tactics and the immigration policy, which may undermine government efforts.

AL QAEDA IN *AL-ANDALUS* 257

This general idea is consistent with counterinsurgency doctrine, which emphasizes the importance of the hearts and minds approach. Internal counterinsurgency is dependent on popular support for long term success. After separating the civilians from the insurgents, according to O'Sullivan and Miller, it is necessary to win popular support through 'protection and the prospect of economic and social progress'.[54] Efforts at normalizing the situation of immigrants to make them less susceptible to recruitment and attempts to increase support of the mosques with an aim of moderation may help accomplish this. The task of identifying and capturing insurgents or terrorists is extremely difficult without accurate local intelligence. This information is much more likely to be obtained if the government enjoys popular support, especially among groups where terrorists try to recruit. However, in practice, especially in cases where the insurgents are a distinct ethnic or religious group, sometimes force and isolation are chosen instead of hearts and minds. If this target population feels it is under attack or being treated unfairly by authorities, neither support nor valuable information will be forthcoming. This recalls the conclusion of the domestic terrorism case studies that security and integration can also be undermined by a repressive state response. The task of strengthening support among the immigrant and Muslim communities may be difficult, but it is nonetheless crucial.

Democratic stability and protection from external threats

There are two fronts to this conflict. In Spain today the Spanish response appears to be broadening the base of support both within and outside of Spain. Although an aggressive counterterrorism effort has resulted in the arrests of 300 people from 2001–2005, the government has not indiscriminately targeted either immigrants or Muslims. The Spanish government has also aimed to gain the support of Muslims and Arabs internationally. For example, in response to the fatal shooting of the Brazilian Jean Charles de Menezes in the British metro in July 2005, British prime minister Tony Blair stated his sincere regret. On the contrary, the president of the Consejo General del Poder Judicial Español, Francisco Jose Hernando, stated that this type of incident was acceptable in the context of a 'third world war against terrorism'. In response, Prime Minister Zapatero replied, 'I do not agree with the statements of the President of the General Council of the Judiciary. This is not a conventional war. The formulas have to be different.'[55] Instead Blair and Zapatero have proposed an idea of the alliance of civilizations to combat radicalization of the young Muslims in Spain and Britain and throughout the world, an idea that was ridiculed by former prime minister José María Aznar. This notion is contrary to the much cited reference to Samuel Huntington's *Clash of Civilizations*. Instead, alliances will be pursued among the majority of moderates to work jointly against fanaticism.

The majority of Spain seems to agree with the overarching view of Zapatero. Whereas previous prime minister Aznar was closely associated with US president Bush, the current prime minister Zapatero is not. Moreover, just as Spaniards lost confidence in Aznar, satisfaction with US policy in regard to the war on terror has also decreased. Interestingly, the evaluations of US policy differ little between Muslim and non-Muslim Spaniards. In 2006, only 19 per cent of the general population approved of the US led war on terror, compared with 12 per cent of Muslim Spaniards. Support has decreased from 63 per cent of the general population in spring 2003.[56] Moreover, among Muslims in Spain, there is more optimism about relations between Muslims and the Western world (49 per cent) than among Spaniards in general (14 per cent).[57] Among those who believe relations to be poor across both groups, there is an understanding of shared blame. Among the general population, 32 per cent blamed Muslims, 10 per cent blamed Western people, and 52 per cent blamed both groups. Among Muslims in Spain, 5 per cent blamed Muslims, 28 per cent blamed Western people, and 40 per cent blamed both.[58] Moreover, there is a significant difference of opinion about the potential success of democracy in Muslim countries between the general population in Spain and the Muslim population in Spain. Only 37 per cent of the general population thought democracy would work well in Muslim countries while 57 per cent of the Muslims in Spain thought so.[59]

In addition to the positive view of democracy in general, this may indicate a satisfaction with democracy locally, even among those with minority status in Spain.

Democracies are judged according to how well they perform. When faced with terrorism, both security and integration should be protected in order to maintain popular support. If the government cannot provide security, people may support those they think will or form their own groups to do so. In Spain, so far, there is little evidence of the emergence of vigilante groups or a broad repressive response to the Muslim or immigrant communities. Instead, the current government of Zapatero has made efforts to regularize and improve the situation of Muslims and immigrants within Spain, both by modifying policies and by expanding collaborative efforts. However, these policies are not supported by the PP opposition. Zapatero's choice of collaboration may succeed in reducing support for Islamic extremists both within Spain and abroad. The continuing divide among the major Spanish political parties threatens to undermine progress, however. Moreover, more attacks could be followed by the emergence of vigilante groups.

Spain has the potential to solidify support among its Muslim and Arab minority groups, minimize recruitment, and maximize intelligence. Historically, in addition to its geographic tie between the two regions, Spain has played a crucial role as mediator between the Islamic world and Europe: Franco spoke Arabic and had a policy of friendship towards the Arab world known as *mozarabidad*; Spain hosted the Arab–Israeli peace conference in Madrid in 1991; and King Juan Carlos restated a pledge of the Hispano-Muslim *convivencia* while in Morocco in 2005. However, just as there are numerous examples of peaceful cooperation and cultural advance, Spain has been the site of some of the sharpest conflicts between the Spaniards and Muslim/Arabs. Historians have noted that the symbolism of *al-Andalus* is interpreted 'through the prisms of contemporary conflicts'.[60] This Hispano-Muslim relationship can be either a symbol of peaceful coexistence and cultural flourishing or of bloody conflict. The success or failure of Spain to prevent the recruitment of those within its borders may rest on the ability of the government to solidify support at home without increasing community divides and suspicion and by successfully utilizing the former interpretation of *al-Andalus*.

Notes

1 It should be noted that previously other international terrorists were active in Spain. For example, attacks linked to Abu Nidal have occurred on Spanish soil. See Fernando Jiménez, 'Spain: The Challenge and the Government's Response', in Alex P. Schmid and Ronald Crenlinsten (eds), *Western Responses to Terrorism* (London: Frank Cass, 1993). Another prominent case is the April 1985 attack near the Torrejón base by Arab terrorists that killed eighteen. See Powell, 2004, p. 376.

2 Fernando Reinares, 'al Qaeda, neosalafistas magrebíes y 11-M: sobre el Nuevo terrorismo islamista en España', in Fernando Reinares and Antonio Elorza (eds), *El Nuevo Terrorismo Islamista* (Madrid: Temas de Hoy, 2004a), p. 31.

3 'Neosalafist' refers to groups committed to a literal interpretation of the Koran and total rejection of Western culture.

4 Whether or not al Qaeda is truly a religiously motivated movement or a politically motivated group, the group tries to mobilize along religious and civilizational lines.

5 Powell, 2004, p. 376.

6 Reinares, 2004a, pp. 15–44, 38.

7 José María Irujo, 'Ceuta y Melilla, la frontera de la "jihad". Informes oficiales advierten de que el paro y la marginalidad alimentan el integrismo radical', *El País* 2 May 2004.

8 Reinares, 2004a, pp. 15–44, 31.

9 Fred Burton, 'Al Qaeda's Pan-Maghreb Gambit', 21 November 2006a, Stratfor.

10 Burton, 2006a.

11 Fred Burton, 'al Qaeda in 2007: The Continuing Devolution', 27 December 2006b, Stratfor.

12 Javier Jordán, and Robert Wesley, 'After 3/11: The Evolution of Jihadist Networks in Spain', *Terrorism Monitor* Vol. 4, Issue 1, 12 January 2006, pp. 1–3.

13 Fidel Sendagorta, 'Jihad in Europe; the Wider Context', *Survival* Vol. 47, Issue 3, 2005, pp. 63–72, p. 66.

14 Respondents are replying to the following question and responding with up to three problems: 'What are, in your view, the three principal problems that exist in Spain?' Various *Barómetro de Opinión*, Centro de Investigaciones Sociológicos.

15 Javier Jordán and Nicola Horsburgh, 'Spain and Islamist Terrorism: Analysis of the Threat and Response 1995–2005', *Mediterranean Politics* Vol. 11, No. 2, 2006, pp. 209–229, pp. 212, 221.

16 'How concerned, if at all, are you about the rise of Islamic extremism in our country these days? Are you very concerned, somewhat con-

cerned, not too concerned or not at all concerned about the rise of Islamic extremism in our country these days?' (Pew Research Center, *Few Signs of Backlash From Western European. Muslims in Europe: Economic Worries Top Concerns about Religious and Cultural Identity* (Washington, DC: Pew Research Center, 2006b), p. 30).

17 'Do you think there is a struggle in [survey country] between moderate Muslims and Islamic fundamentalists or don't you think so? Yes, No' (Pew, 2006b, p. 32).

18 'Which side do you identify with more in this struggle, moderate Muslims or Islamic fundamentalists?' (Pew, 2006b, p. 32).

19 'In your opinion, how many [Muslims] in our country support Islamic extremists like al Qaeda – would you say most, many, just some or very few?' (Pew Research Center, *Europe's Muslims More Moderate. The Great Divide: How Westerns and Muslims View Each Other* (Washington, DC: Pew Research Center, 2006a), p. 58).

20 'Now I'm going to read a list of political leaders. For each, tell me how much confidence you have in each leader to do the right thing regarding world affairs – a lot of confidence, some confidence, not too much confidence, or no confidence at all?' (Pew, 2006a, p. 61).

21 Richard Clutterbuck, *Living with Terrorism* (New Rochelle, New York: Arlington House, 1975), p. 149.

22 David Corkill, 'Immigration, the Ley de Extranjería and the Labour Market in Spain', *International Journal of Iberian Studies* Vol. 3, 2001, pp. 148–150, p. 149.

23 'Los cambios socials de los últimos diez años', Censos de Población y Viviendas 2001, *Boletín informativo Nacional de Estadística* February 2003, p. 4.

24 Human Rights Watch, 'Setting an Example? Counter-terrorism Measures in Spain', 2005 hrw.org/reports/2005/spain0105/4.htm.

25 Boletín informativo Nacional de Estadística, February 2003.

26 Kitty Calavita, 'The Criminalization and Economic Punishment of Immigrants', *Punishment and Society* Vol. 5, No. 4, 2003, pp.399–413, p. 404.

27 Paul Wilkinson, *Terrorism Versus Democracy. The Liberal State Response* (London: Frank Cass, 2001), p. 228.

28 Reinares, 2004a, p. 30.

29 Fernando Reinares, 'Towards a Social Characterisation of Jihadist Terrorism in Spain: Implications for Domestic Security and Action Abroad', Madrid, Real Instituto Elcano study No. ARI 34/2006, 2006. More than 300 people were arrested in that time frame.

30 Irene Delgado and Lourdes Lopez Nieto, 'Spain', *European Journal of Political Research* Vol. 43, 2004, pp. 1138–1143, p. 1139. See also 'Colectivo Ioé, Política migratoria española en el marco europeo' *Studi Emigrazione/Migration Studies* Vol. 38, Issue 144, 2001, pp. 855–868 for a discussion on Spanish immigration policy from 1974–2001.

31 See Boletín de Noticias Especial 2005, Ministry of Labour and Social Affairs, http://empleo.mtas.es/itss/sala_de_comunicaciones/boletin/Boletin_2005.pdf. See Rickard Sandell, 'Spain's Immigration Experience: Lessons to be Learned from Looking at the Statistics' Real Instituto Elcano study Working Paper, No. WWP 30/2006, Madrid, 2006.

32 Human Rights Watch, 2005.
33 For example, see Rickard Sandell, 'Spain's Quest for Regular Immigration', ARI No. 64/2005, Madrid: Real Instituto Elcano, 2005; José Cazorla 'La Frontera sur de Europa: motivaciones y consecuencias sociopolíticas de la migración', REIS Vol. 109, 2005, pp. 239–254.
34 Human Rights Watch, 2005.
35 Luis Aizpeolea, 'El Gobierno estudia una reforma legal para el control de mezquitas e imams', El País 8 May 2004.
36 Patricia Ortega Dolz, 'La mezquita del barrio', El País 9 May 2004.
37 Reinares, 2004a, p. 30.
38 Human Rights Watch, 2005.
39 Elsa Granda and Tomas Barbulo, 'El Gobierno carece de un registro de imames y de mezquitas para controlar a los islamistas', El País 5 May 2004.
40 Patricia Ortega Dolz, 'La mezquita del barrio', El País 9 May 2004. 'Es necesaria una ley para poder controlar a los imames de las pequeñas mezquitas'; author translation. See also Elena Arigita, 'Representing Islam in Spain: Muslim Identities and the Contestation of Leadership', The Muslim World Vol. 96, October 2006, 563–584.
41 'Which of these characteristics do you associate with [Muslims] in Western countries such as the United States and Europe?' Answering yes to fanatical; Pew, 2006a, p. 52.
42 'Do you think it's a good thing or a bad thing that people [INSERT] come to live and work in this country?' a. From the Middle East and North Africa; Pew, 2006b, pp. 25–26.
43 'Do you think of yourself first as [name of country's people] or first as a [Muslim/Christian/Hindu]?' Pew, 2006b, pp. 26–27.
44 'In your opinion, these days do you think there is a growing sense of Islamic identity among Muslims in our country or don't you think so?'; Pew, 2006b, pp. 29–30. 'Do you think this is a good thing or a bad thing for our country?'; Pew, 2006b, p. 29.
45 'Do you think most Muslims coming to our country today want to adopt Spanish customs and way of life or do you think that they want to be distinct from the larger Spanish society?'; Pew, 2006b, p. 28.
46 'In your opinion, how many Europeans do you think are hostile toward Muslims – would you say most, many, just some or very few?'; Pew, 2006b, p. 27.
47 'How concerned, if at all, are you about the future of Muslims in this country – very concerned, somewhat concerned, not too concerned, or not at all concerned?'; Pew, 2006b, p. 31.
48 'In the last two years, have you personally had a bad experience due to your race, ethnicity, or religion, or hasn't this happened to you?'; Pew, 2006b, p. 33.
49 'Please tell me how worried you are about each of the following issues related to Muslims living in Spain. The first one is [READ ITEM]. Are you very worried, somewhat worried, not too worried, or not at all worried about [READ ITEM, ROTATE]?'; Pew, 2006b, p. 31.

50 Anthony N. Celso, 'Spain's Dual Security Dilemma: Strategic Challenges of Basque and Islamic Terror during the Agnar and Zapatero Eras', *Mediterranean Quarterly* Vol. 57, No. 4, 2006, pp. 121–141.

51 Interestingly, al Qaeda has promoted an inclusive community within their ranks and leadership. 'Within al Qaeda, there is a culture of inclusion, and – though the existence of strong Saudi and Egyptian cadres has been noted – commanders have been promoted for the most part on the basis of their faith and merit rather than ethnicity or national origin'; Burton, 2006a.

52 Sir Robert Mark, 'Policing a Britain Under Threat', in Richard Clutterbuck (ed.), *The Future of Political Violence* (New York: St. Martin's Press, 1986), p. 161.

53 Luis Aizpeolea, 'El Gobierno pactara con el PP un plan urgente contra el terrorismo islamista', *El País* 13 May 2004.

54 Patrick O'Sullivan and Jesse W. Miller, *The Geography of Warfare* (New York: St. Martin's Press, 1983), pp. 116–118.

55 'Blair apoya la alianza de civilizaciones propuesta por el presidente Zapatero. El primer ministro británico agradece al jefe del Gobierno español su apoyo tras los atentados' *El País* 27 July 2005. 'No comparto las declaraciones del presidente del Consejo General del Poder Judicial. No hay una guerra convencional. Las formulas tienen que ser distintas', Author translation.

56 'Which of the following phrases comes closer to describing your view? I favor the U.S.-led efforts to fight terrorism, OR I oppose the U.S.-led efforts to fight terrorism'; Pew, 2006b, pp. 24–25.

57 'Do you think that relations these days between Muslims around the world and people in Western countries such as the United States and Europe are generally good or generally bad?'; Pew, 2006a, p. 47.

58 'Who do you think is mostly to blame for this, Muslims or people in Western countries?'; Pew, 2006a, p. 47.

59 'Now on a different subject, some people feel that democracy is a Western way of doing things that would not work in most Muslim countries – others think that democracy is not just for the West and can work well in most Muslim countries. Which comes closer to your opinion?'; Pew, 2006a, p. 46.

60 Hishaam Aidi, 'The Interference of *al-Andalus*; Spain, Islam, and the West', *Social Text* Vol. 24; Issue 2 (2006), pp. 67–88, p.78.

Select bibliography

Abel, Christopher and Nissa Torrents (eds). *Spain: Conditional Democracy*. New York: St. Martin's Press, 1984.

Adrianzén, Alberto. *Democracia, etnicidad y violencia política en los países andinos*. Lima: IEP, 1993.

Agranoff, Robert and Juan Antonio Ramos Gallarin. 'Towards Federal Democracy in Spain: An Examination of Intergovernmental Relations'. *Publius*, Vol. 27, No. 4, Fall 1997, p. 1–39.

Aguero, Felipe, 'Toward Civilian Supremacy in South America'. In Larry Diamond, Marc Plattner, Yun-han Chu, and Hung-mao Tien (eds), *Consolidating the Third World Democracies*. Baltimore: Johns Hopkins University Press, 1997, pp. 176–206.

Aguero, Felipe. *Soldiers, Civilians, and Democracy*. Baltimore: Johns Hopkins Press, 1995.

Aguiar, Cesar. *Uruguay de los setenta: balance de una decada*. Montevideo: CIEDUR, 1981.

Aguilar, Paloma. 'The Memory of the Civil War in the Transition to Democracy: The Peculiarity of the Basque Case'. *West European Politics*, Vol. 21, No. 4, October 1998, pp. 5–25.

Aidi, Hishaam. 'The Interference of *al-Andalus*: Spain, Islam, and the West'. *Social Text*, Vol. 24, Issue 2, 2006, pp. 67–88.

Alisky, Marvin. *Latin American Media: Guidance and Censorship*. Ames: Iowa State University, 1981.

Alisky, Marvin. *Uruguay: A Contemporary Survey*. New York: Praeger Press, 1969.

Alonso, Rogelio and Fernando Reinares. 'Terrorism, Human Rights, and Law Enforcement in Spain'. *Terrorism and Political Violence*, Vol. 17, Nos 1–2, 2005, pp. 265–278.

Alzaga, O. et al. (eds). *Entre Dos Siglos: reflexiones sobre la democracia española*. Madrid: Alianza Editorial, 1996.

Americas Watch. *Peru Under Fire*. New Haven: Yale, 1992.

Americas Watch. *Tolerating Abuses: Violations of Human Rights in Peru*. New Haven: Yale, 1988.

Americas Watch. *A Certain Passivity: Failing to Curb Human Rights Abuses in Peru*. New Haven: Yale University Press, 1987.

Amnesty International. *AI Report 1998: Uruguay*. New York: Amnesty International.

Amnesty International. *Peru: Human Rights During the Government of Alberto Fujimori*. New York: Amnesty International, 1992.

Amnesty International. *Peru: Human Rights in a Climate of Terror*. New York: Amnesty International, 1991.

Amnesty International. *Peru: Human Rights in a State of Emergency*. New York: Amnesty International, 1989.

Amnesty International. *Peru: Violations of Human Rights in the Emergency Zones*. New York: Amnesty International, 1988.

APRODEH, <gopher://gopher.rcp.net.pe:70/00/otros-gopher/nacionales/aprodeh/>.

APRODEH et al. *Los Inocentes Tienen Nombre*. Lima: Grafimace S.A., 1995.

Arango, E. Ramón. *Spain: Democracy Regained*. Boulder: Westview Press, 1995.

Arigita, Elena. 'Representing Islam in Spain: Muslim Identities and the Contestation of Leadership'. *The Muslim World*, Vol. 96, October 2006, pp. 563–584.

Aristotle. *Nicomachean Ethics*. Translated by David Ross. Oxford: Oxford University Press, 1992.

Aristotle. *Nicomachean Ethics*. Translated by Martin Ostwald. New York: Macmillan Press, 1962.

Aristotle. *The Politics of Aristotle*. Translated by Ernest Barker. Oxford: Oxford University Press, 1958.

Aristotle. *Metaphysics*. Translated by Richard Hope. Ann Arbor: University of Michigan Press, 1952.

Arteche, Miguel Castells. *Radiografía de un model represivo*. San Sebastían: Ediciones Vascas, 1982.

Balcells, Albert. *Catalan Nationalism*. New York: St. Martin's Press, 1996.

Banon, Rafael and Manuel Tamayo. 'The Transformation of the Central Administration in Spanish Intergovernmental Relations'. *Publius*, Vol. 27, No. 4, Fall 1997, p. 85 (30).

Barahona de Brito, Alexandra. *Human Rights and Democratization in Latin America*. Oxford: Oxford University Press, 1997.

Barahona de Brito, Alexandra. 'Truth and Justice in the Consolidation of Democracy in Chile and Uruguay'. *Parliamentary Affairs*, Vol. 46, No. 4, October 1986, 579–593.

Barnhurst, Kevin. 'Contemporary Terrorism in Peru: Sendero Luminoso and the Media'. *Journal of Communication*, Vol. 41, No. 4, Autumn 1991, pp. 75–90.

Basombrio, Carlos. *Seguridad ciudadana y actuación del estado: análisis de tendencias de opinion pública*. Lima: Instituto de Defensa Legal, 2004.

Béjar, Héctor. '25 años de Perú'. *Socialismo y Participación*, No. 94, 2002, pp. 17–26.

Bell, David. *Democratic Politics in Spain*. New York: St. Martin's Press, 1983.

Bethel, Leslie (ed.). *Cambridge History of Latin America.* Volume VI: Latin America since 1930: Economy, Society and Politics. Cambridge: Cambridge University Press, 1994.

Bethel, Leslie (ed.). *Cambridge History of Latin America.* Volume VIII: Spanish South America. Cambridge: Cambridge University Press, 1991.

Boletín Informativo Nacional de Estadística. 'Los cambios Socials de los últimos diez años'. Censos de Población y Viviendas 2001, February 2003.

Bollen, Kenneth and Pamela Paxton. 'Subjective Measures of Liberal Democracy'. *Comparative Political Studies,* Vol. 13, No. 1, 2000, pp. 58–86.

Bonime-Blanc, Andrea. *Spain's Transition to Democracy.* Boulder: Westview Press, 1986.

Bonino, Luis Costa. *Crisis de los Partidos Tradicionales y Movimiento Revolucionario en el Uruguay.* Montevideo: Ediciones de la Banda Oriental, 1984.

Bordaberry, Juan Maria. *Las Opciones.* Montevideo: Impresa Rosgal, 1980.

Borzel, Tanja A. 'Shifting or Sharing the Burden? The Implementation of EU Environmental Policy in Spain and Germany'. *European Planning Studies,* Vol. 6, No. 5, 1998, pp. 537–553.

Bourque, Susan C. and Kay B. Warren. 'Democracy Without Peace: The Cultural Politics of Terror in Peru'. *Latin American Research Review,* Vol. 24, No. 1, 1989, pp. 7–34.

Buaquets, Julio, Miguel Angel Aguilar, and Ignacio Puche. *El Golpe.* Barcelona: Editorial Ariel, 1981.

Burt, Jo-Marie and Jose Lopez Ricci. 'Shining Path After Guzman'. *NACLA,* Vol. 28, No. 3, 1996, pp. 6–9.

Burton, Fred. 'Al Qaeda in 2007: The Continuing Devolution'. Stratfor December 27, 2006b, Stratfor Report.

Burton, Fred. 'Al Qaeda's Pan-Maghreb Gambit' 21 November 2006a, Stratfor.

Burton, Fred. 'The Resurgence of Spain's Basque Militants' 17 December 2004, Stratfor.

Calavita, Kitty. 'The Criminalization and Economic Punishment of Immigrants'. *Punishment and Society,* Vol. 5, No. 4, 2003, pp. 399–413.

Cameron, Maxwell. 'Self-coups: Peru, Guatemala, and Russia'. *Journal of Democracy,* Vol. 9, No. 1, 1998, pp. 125–139.

Cameron, Maxwell. *Democracy and Authoritarianism in Peru.* New York: St. Martin's Press, 1995.

Canseco, Javier Diez. *Democracia, militarización y derechos humanos en el Perú 1980–1984.* Lima: Asociación Pro Derechos Humanos: Servicios Populares, 1985.

Carr, Raymond and Juan Pablo Fusi. *Spain: Dictatorship to Democracy.* London: Unwin Hyman, 1981.

Carter Center. 'Statement of the NDI/Carter Center February 2000 Preelection Delegation to Peru'. Lima: 11 February 2000.

Caula, Nelson and Alberto Silva. *Alta el Fuego: FFAA y Tupamaros.* Montevideo: Monte Sexto, 1986.

Cazorla, José. 'La Frontera sur de Europa: motivaciones y consecuencias sociopolíticas de la migración'. *REIS*, Vol. 109, 2005, pp. 239–254.

Ceresole, Norberto (ed.). *Perú: Sendero Luminoso, Ejercito y Democracia.* Buenos Aires: Biblioteca Hispanoamericana, 1987.

Chang-Rodríguez, Eugenio. *Opciones Políticas Peruanas.* Trujillo, Peru: Editorial Normas Legales S.A., 1987.

Chari, Raj S. 'The 2004 Spanish Election: Terrorism as a Catalyst for Change?'. *West European Politics*, Vol. 27, No. 5, November 2004, pp. 954–963.

Chilcote, Ronald (ed.). *Transitions from Dictatorship to Democracy.* New York: Crane Russak, 1990.

Chirinos Soto, Enrique. *Alan García: Análisis de su gobierno.* Lima: Centro de documentación Andina, 1986.

Clark, Robert. *Negotiating with ETA: Obstacles to Peace in the Basque Country, 1975–1988.* Reno: University of Nevada Press, 1990.

Clark, Robert. 'The Basques, Madrid, and Regional Autonomy: Conflicting Perspectives between Center and Periphery in Spain'. In William D. Phillips, Jr. and Carla Rahn Phillips (eds). *Marginated Groups in Spanish and Portuguese History.* Minneapolis: Society for Spanish and Portuguese Historical Studies, 1989.

Clark, Robert. *The Basques: The Franco Years and Beyond.* Reno: University of Nevada Press, 1979.

Clark, Stephen. *Aristotle's Man.* Oxford: Clarendon Press, 1976.

Closa, Carlos. 'Spain: The Cortes and the EU – A Growing Together'. *Journal of Legislative Studies*, Vol. 1, No. 3, Fall 1995, pp. 136–150.

Collier, David and Steven Levitsky. 'Democracy with Adjectives: Conceptual Innovation in Comparative Research'. *World Politics*, Vol. 49, No. 3, April 1997, pp. 430–451.

Collier, Ruth Berins and David Collier. *Shaping the Political Arena.* Princeton: Princeton University Press, 1991.

Comisión de la Verdad y Reconciliación. *Informe* Final. Lima: Comisión de la Verdad y Reconciliacón, 2003.

Comisión Especial de Investigación y Estudio sobre la Violencia y Alternativas de Pacificación. *Violencia y Pacificación en 1991.* Lima: Senado de la República, 1992.

Comisión Especial de Investigación y Estudio sobre la Violencia y Alternativas de Pacificación en el Perú. *Violencia y Pacificación.* Lima: Senado de la República, 1989.

Coordinadora Nacional de Derechos Humanos. *Perú, Informe Anual 1998.* Lima: Coordinadora Nacional de Derechos Humanos, 1999.

Coordinadora Nacional de Derechos Humanos. *Informe Sobre la Situacion de los Derechos Humanos en el Peru en 1997.* Lima: Coordinadora Nacional de Derechos Humanos, 1998.

Coordinadora Nacional de Derechos Humanos. *Informe Sobre la Situacion de los Derechos Humanos en el Peru en 1996.* Lima: Coordinadora Nacional de Derechos Humanos, 1997.

Coordinadora Nacional de Derechos Humanos. *Informe Sobre la Situación de los Derechos Humanos de el Perú en 1995.* Lima: Coordinadora de Derechos Humanos, 1996.

Corkill, David. 'Immigration, the Ley de Extranjería and the Labour Market in Spain'. *International Journal of Iberian Studies*, Vol. 3, 2001, pp. 148–156.

Corr, Edwin and Stephen Sloan (eds). *Low Intensity Conflict: Old Threats in a New World.* Boulder: Westview, 1992.

Costa, Gino and Rachel Neild. 'Police Reform in Peru'. *Australian and New Zealand Journal of Criminology*, Vol. 38, No. 2, 2005, pp. 216–229.

Council on Hemispheric Affairs. 'Uruguay: Keeping the Military in Check'. Report on the Latin American Military, 20 November 2006. http://www.coha.org/2006/11/20/uruguay-keeping-the-military-in-check/.

Cowen, Andrew. 'The Guerrilla War Against Franco'. *European History Quarterly*, Vol. 2, No. 2, April 1990, pp. 227–253.

Crabtree, John. *Peru Under Garcia.* Pittsburgh: University of Pittsburgh Press, 1992.

Craven, Carolyn. 'Wage Determinism and Inflation in Uruguay'. *Journal of Developing Areas*, Vol. 27, No. 4, July 1993, pp. 457–469.

Crenshaw, Martha (ed.). *Terrorism in Context.* University Park: Pennsylvania University Press, 1995.

Davis, William. *Warnings from the Far South: Democracy versus Dictatorship in Uruguay, Argentina, and Chile.* Westport: Praeger, 1995.

Degregori, Carlos Ivan. 'Reflexiones sobre la Comisión de la Verdad y Reconciliación'. *Socialismo y Participación*, No. 94, 2002, pp. 93–98.

del Campo, Salustiano (ed.). *Tendencias Sociales en España Volumen II.* Bilbao: Fundacion BBV, 1993.

del Campo, Salustiano ed. *Tendencias Sociales en España Volumen III.* Bilbao: Fundacion BBV, 1993.

Delgado, Irene and Lourdes Lopez Nieto. 'Spain'. *European Journal of Political Research*, Vol. 43, 2004, pp. 1138–1143.

Diamond, Larry, Marc Plattner, Yun-han Chu, and Hung-mao,Tien (eds). *Consolidating the Third World Democracies.* Baltimore: Johns Hopkins University Press, 1997.

Dietz, Henry. 'Peru's Sendero Luminoso As a Revolutionary Movement'. *Journal of Political and Military Sociology*, Vol. 18, Summer 1900, pp. 123–150.

Douglass, R. Bruce, Gerald M. Mara and Henry S. Richardson (eds). *Liberalism and the Good.* New York: Routledge, 1990.

Douglass, William and Joseba Zulaika. 'On the Interpretation of Terrorist Violence: ETA and the Basque Political Process'. *Comparative Studies in Society and History*, Vol. 32, No. 2, April 1990, pp. 238–257.

Encarnacion, Omar. 'Social Concertation in Democratic and Market Transactions: Comparative Lessons from Spain'. *Comparative Political Studies*, Vol. 30, No. 4, August 1997, pp. 387–420.

Engene, Jan Oskar. 'Five Decades of Terrorism in Europe: The TWEED Dataset'. *Journal of Peace Research*, Vol. 44, No. 1, 2007, pp. 109–121.

Escalante, María and Ana María Vidal, *Los decretos de la guerra: dos año de políticas antisubversivas y una propuesta de paz*. Lima: IDS, 1993.

Farer, Tom (ed.). *Beyond Sovereignty: Collectively Defending Democracy in the Americas*. Baltimore: Johns Hopkins University Press, 1996.

Fernández, Wilson. *El Gran Culpable: la responsabilidad de los E.E.U.I. en el proceso militar uruguayo*. Montevideo: Ediciones Atenea, 1986.

Ferreira Aldunate, Wilson. *El exilio y la lucha*. Montevideo: Ediciones de la Banda Oriental, 1986.

Finch, Henry. *Contemporary Uruguay*. University of Liverpool, Institute of LA Studies, Working Paper No. 9, 1989.

Finch, M. H. J. *A Political Economy of Uruguay Since 1870*. New York: St. Martin's Press, 1981.

Finley, M. I. *Politics in the Ancient World*. Cambridge: Cambridge University Press, 1983.

Fishman, Robert. *Working Class Organization and the Return to Democracy in Spain*. Ithaca: Cornell University Press, 1990.

Fitch, J. Samuel. *The Armed Forces and Democracy in Latin America*. Baltimore: Johns Hopkins University Press, 1998.

Fitzgibbon, Russell. *Uruguay: Portrait of a Democracy*. New Brunswick: Rutgers University Press, 1954.

Fitz-Simons, Daniel W. 'Sendero Luminoso: Case Study in Insurgency'. *Parameters*, Vol. 23, No. 2, Summer 1993, pp. 64–73.

Forgues, Rolando (ed.). *Perú: entre el desafío de la violencia y el sueño de lo posible*. Lima: Minerva, 1993.

'Fujimori and the Business Class'. *NACLA*, Vol. 30, No. 1, July/August 1996, pp. 25–30.

'Fujimori and the Military'. *NACLA*, Vol. 30, No. 1, July/August 1996, pp. 31–36.

Gallup. *Informe Gallup 1970: Futuro Inmediato y Previsible del Uruguay*. Montevideo: Gallup Uruguay, 1970.

'García's Peru'. *NACLA*, June 1986, Vol. 20, No. 3, pp. 34–46.

Gardels, Nathan and Abraham Lowenthal. 'Saving the State in Peru'. *New Perspectives Quarterly*, Autumn 1993, pp. 10–12.

Gellner, Ernest. *Legitimation of Belief*. London: Cambridge University Press, 1974.

Generals and Tupamaros: The Struggle for Power in Uruguay 1969–1973. London: Latin American Review of Books, 1974.

Gillespie, Charles Guy. *Negotiating Democracy: Politicians and Generals in Uruguay*. Cambridge: Cambridge University Press, 1991.

Gillespie, Richard. 'The Continuing Debate on Democratization in Spain'. *Parliamentary Affairs*, Vol. 46, October 1993, pp. 534–548.

Glewwe, Paul and Gillette Hall. 'Poverty, Inequality, and Living Standards During Unorthodox Adjustment: The Case of Peru, 1985–1990'. *Economic Development and Cultural Change*, Vol. 42, No. 4, July 1994, pp. 689–718.

González Casanova, Pablo and Marcos Roitman Rosenmann (eds). *La Democracia en América Latina: actualidad y perspectivas*. Mexico D.F.: La Jornada, 1995.

Gorriti, Gustavo Ellenbogen. *Sendero: Historia de la guerra milenaria en el Perú.* Lima: Editorial Apoyo, 1990.

Gowan, Peter and Perry Anderson (eds). *The Question of Europe.* New York: Verso, 1997.

Graham, Carol. *Peru's APRA.* Boulder: L. Rienner Publishers, 1992.

Gunther, Richard (ed.). *Politics, Society and Democracy: The Case of Spain.* Boulder: Westview Press, 1993.

Gunther, Richard, P. Nikiforos Diamandouros, and Hans-Jurgen Puhle, eds. *The Politics of Democratic Consolidation.* Baltimore: Johns Hopkins University Press, 1995.

Gunther, Richard, Giancomo Sani, and Goldie Shabad. *Spain After Franco.* Berkeley: University of California Press, 1988.

Gutiérrez, Gustavo. *A Theory of Liberation: History, Politics and Salvation.* Maryknoll: Orvis Books, 1973.

Handelman, Howard. 'Labor–Industrial Conflict and the Collapse of Uruguayan Democracy'. *Journal of Interamerican Studies and World Affairs*, Vol. 23, No. 4, November 1981, pp. 371–394.

Harrison, Joseph. *The Spanish Economy in the Twentieth Century.* London: Croom Helm, 1985.

Herrera, Javier. 'Gobernabilidad, corrupción, participación ciudadana y pobreza en el Perú, 2002'. Working paper of the Ministerio de Economía y Finanzas. http://www.mef.gob.pe/propuesta/ESPEC/Gobernabilidad_en_el_Peru_2002.pdf pp. 13–14.

Herz, John ed. *From Dictatorship to Democracy.* Westport: Greenwood Press, 1982.

Hispania Service. *La imagen de las instituciones políticas en la opinión pública.* Madrid: Hispania Service, 1981.

Human Rights Watch. 'Setting an Example? Counter-terrorism Measures in Spain'. www.hrw.org/reports/2005/spain0105/4.htm.

Human Rights Watch. 'In the Name of Counter-terrorism: Human Rights Abuses Worldwide: A Human Rights Watch Briefing Paper for the 59th Session of the United Nations Commission on Human Rights'. 25 March 2003.

Human Rights Watch. *World Report 1999.* New York: Human Rights Watch.

Human Rights Watch. *Torture and Political Persecution in Peru.* New York: Human Rights Watch, 1998.

Human Rights Watch. *Peru: Presumption of Guilt.* Washington: Human Rights Watch, 1996.

Huntington, Samuel. *The Third Wave: Democratization in the late 20th Century.* Norman, OK: University of Oklahoma Press, 1991.

Instituto Nacional de estadistica e informatica. *Perú en Cifras.* Lima: Prompens, INEI,1994.

Instituto Nacional de estadistica e informatica. *Peru: compendio estadístico 1995–6.* Lima: Dirección Ejecutiva de Coyuntura, 1996.

Inter-Church Committee on Human Rights in Latin America. *Violations of Human Rights in Uruguay (1972–1976).* Toronto: Inter-Church Committee on Human Rights in Latin America, 1978.

Jaime Barreto, Wilson. *Marketing político: elecciones 1990.* Lima: Universidad del Pacifico Centro de Investigacion, 1991.

Janke, Peter. *Spanish Separatism: ETA's Threat to Basque Democracy.* London: Institute for the Study of Conflict, 1980.

Jellinek, Sergio and Luis Ledesma. *Uruguay: Del Consenso Democratico a la Militarismo Estatal.* Part 1, Paper #19, November 1979. Stockholm: Institute of Latin American Studies, 1979a.

Jellinek, Sergio and Luis Ledesma. *Uruguay: Del Consenso Democratico a la Militarismo Estatal.* Part 2, Paper No. 19, November. Stockholm: Institute of Latin American Studies, 1979b.

Jiménez, Fernando. 'Spain: The Challenge and the Government's Response'. In Alex P. Schmid and Ronald Crenlinsten (eds), *Western Responses to Terrorism.* London: Frank Cass, 1993.

Jordán, Javier and Nicola Horsburgh. 'Spain and Islamist Terrorism: Analysis of the Threat and Response 1995-2005'. *Mediterranean Politics*, Vol. 11, No. 2, 2006, pp. 209-229.

Jordán, Javier and Robert Wesley. 'After 3/11: The Evolution of Jihadist Networks in Spain'. *Terrorism Monitor*, Vol. 4, Issue 1, 12 January 2006, pp. 1-3.

Jugo, Miguel. 'Panoram sobre derechos humanos'. *Actualidad Peruana*, Vol. 8, No. 1, February 1999.

Kaufman, Edy. *Uruguay in Transition: From Civilian to Military Rule.* New Brunswick: Transaction Books, 1979.

Klaren, Peter. 'Peru's Great Divide'. *The Wilson Quarterly*, Vol. 14, No. 3, Summer 1990, pp. 23-33.

Kohl, James and John Litt. *Urban Guerrilla Warfare in Latin America.* Cambridge: MIT Press, 1974.

Krasikov, Anatoly. *From Dictatorship to Democracy: Spanish Reportage.* Oxford: Pergamon Press, 1984.

Kraut, Richard. *Aristotle on the Human Good.* Princeton: Princeton University Press, 1991.

Labrousse, Alain. *The Tupamaros: Urban Guerrillas in Uruguay.* Harmondsworth: Penguin Books, 1970.

Lancaster, Thomas D. and Gary Prevost (eds). *Politics and Change in Spain.* New York: Praeger, 1985.

Langguth, A. J. *Hidden Terrors.* New York: Pantheon, 1978.

Lannon, Frances and Paul Preston (eds). *Elites and Power in Twentieth-Century Spain: Essays in Honour of Sir Raymond Carr.* Oxford: Clarendon Press, 1990.

Levander, Sandro Macassi. 'Cultura politica de la eficacia'. *Socialismo y participacion*, No. 58, June 1992, pp. 65-75.

Li, Peiyin Patty, 'Will It Hold?'. *Harvard International Review*, Vol. 21, Issue 1, Winter 1998/1999, pp. 10-11.

Linz, Juan. 'Church and State in Spain from the Civil War to the Return of Democracy'. *Daedalus*, Vol. 120, No. 2, Summer 1991 pp. 159-179.

Linz, Juan (ed.). *Un presente para el futuro.* Madrid: Instituto de Estudios Economicos, 1985.

Linz, Juan. *Breakdown of Democratic Regimes: Crisis, Breakdown and Reequilibration*. Baltimore: Johns Hopkins University Press, 1978.

Linz, Juan and Alfred Stepan. 'Toward Consolidated Democracies'. In Larry Diamond, Marc Plattner, Yun-han Chu, and Hung-mao Tien (eds), *Consolidating the Third Wave Democracies: Themes and Perspectives*. Baltimore: Johns Hopkins University Press, 1997, pp. 14–33.

Linz, Juan and Alfred Stepan (eds). *Problems of Democratic Transition and Consolidation: Southern Europe, South America and Post-Communist Europe*. Baltimore: Johns Hopkins University Press, 1996.

Linz, Juan and Alfred Stepan. 'Political Identities and Electoral Sequences: Spain, the Soviet Union, and Yugoslavia'. *Daedalus*, Vol. 121, No. 2, Spring 1992, pp. 123–140.

Llera, Francisco J., José M. Mata, and Cynthia L. Irvin. 'ETA: From Secret Army to Social Movement – the Post Franco Schism of the Basque National Movement'. *Terrorism and Political Violence*, Vol. 5, No. 3, Fall 1993, pp. 106–134.

López Pintor, Ratael. *La Opinión Pública Española del Franquismo a la Demcracia*. Madrid: CIS, 1982.

Loveman, Brian. '"Protected Democracies" and Military Guardianship: Political Transitions in Latin America'. *Journal of Interamerican Studies and World Affairs*, Vol. 36, Summer 1994, pp. 105–189.

McClintock, Cynthia. 'The Prospects for Democratic Consolidation in a "Least Likely" Case: Peru'. *Comparative Politics*, Vol. 21, No. 2, January 1989, pp. 127–149.

McClintock, Cynthia. 'The War on Drugs: The Peruvian Case'. *Journal of Interamerican Studies and World Affairs*, Vol. 30, No. 23, Summer/Fall 1988, pp. 127–142.

McClintock, Cynthia and Abraham F. Lowenthal (eds). *The Peruvian Experiment Reconsidered*. Edited by Princeton: Princeton University Press, 1983.

McCormick, John. *The European Union: Politics and Policies*. Boulder: Westview, 1999.

McDonald, Ronald. 'Confrontation and Transition in Uruguay'. *Current History*, Vol. 84, February 1985, pp. 25–44.

McDonald, Ronald H. 'The Rise of Military Politics in Uruguay'. *Inter-American Economic Affairs*, Vol. 27, No. 4, Spring 1975, pp. 25–44.

McDonald, Ronald H. 'Electoral Politics, and Uruguayan Political Decay'. *Inter-American Economic Affairs*, Vol. 26, No. 1, Summer 1972, pp. 25–46.

McDonough, Peter, Samuel Barnes, and Antonio López Pina. 'The Growth of Democratic Legitimacy in Spain'. *APSR*, Vol. 80, No. 3. September 1986, pp. 735–760.

MacIntyre, Alasdair. *After Virtue*. Notre Dame: University of Notre Dame Press, 1984.

Mainwaring, Scott. 'Political Parties and Democratization in Brazil and the Southern Cone'. *Comparative Politics*, Vol. 21, No. 1, October 1988, 91–120.

Maravall, José. *The Transition to Democracy in Spain*. London: St. Martin's Press, 1982.

Masterson, Daniel. 'In the Shining Path of Mariátegui, Mao Zedong or President Gonzalo? Peri's Sendero Lureinoso in Historical Perspective'. *Journal of Third World Studies*, Vol. 11, No. 1, Spring 1994, pp. 154–179.

Mauceri, Philip. *State Under Siege: Development and Policy Making in Peru*. Boulder: Westview, 1996.

Mauceri, Philip. 'State Reform, Coalitions, and the Neoliberal Autogolpe in Peru'. *Latin American Research Review*, Vol. 30, No. 1, Winter 1995, pp. 256–266.

Mauceri, Philip. 'Military Politics and Counter-insurgency in Peru'. *Journal of Interamerican Studies and World Affairs*, Vol. 33, No. 4, Winter 1991, pp. 83–109.

Mayer, Enrique. 'Patterns of Violence in the Andes'. *Latin American Research Review*, Vol. 29, No. 2, 1994, pp. 141–171.

Medrano, Juan Díez. *Divided Nations: Class, Politics, and Nationalism in the Basque Country and Catalonia*. Ithaca: Cornell University Press, 1995.

Mees, Ludger. *Nationalism, Violence and Democracy: The Basque Clash of Identities*. London: Palgrave Macmillan, 2004.

Méndez, Juan. *Human Rights in Peru after President Garcia's First Year*. New York: Americas Watch Committee, 1986.

Mieres, Paolo. 'Elecciones de 1989 en Uruguay'. *Sintesis*, Vol. 13, April–June 1991, pp. 205–228.

Miller, George. 'A Lesson Learned in Uruguay'. *New Leader*, Vol. 76, No. 10, August 9, 1993, pp. 7–10.

Ministry of Labour and Social Affairs. *Boletín de Noticias Especial 2005*, http://empleo.mtas.es/itss/sala_de_comunicaciones/boletin/Boletin_2005.pdf.

Moreno, Luis. 'Federalization and Ethnoterritorial Concurrence in Spain'. *Publius*, Vol. 27, No. 4, Fall 1997, pp. 65 (20).

Muller, Edward, Henry Dietz, and Steven Finkel. 'Discontent and the Unexpected Utility of Rebellion: The Case of Peru'. *American Political Science Review*, Vol. 85, No. 4, December 1991, pp. 1261–1283.

Munck, Geraldo and J. Verkuilen. 'Conceptualizing and Measuring Democracy: Evaluating Alternative Ideas'. *Comparative Political Studies*, Vol. 35, No. 1, 2002, pp. 5–34.

Nef, Jorge and J. Vanderkop. 'The Spiral of Violence: Insurgency and Counter-insurgency in Peru'. *Canadian Journal of Latin American and Caribbean Studies*, Vol. 9, No. 17, 1988, pp. 53–72.

Nelsen, Brent and Alexander C.-G. Stubb (eds). *The European Union: Readings on the Theory and Practice of European Integration*. Boulder: Lynne Rienner, 1994.

Nelson, Caulo and Alberto Silva. *Alto el Fuego*. Montevideo: Montesexio, 1986.

Newton, Michael T. with Peter J. Donaghy. *Institutions of Modern Spain*. Cambridge: Cambridge University Press, 1997.

Nussbaum, Martha. 'Human Functioning and Social Justice: In Defense of Aristotelian Essentialism'. *Political Theory*, Vol. 20, No. 2, May 1992, pp. 202–246.

Nussbaum, Martha and Amartya Sen (eds). *The Quality of Life*. Oxford: Clarendon Press, 1993.

O'Donnell, Guillermo. 'Illusions about Consolidation'. In Larry Diamond, Marc Planer, Yun-han Chu and Hung-Mao Tien (eds), *Consolidating the Third Wave Democracies: Themes and Perspectives*. Baltimore: Johns Hopkins University Press, 1997, pp. 40–57.

O'Donnell, Guillermo, Philippe Schmitter, and Laureñce Whitehead. *Transitions from Authoritarian Rule: Tentative Conclusions about Uncertain Democracies*. Baltimore: Johns Hopkins University Press, 1986.

Organization of American States. *Report on the Situation of Human Rights in Peru*. Washington, DC: OAS, 1992.

O'Sullivan, Patrick and Jesse W. Miller. *The Geography of Warfare*. New York: St. Martin's Press, 1983.

Palmer, David Scott. '"Fujimpopulism" and Peru's Progress'. *Current History*, February 1996.

Palmer, David Scott. 'Peru, the Drug Business and Shining Path: Between Scylla and Charybdis?'. *Journal of Interamerican Studies and World Affairs*, Vol. 34, No. 3, Fall 1992, pp. 65–89.

Palmer, David Scott. 'Rebellion in Rural Peru'. *Comparative Politics*, Vol. 18, No. 2, January 1986, pp. 127–146.

Paloma, Román Marugán. Sistema político español Ninou, Carmen. Madrid: McGraw-Hill, 1995.

Payne, Stanley. 'Political Violence During the Spanish Second Republic'. *Journal of Contemporary History*, Vol. 25, 1990, pp. 269–288.

Payne, Stanley (ed.). *The Politics of Democratic Spain*. Chicago: Chicago Council of Foreign Relations, 1986.

Payne, Stanley. *Basque Nationalism*. Reno: University of Nevada Press, 1975.

Pease García, Henry. *America Latina 80: Democracia y Movimiento Popular*. Lima: Centro de Estudios y Promocion del Desarrollo, 1981.

Peckenham, Nancy. 'Ayacucho Under Siege'. *NACLA*, Vol. 19, No. 3, May/June 1985, pp. 6–8.

Penniman, Howard R. and Eusebio M. Mujal-Leon (eds). *Spain at the Polls 1977, 1979, and 1982*. Chapel Hill: Duke University Press, 1985.

Perelli, Carina. 'From Counterrevolutionary Warfare to Political Awakening: The Uruguayan and Argentine Armed Forces in the 1970's'. *Armed Forces and Society*, Vol. 20, No. 1, Fall 1993, pp. 25–49.

Pérez-Díaz, Víctor M. *The Return of Civil Society*. Cambridge: Harvard University Press, 1993.

Pérez Díaz, Víctor (ed.). *El Retorno de la sociedad civil*. Madrid: Instituto de Estudios Económicos, 1987.

Pew Research Center. *Europe's Muslims More Moderate. The Great Divide: How Westerners and Muslims View Each Other*. Washington DC: Pew Research Center, 2006a.

Pew Research Center. *Few Signs of Backlash From Western Europeans. Muslims in Europe: Economic Worries Top Concerns about Religious and Cultural Identity*. Washington DC: Pew Research Center, 2006b.

Pion-Berlin, David. 'To Prosecute or to Pardon? Human Rights Decisions in the Latin American Southern Cone', *Human Rights Quarterly*, Vol. 16, No. 1, February 1994, pp. 3–4.

'Política migratoria española en el marco europeo'. *Studi Emigrazione/ Migration Studies*, Vol. 38, Issue 144, 2001, pp. 855–868.

Poole, Deborah (ed.). *Unruly Order: Violence, Power and Cultural Identity in the High Provinces of Southern Peru*. Boulder: Westview, 1994.

Poole, Deborah and Gerardo Renique. 'The New Chroniclers of Peru: US Scholars and their "Shining Path" of Peasant Revolution'. *Bulletin of Latin American Research*, Vol. 10, No. 2, 1991, pp. 133–191.

Porzencanski, Arturo. *Uruguay's Tupamaros*. New York: Praeger, 1973.

Powell, Charles. 'Did Terrorism Sway Spain's Election?'. *Current History*, November 2004, pp. 376–382.

Powell, Charles. *El piloto del cambio*. Barcelona: Editorial Planeta, 1991.

Powell, G. Bingham. *Contemporary Democracies: Participation, Stability and Violence*. Cambridge: Harvard University Press, 1982.

Pridham, Geoffrey. *Securing Democracy: Political Parties and Democratic Consolidation in Southern Europe*. London: Routledge, 1990.

Pridham, Geoffrey ed. *The New Mediterranean Democracies*. London: Frank Cass, 1984.

Reinares, Fernando. 'Towards a Social Characterisation of Jihadist Terrorism in Spain: Implications for Domestic Security and Action Abroad'. Madrid: Real Instituto Elcano, Study No. ARI 34/2006, 2006.

Reinares, Fernando. 'al Qaeda, neosalafistas magrebíes y 11-M: sobre el Nuevo terrorismo islamista en España'. In Fernando Reinares and Antonio Elorza (eds), *El Nuevo Terrorismo Islamista*. Madrid: Temas de Hoy, 2004a, pp. 15–44.

Reinares, Fernando. 'Who are the Terrorists? Analyzing the Changes in Sociological Profile among Members of ETA'. *Studies in Conflict and Terrorism*, Vol. 27, No. 6, 2004b, pp. 465–488.

'Report on Peru': Privilege and Power in Fujimori's Peru'. *NACLA*, Vol. 20, No. 1, July/August 1996, p. 15.

Republica Oriental del Uruguay Junta de Comandantes en Jefe. *Volumen 2. El Proceso Politico*. Montevideo: Las Fuerzas Armadas al Pueblo Oriental, 1978.

Republica Oriental del Uruguay Junta de Comandantes en Jefe. *La Subversion*. Montevideo: Las Fuerzas Armadas al Pueblo Oriental, 1977.

Revista Española de la Opinion Publica. Madrid: Instituto de la Opinion Publica.

Rial, Juan. 'Los Partidos Traditionales: restauración o renovación'. Documentos de Trabajo CIEDSU/DT 77/84. Montevideo: CIESU.

Roberts, Kenneth M. and Moises Arce. 'Neoliberalism and Lower Class Voting Behavior in Peru'. *Comparative Political Studies*, Vol. 31, No. 2, April–May 1998, pp. 217–247.

Roniger, Luis and Mario Sznajder. 'The Legacy of Human Rights Violations and the Collective Identity of Redemocratized Uruguay'. *Human Rights Quarterly*, Vol. 19, No. 1, February 1997, pp. 5–77.

Rorty, Amelie Oksenberg ed. *Essays on Aristotle's Ethics*. Berkeley: University of California Press, 1980.

Ross, Chris. 'Nationalism and Party Competition in the Basque Country and Catalonia'. *West European Politics*, Vol. 19 No. 3, July 1996, pp. 488–506.

Salkever, Stephen. *Finding the Mean: Theory and Practice in Aristotelian Political Philosophy*. Princeton: Princeton University Press, 1990.

Salkever, Stephen. 'Aristotle's Social Science'. *Political Theory*, Vol. 9, No. 4, November 1981, pp. 479–508.

Sanchez, W. Alejandro. 'The Rebirth of Insurgency in Peru'. *Small Wars and Insurgencies*, Vol. 14, No. 3, autumn 2003, pp. 185–198.

Sandell, Rickard. 'Spain's Immigration Experience: Lessons to be Learned from Looking at the Statistics. Madrid: Real Instituto Elcano,Working Paper' 2006, WWP 30/2006.

Sandell, Rickard. 'Spain's Quest for Regular Immigration'. Madrid: Real Instituto Elcano, 2005, ARI No. 64/2005.

Santos, Julia, Javier Pradera and Jaoquin Prieto (eds). *Memoria de la transicion*. Madrid: Taurus, 1996.

Savater, Fernando and Gonzalo Martínez-Fresneda. *Teoría y presencia de la tortura en España*. Barcelona: Editorial Anagrama, 1982.

Sawyer, Katherine, 'Comment: Rejection of the Weimarian Politics or Betrayal of Democracy? Spain's Proscription of Batasuna under the European Convention of Human Rights'. *American University Law Review*, Vol. 52, No. 6, August 2003, pp. 1540–1552.

Schmidt, Gregory. 'Fujimori's 1990 Upset Victory in Peru'. *Comparative Politics*, Vol. 28, No. 3, April 1996, pp. 321–354.

Schmitter, Phillippe. 'Interest Intermediation and Regime Governability in Contemporary Western Europe and North America'. In Suzanne Berger (ed.), *Organizing Interests in Western Europe*. New York: Cambridge University Press, 1981, pp. 285–327.

Schultz, Frederick. 'Breaking the Cycle: Empirical Research and Postgraduate Studies on Terrorism'. In Andre Silke (ed.), *Research on Terrorism: Trends, Achievements and Failures*, New York: Routledge, 2004, pp. 161–185.

Sendagorta, Fidel. 'Jihad in Europe; the Wider Context'. *Survival*, Vol. 47, Issue 3, 2005, pp. 63–72.

Seregni, General Liber. *Discursos*. Montevideo: Bolsilibros ARCA 86, 1971.

Servicio Paz y Justicia: Uruguay. *Nunca Más: Human Rights Violations, 1972–1985*. Senicio Paz y Justicia, *Uruguay: Nunca Más*. Philadelphia: Temple Press, 1992. Philadelphia: Temple University Press, 1986.

Shabad, Goldie. 'After Autonomy: The Dynamics of Regionalism in Spain'. In Stanley G. Payne (ed.), *The Politics of Democratic Spain*. Chicago: Chicago Council on Foreign Relations, 1986, pp. 111–180.

Shady, Norbert. 'Seeking Votes: The Political Economy of Expenditures by the Peruvian Social Fund (FONCODES), 1991–95', Policy Research Working Paper no. WPS 2166, World Bank.

Share, Donald. *The Making of Spanish Democracy*. New York: Westport, 1986.

Shepard, William. 'The ETA: Spain Fights Europe's Last Active Terrorist Group'. *Mediterranean Quarterly*, Vol. 13, No. 1, 2002, pp. 54–68.

Shifter, Michael. 'Human Rights: Peruvian Responses'. *Hemisphere*, Winter/Spring 1990, pp. 6–9.

Shub, Joyce Lasky and Raymond Carr (eds). *Spain: Studies in Political Security*. New York: Praeger, 1985.

Skopol, Theda and Margaret Somer. 'The Uses of Comparative History in Macrosocial Inquiry'. *Comparative Studies in Society and History*, Vol. 22, No. 2, April 1980, pp. 174–197.

Soldevilla, Fernando Tuesta. *Perú Político en Cifras*. Lima: Fundacion, 1994.

Sosnowski, Saúl and Lousie Popkin (eds). *Repression, Exile, and Democracy: Uruguayan Culture*. Durham: Duke University Press, 1993.

Starn, Orin. 'To Revolt Against the Revolution: War and Resistance in Peru's Andes'. *Cultural Anthropology*, Vol. 10, No. 4, November 1995, pp. 547–581.

Starn, Orin, Carlos Ivan Degregori, and Robin Kirk (eds). *The Peru Reader: History, Culture, Politics*. Durham: Duke University Press, 1995.

Stokes, Susan. *Cultures in Conflict*. Berkeley: University of California Press, 1995.

Strauss, Leo. *Natural Right and History*. Chicago: University of Chicago Press, 1965.

Strauss, Leo. *The City and Man*. Chicago: University of Chicago Press, 1964.

Tamames, Ramon. *Una Idea de España*. Madrid: Plaza & Janes Editores, 1985.

Tejerina, Benjamín. 'Protest Cycle, Political Violence and Social Movements in the Basque Country'. *Nations and Nationalism*, Vol. 7, No. 1, 2001, pp. 39–57.

Tezanos, José Feliz, Ramón Cotarelo, and Andrés De Blas. *La Transición Democrática Española*. Madrid: Editorial Sistema, 1989.

Treverton, Gregory. *Spain: Domestic Politics and Security Policy*. Adelphi Papers 204, London: International Institute for Strategic Studies, 1986.

Tucker, H. H. (ed.). *Combating the Terrorists: Democratic Responses to Political Violence*. New York: Facts on File, 1988.

Tulchin, Joseph and Gary Bland eds. *Peru in Crisis: Dictatorship or Democracy?* Boulder: Lynne Rienner, 1994.

Turano, Leslie. 'Spain: Banning Political Parties as a Response to Basque Terrorism'. *International Journal of Constitutional Law*, Vol. 1, No. 4, October 2003, pp. 732–738.

United Nations Development Programme, *Human Development Report 1999*. New York: Oxford University Press, 1999.

Uruguay: A Country Study. United Stated: Federal Research Division Library of Congress, 1990.

Uruguay. Ministro del Interior. *Siete meses de la lucha antisubversiva*. Montevideo: Ministro del Interior, 1972.

Uruguay: Poder, Ideologia y Clases Sociales. Montevideo: Facultad de Derecho, 1970.

US Department of State. Bureau of Democracy, Human Rights, and Labor. *Country Reports on Human Rights Practices 2006*, 6 March 2007.

US Department of State. *Human Rights Practices*. Washington, DC: United States. Department of State, 1998.

US Department of State. *Spain Country Report on Human Rights Practices for 1997*. Washington, DC: United States. Department of State, 1998.

US Department of State. *Human Rights Practices*. Washington, DC: United States. Department of State, 1997.

US Department of State. *Uruguay Country Report on Human Rights Practices for 1996*. Washington, DC: United States. Department of State, 1997.

US Department of State. *Human Rights Practices*. Washington, DC: United States. Department of State, 1996.

US Department of State. *Human Rights Practices*. Washington, DC: United States. Department of State, 1994.

US House of Representatives and Committee on Foreign Relations. US Senate by the Department of State. *Report Submitted to the Committee on International Relations* 1978–1986.

US Senate, *Committee Report of Human Rights Practices 1979–1986* (Washington, DC: US Senate).

Van Biezen, Ingrid. 'Terrorism and Democratic Legitimacy: Conflicting Interpretations of the Spanish Elections'. *Mediterranean Politics*, Vol. 10, No. 1, 2005, pp. 99–108.

Van Den Broek, Hanspeter. 'Borroka – the Legitimation of Street Violence in the Political Discourse of Radical Basque Nationalists'. *Terrorism and Political Violence*, Vol. 16, No. 4, 2004, pp. 714–736.

Villanueva, Victor. 'Peru's New Military Professionalism: The Failure of the Technocratic Approach'. In Steven M. Gorman (ed.), *Post Revolutionary Peru*, Boulder: Westview, 1982, pp. 157–178.

Watters, R. F. *Poverty and Peasantry in Peru's Southern Andes, 1963–1990*. Pittsburgh: University of Pittsburgh Press, 1994.

Weinstein, Martin. *Uruguay: Democracy at the Crossroads*. Boulder: Westview Press, 1988.

Werlich, David. 'Peru: The Shadow of the Shining Path'. *Current History*, Vol. 83, February 1984, pp. 78–84.

Weyland, Kurt. 'Latin America's Four Political Models'. *Journal of Democracy*, Vol. 6, No. 4, October 1995, pp. 125–140.

Wiarda, Howard. *The Transition to Democracy in Spain and Portugal*. Washington, DC: American Enterprise Institute for Public Policy Research, 1988.

Wilkinson, Paul. 'Maintaining the Democratic Process and Public Support'. In Richard Clutterbuck (ed.), *The Future of Political Violence*. New York: St. Martin's Press, 1986.

Woodworth, Paddy. 'Spain Changes Course: Aznar's Legacy, Zapatero's Prospects'. *World Policy Journal*, Vol. 21, No. 2, Summer 2004, pp. 7–26.

Woy-Hazleton, Sandra and William A. Hazleton. 'Sendero Luminos and the Future of Peruvian Democracy'. *Third World Quarterly*, Vol. 12, No. 2, 1990, pp. 21–35.

Yack, Bernard. *The Problems of a Political Animal: Community, Justice and Conflict in Aristotelian Political Thought*. Berkeley: University of California Press, 1993.

Yack, Bernard. 'Natural Right and Aristotle's Understanding of Justice'. *Political Theory*, Vol. 18, No. 2, May 1990, pp. 216–237.

Yehude, Simon Munaro. *Estado y Guerrillas en el Peru de los '80*. Lima: EES Asociación Instituto de los Estudios Estratégicos y Sociales, 1988.

Zirakzadeh, Cyrus. *A Rebellious People: Basques, Protests and Politics*. Reno: University of Nevada Press, 1991.

Index

Acción Popular (AP) 12
Acuerdo de Cooperación 237, 254
Acuerdo de Lazarra 229
agrarian Reform 5
Al-Andalus 248, 259–260
Al Qaeda 6, 8, 234, 235, 247–252
Alfonso XIII, King of Spain 65–66
Alianza Apostólica Anticomunista (AAA) 98
Alianza Popular Revolucionaria Americana (APRA) 7, 11, 59, 61–62, 76, 157
Amnesty 114–115, 121–122, 199, 200–201, 210, 214
Arce, Liber 107, 154
Argentina 14, 111
Arias Navarro, Carlos 66
Aristotelian approach 31, 35–42, 44–48
Aristotle 1, 2, 24, 36–39
Atocha 248
autogolpe 5, 7, 17, 37, 63–64, 117, 205
autonomy 69, 122, 150, 162, 235
Aznar, José María 229, 235, 248, 258

Bardesio, Nelson 111
Batasuna (see also HB) 230, 234, 236
Batlle, Jorge 54, 200
Belaúnde, Fernando 12, 62, 97, 113–114, 117, 158, 172
Blanco Party 7, 9, 13, 53–55, 73, 154

Boiso Lanza agreement 58–59
Bordaberry, Juan Maria 9, 13, 56–58, 94, 96, 109, 155, 168–171

Carrero Blanco, Admiral Luis 66, 92
Catalan Convergence and Union (CiU) 67
Catholic Church 5, 53, 65–66, 159–161, 218
Caza Tupamaro 96, 111, 134
Centro de Estudios Militares de Peru (CAEM) 60
citizen confidence 39, 40–42, 49
  Peru 156–162
  Spain 162–165
  Uruguay 152–156
Club Naval Talks 199
Colegiado 54
Colorados 7, 9, 13, 53–55, 73, 155
Comisión de la Verdad y Reconciliación 115, 135, 137, 215
Communist Party 66–67, 144
Concordat 5
Consejo de Seguridad Nacional (COSENA) 59, 195–196
coparticipación 11, 53–54
corruption 61, 64, 205, 220–221

democratic stability
  Peru 171–175
  Spain 175–177
  Uruguay 167–171

INDEX

desencanto 175
dictablanda/dictadura 36
Double simultaneous vote 13

ELP (National Liberation Army) 60
Ertzaintza 123, 231
Estatuto de Guernica 122, 229
European Economic Community, European Union 18–20, 223–224
Euzkadi ta Askatasuna (ETA) 6, 19, 66–67, 91–93, 101, 122, 142–143, 177, 223–247
Expiry law 200

Fraga, Manuel 176–177
Franco, Comando Rodrigo 119
Franco, General Francisco 5, 12, 18, 65–66, 68, 77, 165, 176, 259
Frente Amplio 9, 11, 13, 94, 112, 155, 194, 199, 200
Frente Democrático (FREDEMO) 139
Fujimori, Alberto 5, 7, 10–12, 17, 37, 62–64, 74–76, 97–98, 115, 118, 157–162, 172–173, 206–209, 214–215, 217–220

GAL 125–126, 228
Garcia, Alan 12, 16, 62, 74, 76, 97, 113–115, 117–118, 157–159
González, Felipe 67, 92, 165, 228
Grupo Salafista para la Predicación y el Combate (GSPC 247–249)
Grupos de Resistencia Antifascista Primero de Octubre (GRAPO) 93, 98
Guevara, Che 90
Guzmán, Abimael 89, 98, 210

Herri Batasuna (HB) 67, 91–92, 124, 229, 230–231

immigrants 248–256
Inter-American Court of Human Rights 214–215
Ivcher, Baruch 214

Játiva conspiracy 69
Juan Carlos I, King of Spain 5, 10, 66, 70–71, 121–122, 259
JUJEM 69
Junta de Comandantes en Jefe 59
justice 39–41, 47
Juventud Uruguaya de Pie (JUP) 111, 134

Kale Borroka 226

Law of Political Reform 66
leadership 9–10, 21
legitimacy 1, 2, 22–23, 32–35
Lema system (DSV) 13
Ley Orgánica de Partidos Políticos 230

MANO 111, 134
military 20–21, 48, 45–66, 37, 55–56, 155–156, 159–161, 173, 194–198
MIR (Movement of the Revolutionary Left) 60
Mitrione, Dan 88
Moncloa Pact 67–68
Montesinos, Vladimiro 63, 81n33, 208–209, 218
Morales Bermúdez, Francisco 6, 61
Movimiento Revolucionario Tupac Amaro (MRTA) 5, 80–81, 115, 118–119, 134–138, 172, 212
MPS (prompt security measures) 56, 106, 108–109, 153–154

National Security Doctrine 15, 16
North Atlantic Treaty Organization (NATO) 18

Odria, Manuel 4, 60
Operation Condor 201
Operation Galaxia 70
Operation Zen 124
Organization of American States 17–18, 205, 222

Pacheco Areco, Jorge 106–109, 155
Pact of Chinchulín (Pork Barrel Pact) 73
Pacto de Ajuria Enea 228

Paniagua, Valentín 215
Partido Popular 235–236, 248, 253, 259
Partido Popular Cristiano 11
party system 11–13, 22, 55
Plan Ibarretxe 236
PNV 12, 67, 92–93
Polay Campos, Víctor 91, 98
Primo de Rivera, General Miguel 64
PSOE 12, 18, 67, 229, 235–236
purposes of the state 2, 38, 40, 42, 44, 48–49, 133–154

repression 8, 41–48
    Peru 113–121, 140
    Spain 124–126
    Uruguay 106–113, 154
restitution 200, 215, 228
rondas 115, 117–118

Sanguinetti, Julio 10, 199, 202
Saudi Arabia 254
Second Republic 64–65, 68
Sendero Luminoso 5, 7, 62–64, 89–90, 97–98, 118–119, 135–141, 146–149, 172, 210–212
Seregni, General Liber 9, 16, 168–170, 194

SIN 116, 208
Sinchis 113
Soldados de Alá 249
state 12, 13, 15, 19
state of exception or state of siege 114–116, 213
strategic hamlet plan 16
Suárez, Adolfo 67, 70–71, 165

teleology 37–38
Toledo, Alejandro 208–209, 215, 221–222
Tupamaros 4, 7, 56, 78, 86–89, 94–96, 110–111, 112–113, 133–134, 152–153, 168–169, 200–201

Union of the Arab Maghreb 249
Union of the Democratic Centre (UCD) 12, 18, 67, 69, 71
United States 7, 13–17, 20, 258

Vázquez, Tabaré 200–201
Velasco Alvarado, Juan 5, 60–61, 196

Weber, Max 31–32

Zapatero, José Luis Rodríguez 235–236, 258–259

EU authorised representative for GPSR:
Easy Access System Europe, Mustamäe tee 50,
10621 Tallinn, Estonia
gpsr.requests@easproject.com

www.ingramcontent.com/pod-product-compliance
Ingram Content Group UK Ltd.
Pitfield, Milton Keynes, MK11 3LW, UK
UKHW021832140426
5217IPUK00021B/1404